Programming Applications with the Wireless Application Protocol

Programming Applications with the Wireless Application Protocol

The Complete Developer's Guide

Steve Mann

Wiley Computer Publishing

John Wiley & Sons, Inc.

NEW YORK • CHICHESTER • WEINHEIM • BRISBANE • SINGAPORE • TORONTO

Publisher: Robert Ipsen

Editor: Carol A. Long

Managing Editor: Angela Murphy

Associate New Media Editor: Mike Sosa

Text Design & Composition: North Market Street Graphics, Lancaster, Pennsylvania

This publication is designed to provide accurate and authoritative information in regard to the subject matter covered. It is sold with the understanding that the publisher is not engaged in professional services. If professional advice or other expert assistance is required, the services of a competent professional person should be sought.

Library of Congress Cataloging-in-Publication Data:

Mann, Steve
    Programming applications with the wireless application protocol: the complete
  developer's guide / Steve Mann.
      p.   cm.
  Includes bibliographical references.
  ISBN 0-471-32754-9 (cloth)
    1. Computer network protocols.   2. Wireless communication systems. I. Title.

TK5105.55.M36   1999
004.6'2—dc21   99-042181

Printed in the United States of America.

10 9 8 7 6 5 4 3 2 1

CONTENTS

Chapter 3   WMLScript

Chapter 4   WorldFAQ

Chapter 5   Caching

Phone.com is pleased to have contributed to the creation of this valuable book. We are dedicated to supporting you, the developer of Web-based content, in your efforts to bring your information and applications to the most exciting new information delivery platform since the inception of the World Wide Web. Our support does not stop with this book. The Phone.com Software Developer's Kit (SDK) on the accompanying CD-ROM will allow you to instantly practice what you learn in the book, and quickly bring your own content to the screen of wireless telephones around the world.

Wireless telephones are rapidly changing the way people communicate around the planet. Industry analysts predict over a billion wireless phones in operation by the year 2003. The Wireless Application Protocol (WAP) Forum, founded in 1997 by Phone.com, Ericsson, Motorola, and Nokia, is an industry group dedicated to the goal of enabling sophisticated telephony and information services on handheld wireless devices. WAP is the de facto world standard for wireless information and telephony services on digital mobile phones and other wireless terminals. Handset manufacturers representing over 95 percent of the world market across all digital standards have committed to shipping WAP-enabled devices. Carriers representing hundreds of millions of subscribers worldwide have joined WAP. This commitment will provide tens of millions of WAP browser–enabled products to consumers by the end of 2000.

As a leader in the WAP Forum, and a leading provider of WAP microbrowsers and infrastructure software, Phone.com is happy to welcome you to the exciting world of Wireless Internet. Please visit us at www.phone.com for the latest in WAP developments.

Chuck Parrish
Executive Vice President, Phone.com Inc.
Vice-chairman of the WAP Forum Board of Directors
Chuck@corp.phone.com

There are more than 300 million cell phone users in the world. There are also millions of Internet users in the world. These two markets are rapidly converging on the same spot: small, lightweight, inexpensive mobile computing devices that are equally suitable for high-quality voice communication, modest-bandwidth (5 to 10 Kbps) data communication, seamless Internet connectivity, access to Internet services such as e-mail and content, and general-purpose, programmable computing devices that can run custom applications. Just to simplify our descriptions, let's call these devices smart phones.

There is an organization, the WAP Forum, whose members predicted this convergence a few years ago. The founding members, Ericcson, Motorola, Nokia, and Phone.com (formerly Unwired Planet), started collaborating to design an architecture for delivering advanced data services to smart phones. This architecture, which draws heavily from existing Internet technologies, is based on a protocol stack called the Wireless Application Protocol (WAP).

WAP sits on top of a variety of wireless carriers. It provides services such as compression, encryption, the integration of telephony and data services, and, most important, the Wireless Application Architecture (WAE) for building application programs that run on smart phones—WAP apps.

WAP apps are the key to making smart phones really smart. Hardware doesn't really solve user problems or provide users with advanced intelligent capabilities. Software does. To that end, we're pleased to present you with *Programming Applications with the Wireless Application Protocol: The Complete Developer's Guide.*

Road Map

This book has eight chapters. The first chapter, "Introducing WAP," sets the stage for the rest of the book. It describes the markets and the technologies that WAP addresses and includes an overview of the major components of WAE. Most important, it addresses the question: Why WAP? It also describes the similarities and differences between developing applications for the World Wide Web and for WAP.

Chapter 2, "Wireless Markup Language," describes the Wireless Markup Language, the primary programming vehicle for creating WAP apps. WML is an XML-conforming markup language that has a tagged syntax much like HTML. You create WAP apps by creating WML documents, either statically or dynamically, and delivering them to a WAP device. We include short code snippets as examples.

Chapter 3, "WMLScript," describes the scripting language that is part of the WAE. WMLScript adds lightweight procedural capabilities and function libraries to WML. Together they provide you with a rich, robust application development environment. We include in this chapter a fairly complex application that combines WML and WMLScript.

Chapter 4, "WorldFAQ" (WorldFAQ is a trademark of Creative Digital Publishing, Inc.) takes you step by step through the process of creating a real-world WAP application. It includes both static and dynamic content. The dynamic content is created using a Java servlet, a powerful and flexible technology that is well suited to building WAP applications.

Chapter 5, "Caching," describes techniques for optimizing WAP apps by managing the cache in a WAP device. Applications that use wireless networks must be small and fast. The best way to achieve those goals is to use the network as little as possible. Caching is the key.

Chapter 6, "Graphics and Multipart Responses," shows you how to create more sophisticated and interesting applications using graphics. In this chapter we modify WorldFAQ to include graphics, and we deliver the graphics using MIME multipart documents served up by our Java servlet. Although graphics and multipart documents are not directly related topics, they complement each other nicely.

Chapter 7, "Internationalization (I18N)," describes issues you need to be aware of to build WAP applications that can work throughout the world. As a global standard developed by an international group of companies, the WAP Forum's work focuses on internationally useful solutions. This chapter introduces you to character sets, character encodings, and languages, and how they affect the operation of WAP applications.

Chapter 8, "Beyond WAP 1.1," describes some of the advanced extensions to WAP that have been developed by Phone.com. As the originator of much of the technology that went into WAP 1.0, and as active participants in the WAP Forum's ongoing efforts, Phone.com has a unique perspective on WAP. This chapter gives you a look at what they think is important, and suggests directions in which WAP may evolve.

We conclude with a bibliography and several appendixes that are very helpful quick references to WML and other WAP characteristics. Upon first reading,

WML can be a bit confusing. Appendixes A ("WML Elements"), B ("WML Elements Cross Reference"), and C ("WML Attributes Cross Reference") are concise tools for quickly getting your arms around all that is WML. Appendix D, "WMLScript Library Functions," is also a concise summary of all the WMLScript libraries. These four appendixes are your quick-start WAP app tools.

Who Should Read This Book

This book is, first and foremost, for application developers. Wireless application development is a fairly new discipline that combines an understanding of traditional programming using third-generation languages, Web content development using tagged languages, and an understanding of how HTTP works, an area that until now was primarily the domain of Web server and application developers. We assume that you know how to program. If you know C, C++, Basic, Java, or any one of a number of modern programming languages, you should be able to read this book and understand it without much difficulty.

We don't, however, assume that you are familiar with Web applications development. When important, we explain the underpinnings of the Internet and WAP: HTTP, MIME, and more. This book is not a detailed explanation of all things Internet—just the things you need to know to build WAP applications.

Despite our applications focus, this book is well suited for technical managers who need to get an overview of the reality of WAP. We cover the high-level architecture more than the low-level details. Web content developers should also find it useful, even if they don't know much about programming. In one sense, a WAP application is just the delivery of WML-tagged, instead of HTML-tagged, documents to a browser. What goes on in a WAP application is very similar to what goes on in a WEB application.

Throughout this book, we try to focus on what's practical and useful to application developers. To that end, we try to include lots of useful code snippets and complete applications. We don't, however, include lots of gratuitous samples just for the heck of it. If something is obvious, we assume that we've explained it reasonably well and that you are capable of understanding it. If we've failed, our apologies.

The CD-ROM

This book includes a companion CD-ROM that contains all the source code from each chapter, except for simple one- and two-line examples. Whenever we use source code that is also on the CD-ROM, we include the source file name in the text enclosed in square brackets. For instance, the WML source code file for the first version of WorldFAQ can be found in [wfaq1.wml].

What's Next

To get started with WAP, you should read Chapter 1, "Introducing WAP," which sets the stage for the rest of the book. Then, we recommend that you read Chapter 2, "Wireless Markup Language." WML is the primary language for creating WAP documents. From there you can skip directly to Chapter 4, "WorldFAQ," to look at a complete example. Chapter 3, "WMLScript," can be treated as a stand-alone chapter; you don't need to read it to understand any of the other examples in the book.

In Chapter 5, "Caching," we discuss a lot of HTTP basics. It's a good idea to read that before going on to Chapters 6 through 8. If you already know a bit about how HTTP works, you can probably read any of Chapters 5 through 8 independently. They are, for the most part, self-contained.

ACKNOWLEDGMENTS

As with any project of this size, there are a variety of people to thank:

- Ben Linder at Phone.com, for initiating this project

- Carol Long, Wiley senior editor extraordinaire, for her patience and grace under fire

- My coauthors, Bruce Martin and Peter King (particularly Bruce), for continued patience in answering questions and providing commentary under bone-crushing workloads

- Several excellent folks at Phone.com, for their comments, tech support, and assistance: Don Schuerholz, Ron Mandel, Avi Weiss, Peter Stark, Kathryn Malm, and Jeff Stock

- Finally, my wife Betty, for her continued support and good humor

This project would not have been possible without all of these people.

Programming Applications with the Wireless Application Protocol

Introducing WAP

T here are more than 300 million cell phone users in the world. There are also millions of Internet users in the world. According to all the experts, the number of users of both of these technologies will continue to grow rapidly for several years.

Cell phones are ideal for staying in touch with the rest of the world (assuming you have coverage, but that's another story). They are small, lightweight, and inexpensive. Most countries have one or more cellular voice networks. Less-developed countries are also building cellular telephone infrastructures because it's easier and quicker to deploy a cellular network than a traditional wired network. Clearly, wireless telephony will become the dominant form of voice communication in the world.

Internet access is also transforming the way the world operates. E-mail and the World Wide Web are becoming the lingua franca of modern living. Families use e-mail to stay in touch. Businesses use the Web to market and sell products. You can have focused, timely news delivered to your computer. You can sell personal items at one of the many auction sites, conducting a virtual garage sale. You can buy and sell stocks, and check airline schedules, international weather, and local movie listings. There are literally tens of thousands of resources on the Internet.

Cellular telephony is a mobile technology. You carry the phone with you, placing and receiving calls from around the world. To date, Internet access has primarily been a desktop activity done with a physical telephone line and a modem. Mobile Internet access has been a dream but not a reality. Although it's possible to achieve wireless Internet access using a wireless modem with a laptop or handheld computer, or with certain types of two-way pagers, these solutions are not ideal for many reasons: device size and weight, battery life, and cost, for instance.

There are a variety of forces at work that are causing a convergence of cell phone and Internet technologies:

- The cost of buying and using cell phones is decreasing. In many parts of the world, wireless voice communication is less expensive than traditional wired voice communication. As a result, cell phone usage is surging.

- Both computer and cell phone technologies are becoming more powerful. We are witnessing tremendous improvements in memory, battery, and central processing unit (CPU) technologies, making it possible for both telephone and computer manufacturers to deliver substantially more horsepower for less money.

- Internet use is surging. More and more people are realizing that there is tremendous value to using the Internet, both for communication and for content. It's natural to want access to that value, all the time, without having to carry a full-blown computer or deal with the complexities of figuring out how to add wireless capabilities to that computer.

- People want information when they need it, not just when they are near a desktop computer. The cell phone is the most appropriate device for receiving information on demand. Also, more than 300 million people already carry them and millions of new cell phone users are signing up each year.

- Cell phones are becoming smarter. They are no longer just devices for voice communication. Manufacturers are starting to put more memory and more powerful processors in cell phones. Once you do that, it's natural to include more powerful applications such as contact management programs, to-do lists, and other personal productivity software.

- Cellular networks are becoming more capable. For several years now, it's been possible, with some difficulty, to use analog cellular networks for data communications. The new digital cellular networks are much more suited for both voice and data traffic.

- Internet and cell phone use is converging on flat-rate pricing. Both markets previously charged in increments of minutes (cell phones) or hours (Internet). Flat-rate, unlimited Internet pricing is now the norm. Flat-rate wireless voice and data pricing is starting to emerge in the United States;

it has been available for certain types of services for several years in parts of Europe and Asia. Predictable fixed costs make it much easier for potential wireless data consumers to take the plunge.

As a result of all these trends, cell phone manufacturers are starting to deliver smart phones, telephones with full-blown programmable computers embedded in the hardware. Computer device manufacturers are starting to build handheld computers with wireless communications capabilities. Both markets are converging on the same spot: small, lightweight, inexpensive mobile computing devices that are equally suitable for high-quality voice communication; modest-bandwidth (5–10 Kbps) data communication; seamless Internet connectivity; access to Internet services like e-mail and content; and general-purpose, programmable computing devices that can run custom applications.

The WAP Forum

Long ago, and far away in Internet years, in the early 1990s, it was becoming clear to the major cell phone manufacturers that wireless voice and data and the Internet would eventually converge. They started working on technologies to foster that convergence. At the same time, a Silicon Valley start-up, formerly Unwired Planet, now called Phone.com, also started working on technologies for that convergence.

Phone.com's HDML (Handheld Device Markup Language) served as the basis for Wireless Markup Language (WML). The company, headquartered in Silicon Valley, with overseas operations in Japan and the United Kingdom, is currently a publicly held provider of WAP-compatible microbrowser and WAP gateway technologies. Phone.com's products are in use by leading global wireless vendors, including AT&T Wireless, Bell Atlantic-Mobile, GTE Wireless, Mitsubishi, Panasonic, QUALCOMM, Samsung, Siemens, and others.

In June of 1997, the three largest cell phone manufacturers—Ericsson, Motorola, and Nokia—and Unwired Planet announced the WAP (Wireless Application Protocol) Forum, a nonprofit organization for creating standards for delivering Internet access to consumer-class wireless devices. Open to all interested parties, particularly content developers, device manufacturers, carriers, and infrastructure providers, the WAP Forum's goals are to:

- Foster the delivery of Internet content and advanced data services to wireless telephones and other mobile wireless devices. These services can be simple generic services like wireless e-mail and Web access. They also include specific solutions for vertical markets like dispatching and field service.

- Create a global protocol specification that works on all wireless networks in all parts of the world. WAP includes a protocol stack definition that is easily adapted to Short Message Service (SMS), GSM Unstructured Supplementary Service Data (USSD), Cellular Digital Packet Data (CDPD), and other networks.

- Enable the creation of content and applications that scale across a wide range of networks and devices. The WAP Application Environment (WAE) includes definitions for user interface (UI) independent applications that can run, unchanged, on a variety of devices with different characteristics.

- Embrace and extend existing standards and technologies whenever possible and appropriate. Specifically, the WAP Forum borrows heavily from existing Internet standards while solving problems specific to wireless networks. This includes a strong focus on making all WAP technologies and applications readily internationalizable.

In order to meet these goals, the WAP Forum had to carefully consider the characteristics of the target devices and the wireless environment in which they operate. Despite the increasing power and capabilities of cellular telephones, they are still consumer devices selling in a very price-sensitive market. Every manufacturing dollar that can be saved is critical.

WAP Device Characteristics

While working on their initial specifications, the WAP Forum made certain assumptions about a typical WAP device. They did not create any reference designs, as Microsoft does for Windows CE consumer devices, for instance, that dictate the minimum RAM and ROM, the number and types of communications ports, the data entry mechanisms, and so on. Instead, based on the current crop of cell phones, two-way pagers, and handheld computers, they specified a set of likely device characteristics.

First and foremost, a WAP device has limited CPU, random access memory (RAM), read-only memory (ROM), and processing speed. There are no hard-and-fast rules that spell out the hardware requirements in more detail. *Limited* means enough to get the job done but no more.

Second, since WAP devices are mobile wireless devices, they have limited battery life. Again, there are no hard-and-fast rules. If you look at cell phones today, they have talk times ranging from approximately 2 to as many as 10 hours. Although battery technologies are improving, don't expect to see an order-of-magnitude improvement every 18 months, as Moore's law predicts for CPU processing power. The important point is that manufacturers and application developers should do everything they can to preserve battery life, by writing short, fast, efficient programs and using good power conservation techniques. It also means that you should use the network as little as possible. Wireless messaging uses battery power much faster than plain old CPU processing.

Third, WAP bearer networks are likely to be low-power networks with modest bandwidth, less than 10 Kbps for now. This ties in with battery life issues—the more bandwidth you use, the more power you need. The more power you need, the shorter your battery life. As 3COM has shown with its very popular Palm computing devices, users prefer to change their batteries as infrequently as possible.

Fourth, wireless voice and data networks are inherently unreliable, unstable, and unpredictable. The WAP protocols, and the applications running on WAP devices, need to be robust and reliable. They need to be able to cope with service interruptions, broken connections, and loss of service. Fortunately, the WAP protocol designers have dealt with those issues so that applications designers don't have to.

Fifth, WAP devices will typically have small screens and limited data entry capabilities. This is a natural side effect of the need to minimize manufacturing costs. The smaller the screen, the lower the cost. If you forgo a full QWERTY keyboard and use a telephone keypad instead, you lower the cost some more. So far, all the WAP devices that have been announced or manufactured have been essentially cell phones with a few extra keys and some additional software-based features. The screens are as small as four lines of 12 characters; the input mechanism, a telephone keypad. Look for larger displays, touchscreen-based keyboards, voice recognition, and other enhancements in future models. At the same time, expect things to stay small, simple, and minimalist.

In addition to considering device characteristics, the WAP Forum focused on the user experience. The foremost consideration is the nature of wireless networks. Wireless networks have high latency, meaning there is a perceptible pause between the times a user requests an action, the device transmits that request over a wireless network, and the response comes back to the device for the user to view. The WAP user paradigm is one where users are able to make small, specific, focused requests for small chunks (typically less than 1000 bytes) of data—telephone numbers, addresses, concise driving directions, movie listings, world times, and so on—not browse random Web sites. The more concise the request and response, the lower the latency.

Many cell phone designs are just too complicated, containing features that are never used. In addition, a typical cell phone user moves from place to place and does several things simultaneously (such as, unfortunately, drive a vehicle, talk on the telephone, and listen to the radio). There's no reason to think that a WAP device user will be any different. Since a WAP device has more capabilities than a cell phone, it's important that the device be as simple to use as possible.

The WAP Specification

Less than one year after the WAP Forum was founded, the organization released the WAP 1.0 specification. As of this writing, the WAP 1.1 specification is currently in development. As you will see as you read through this book, the 1.1 specification draws heavily on existing Internet standards, including Hyper Text Markup Language (HTML), Transmission Control Protocol/Internet Protocol (TCP/IP), Hyper Text Transport Protocol (HTTP), Extensible Markup Language (XML), Secure Sockets Layer (SSL), JavaScript, vCard and vCalendar, and Multipurpose Internet Mail Extensions (MIME), to name a few. The ultimate goal of the WAP Forum is to merge with current standardization efforts within the Internet community as much as possible in the coming years. To that end, the WAP Forum is having ongoing discussions with the Internet Engineering Task Force (IETF).

The WAP specification has the following key components:

A programming model based heavily on the existing Web programming model. Much like a Web browser, a WAP device engages in a series of individual request/response transactions with content servers that deliver both static and dynamic content. This lets you leverage your existing knowledge of how the Web works and allows you to use many existing Web tools to create WAP software.

An XML-conforming markup language designed for creating device-independent WAP applications. This language, the Wireless Markup Language (WML), has a limited number of XML elements (called tags in HTML). It makes very few a priori assumptions about the device executing the program. Applications are divided into small units of execution that can readily be moved across a wireless network. Much like HTML, WML focuses on presenting formatted content and limited execution options to users.

The WMLScript scripting language, based on the ECMA (European Computer Manufacturers Association) ECMAScript language for extending the power of WML. Unlike WML, which focuses on what the user sees, WMLScript has very few user interface capabilities. Instead, it is designed for adding robust computational capabilities to WML.

A microbrowser specification that defines how WML and WMLScript should be interpreted in the handset and presented to the user. It details key algorithms that the user agent must implement. It does not, however, suggest how content should be displayed. This is left to the discretion of each device manufacturer. It also defines the minimal functionality and basic user interface a WAP-compliant device must have. WAP Forum members are free to add additional capabilities to suit the specific needs of their customers.

A framework for wireless telephony applications (WTA), providing functions that carriers can use to integrate the telephone and microbrowser functions of a WAP device. For instance, carriers can write software in WML to handle incoming calls, voice mail retrieval, and call forwarding, or to make changes in the telephone's address book. Only two WTA functions are available to all application developers: You can make calls and send Dual Tone Multi-Frequency (DTMF) tones during a telephone call.

A lightweight protocol stack designed to minimize bandwidth requirements, work with a variety of wireless transports, and provide secure connections. It includes automatic compression of all transactions and content, plus support for interacting with and mapping to common Internet protocols.

As application developers, you don't need to know much about the WTA framework or the protocol stack to write good WAP software. You do, however, need to intimately understand the basic application model, the microbrowser specification, and WML and WMLScript.

Throughout the remainder of this book we refer to the WAP specification [WAP], which is formalized in *Official Wireless Application Protocol, The Complete Standard with Searchable CD-ROM,* by the Wireless Application Protocol Forum Ltd. (John Wiley & Sons, Inc., 1999, ISBN 0-471-32755-7). In addition to containing the WAP 1.0 specifications in printed form and in an extensive CD-ROM infobase, there is also a Web site at www.wiley.com/compbooks/WAP that contains updates to the specification, including the version 1.1 documents.

The Web Programming Model

The WAP programming model is based on the World Wide Web programming model. In the Web model, using a Web browser, a user requests a Uniform Resource Locator (URL). Figure 1.1 shows how you might request the site www.worldfaq.com using the URL field on Internet Explorer 4.5.

The Web browser parses that URL and sends an HTTP or HTTPS (Hyper Text Transfer Protocol Secure) request to a Web server. In this case, it sends a GET

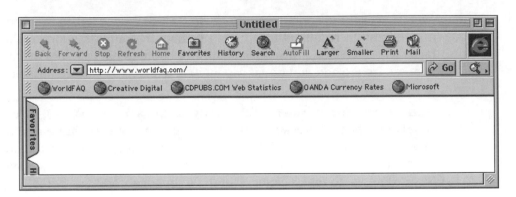

Figure 1.1   Requesting a URL.

request to the worldfaq server (see Chapter 5 for a more detailed explanation of GET requests):

```
GET / HTTP/1.1
```

requesting the root document from the server. The browser asks for the root document because the user specifies no specific document in the URL. The root is the Web-standard default document.

NOTE

The browser may send quite a bit of extra information along with the GET request in the form of HTTP headers. These headers might specify the name and version number of the browser, the content formats it can accept, and the date and time of the request. We don't show the headers here just to keep things simple for the moment. See Chapter 5, "Caching," for a more detailed explanation of HTTP headers.

The Web server receives and parses the request. If the request is legitimate, the server takes the contents of a static file, or the output from a CGI (Common Gateway Interface) program, and returns it as part of an HTTP response. The content part of the response is in HTML—the formatting and display language that Web browsers understand. In this case, the server retrieves the contents of the file index.html and appends it to a typical HTTP response.

NOTE

Web servers are set up to deliver a default file if none is specified. The most frequent defaults are typically index.htm and index.html, although they can be anything.

The response indicates the status of the request (in this case, an OK).

```
HTTP/1.1 200 OK

<HTML>
  <BODY>
```

```
    <P>WorldFAQ is a web site that provides information about places
       around the world. It is currently under construction.
    </P>
  </BODY>
</HTML>
```

The browser receives this message, parses the message body, and displays the contents of the file index.html on the browser's screen, formatted according to whatever conventions it uses. Figure 1.2 shows this response as displayed by Internet Explorer 4.5.

NOTE

Just like the GET request, the server might send back quite a bit of extra information to the browser in the form of HTTP headers. We've omitted them from this example for the sake of clarity. You can find more details on HTTP headers in Chapter 5, "Caching."

The World Wide Web, in a simplified nutshell, uses a basic transaction model whereby a Web browser (or some other program) requests a specific piece of information, using HTTP, and waits for a response to that request. Figure 1.3 summarizes the Web programming model. All the HTTP messages are text messages, not the most compact message format.

The entity requesting information from a server can be almost any type of program running on almost any type of hardware. As long as that entity can create a TCP/IP connection and generate a valid HTTP request, it can initiate a Web transaction. The commonly accepted term for entities that can originate HTTP requests is user agent.

Similarly, the computing entity that responds to a valid HTTP request can be any one of a wide variety of programs running on a wide variety of hardware. To reflect the general nature of responders, the commonly accepted term for an entity that responds to HTTP requests is content server.

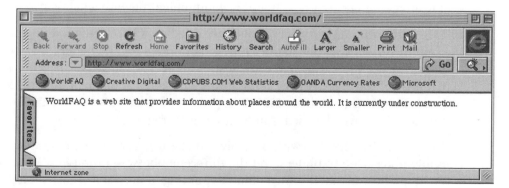

Figure 1.2 The formatted response.

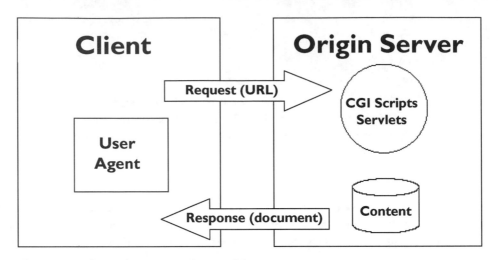

Figure 1.3 The Web programming model.

Of course, things are usually not as simple as they might appear at first glance. For instance, there are more than just HTTP and HTTPS protocols. There are many different types of URLs. There are several different types of requests a browser can make. Both the user agent and the content server can include lots of extra, optional information in special message headers. For all the gory details, you should read the official HTTP 1.1 specification [RFC2616]. Other useful references are [ROBERTS], [WONG], [STEVENS], and [NAIK].

Complicating matters is the possibility that there may be one or more gateways or proxy servers between the user agent requesting information and the server responding to that request. A gateway acts as an intermediary for some other server. The most common example of a gateway is a corporate firewall. It forwards requests from user agents outside a corporation's internal network, but only if they have permission to access the network. A gateway may or may not use HTTP to communicate with the server on whose behalf it's operating. Also, a user agent may not know that it is communicating with a gateway.

Like a gateway, a proxy server also intermediates between a user agent and a content server. Unlike a gateway, which operates for the benefit of a server, a proxy server's job is to make requests to a server on behalf of other clients. Because of this role, a proxy server generally has to implement both the request and response capabilities of HTTP. A proxy server can also be the final destination server, in which case it fulfills user agent requests internally.

Unless you're charged with actually writing a gateway or proxy server, you really don't need to understand the difference between the two. What you do need to know is that there's a computer sitting in between your user agent and your content server and that it provides certain functions.

NOTE

It's common to use the terms proxy server and gateway interchangeably, and we take that liberty throughout the rest of this book. In this chapter we favor proxy server because it's the correct term. In subsequent chapters we favor WAP gateway because it's shorter and rolls off the tongue more easily. If you're ever quizzed, just remember that a WAP gateway is actually a proxy server.

The WAP Programming Model

The WAP programming model, shown in Figure 1.4, is similar to the Web model, but with two crucial differences:

- There is always at least one WAP-cognoscente proxy server between the user agent and the content server. This proxy server's primary job is to translate WAP protocols from the user agent into HTTP to communicate with the content server and vice versa. It may also need to compile dynamically-generated WML and WMLScript programs coming from the content server prior to sending them back to the user agent.

- The communication between the user agent and the WAP proxy server is done with WAP protocols. The most important of these protocols is the Wireless Session Protocol (WSP), which is essentially a compact, binary form of HTTP 1.1.

The proxy is also key in managing other aspects of each transaction. For instance, the WAP proxy server is responsible for knowing the languages and character sets each WAP device understands and the languages the content server likes, and arbitrating between the two so that the user receives a coherent message. The WAP proxy may also provide additional optional services, services not included as part of the WAP specification, such as storing subscriber preferences, and e-mail management.

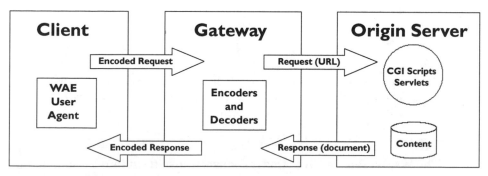

Figure 1.4   The WAP programming model.

NOTE The WAP proxy server and the content server needn't be located on separate machines or even in separate processes on the same machine. A content server may include WAP proxy capabilities. This might be suitable for configurations where you need to guarantee end-to-end transaction security without the overhead of a full-blown HTTPS connection, customized vertical solutions for a select audience, or applications that require guaranteed maximum response times, for instance.

Let's take the same transaction we discussed in the preceding section and look at the WAP equivalent.

Users request the URL www.worldfaq.com by entering the URL on their WAP device and pressing a special key signaling the device to fetch that URL, or perhaps by executing a program that makes the request on their behalf. Just like our previous example, the WAP user agent generates a GET request for www.worldfaq.com:

```
GET / HTTP/1.1
```

The user agent sends the GET request out over the airwaves to the WAP server, but first it transforms the message into a compact, binary format that is more suited to quick transmission over a wireless link than the ASCII text format of HTTP. When the WAP server receives the message, it parses it and realizes it needs to forward the message to the www.worldfaq.com server. It converts the message to a text-based HTTP GET and sends it on to www.worldfaq.com. The worldfaq server receives the request, parses it, and sends its response. In this case, the response is an HTTP OK message similar to the previous example, but with a Wireless Markup Language document, not an HTML document, as the message body. [ex1-01.wml]

```
HTTP/1.1 200 OK

<?xml version="1.0"?>
<!DOCTYPE <WML> PUBLIC "-//WAPFORUM//DTD <WML> 1.1//EN"
  "http://www.wapforum.org/DTD/wml_1.1.xml">

<wml>
  <card>
    <p>
      WorldFAQ is a web site that provides information about places
      around the world. It is currently under construction.
    </p>
  </card>
</wml>
```

The WAP server receives this response, translates it into a compact binary message and sends it out over the airwaves to the requesting device. The WAP device receives the response, parses the message body, and displays the con-

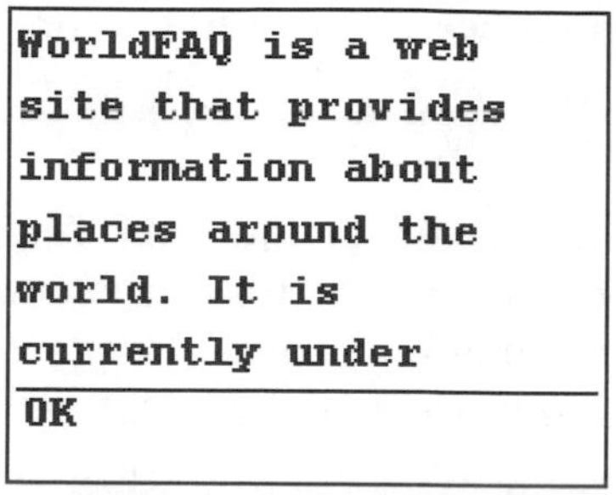

```
WorldFAQ is a web
site that provides
information about
places around the
world. It is
currently under
OK
```

Figure 1.5 The formatted WAP response.

tents of index.wml on the WAP user agent's screen. Figure 1.5 shows how it looks on the Phone.com browser.

The Web and WAP programming models are similar because of the WAP Forum's work at leveraging existing standards whenever possible. This gives application developers some significant advantages:

- The WAP model is simple and easy to understand. You can use all your current knowledge about how the Web works to create WAP applications.

- You can use a lot of existing software development tools. In fact, for creating dynamic content, you can use all existing CGI tools, available in a variety of programming languages, to serve up WAP documents to a user agent.

- WAP user agents are very simple. Consequently, WAP applications are also relatively simple. They focus on content presentation not content creation. You can isolate the bulk of the application logic and complex processing on the server. This separation makes it easier to create and maintain applications than many traditional programming models.

- If you have existing Web-based applications, you can preserve your investments in databases, proprietary content, application logic, and Application Programming Interfaces (APIs). In fact, there are commercially available WAP proxy servers that can take existing Web-based applications and automatically convert them to WAP applications on the fly by converting HTML responses to their WML equivalents. These proxy servers often generate suboptimal content for cell phones, however, and are usually not the best choice.

The WAP Architecture

Now that you have a basic understanding of the WAP programming model, let's take a more detailed look at the overall WAP architecture, which is illustrated in Figure 1.6. [WAP] provides more details on the WAP architecture as well.

WAP has a layered architecture similar to the well-known International Standards Organization (ISO) network model. You can find detailed descriptions of all of the layers in [WAP]. Here's a quick overview.

As application developers, we're most interested in the WAP Application Environment (WAE), the topmost layer of the architecture. It encompasses general device specifications, the programming languages (WML and WMLScript) needed to write WAP applications, the telephony APIs (WTA) for accessing telephony functions from WAE programs, and a set of well-defined content formats including graphics, phone book records, and calendar information. We cover the Application Environment in much more detail in the next section.

The next layer of the WAP architecture is the Wireless Session Protocol. The simplest description of WSP is that it is a binary, tokenized version of HTTP 1.1 designed specifically for browser-like transactions on low-bandwidth wireless networks that have relatively long latency. In addition, the WAP Forum went beyond what HTTP can do and added the ability to quickly suspend and resume connections.

Perhaps most important, they also added reliable (guaranteed delivery) and unreliable content push, enabling a server to send messages and documents to a user agent without being asked. In our description of both the Web and WAP programming models, the user agent initiates the transaction. However, it can be very useful for a server to notify a WAP device of an incoming telephone call, e-mail, fax, or paging message. Content push is designed to provide those types of services.

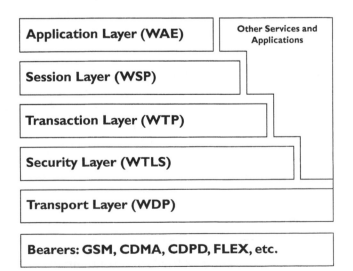

Figure 1.6 The WAP Architecture.

The third layer of the WAP architecture is the Wireless Transaction Protocol (WTP), a lightweight transaction protocol that supports the following types of messages: unreliable one-way requests (unguaranteed push), reliable one-way requests (guaranteed push), and reliable two-way request/response (browser-like) transactions. It has been optimized for wireless networks by eliminating the overhead, such as packet sequencing, used by TCP/IP.

The Wireless Transport Layer Security (WTLS) is a security protocol based on the industry-standard Transport Layer Security (TLS), formerly know as Secure Sockets Layer (SSL). It provides data integrity, privacy, authentication, and denial-of-service protection services. As a developer, you can activate WTLS the same way you do a Web browser: use HTTPS as your protocol in a URL instead of HTTP.

The final layer of the WAP architecture is the Wireless Datagram Protocol (WDP). This is the layer that provides a consistent interface between multiple wireless carriers and the higher layers of the architecture. Underneath the WDP are a number of networks, including CDPD (Cellular Digital Packet Data), GSM (Global System for Mobile Communication), iDEN (Integrated Digital Enhanced Network), and CDMA (Code Division Multiple Access).

The WAP Application Environment

The WAP Application Environment is that part of the overall WAP architecture that is available to application developers for creating WAP applications. It has several components:

- **A microbrowser specification** that defines how WML and WMLScript should be interpreted in the handset and presented to the user.

- **A markup language** (WML) designed for creating device-independent WAP applications.

- **The WMLScript scripting language** for extending the power of WML.

- **A framework for Wireless Telephony Applications,** providing mechanisms that carriers can use to implement functions that integrate the telephone and microbrowser functions of a WAP device.

In addition, the WAE assumes that there is a WAP-compatible proxy server available that translates between WAP and Internet communications protocols as well as between WAP and HTTP-formatted requests and responses. It may also provide caching servers to speed up access to content, in addition to compiling WML and WMLScript programs into their binary equivalents for delivery to and execution by a WAP-compatible device. The WAP proxy server may pro-

vide other services such as translating Internet graphics into formats under-
stood by a WAP device.

NOTE
A properly deployed WAP network must include a proxy server. The server may reside on a separate system, or it may be part of a content server.

The Microbrowser

We already described the basic characteristics of the WAP microbrowser—it's
a process that implements the WAP programming model. That means that, like
an HTML browser, it manages the mechanics of submitting requests and receiving and parsing responses, and all the secondary tasks associated with that job.

The microbrowser includes the WML and WMLScript interpreters. It knows
how to interpret those languages' bytecodes and decides exactly how to display
WML and WMLScript language constructs on the device's display. It also needs
to have an exact, detailed understanding of URLs, because that's how WAP
applications are requested. To manage each transaction, the microbrowser also
needs to know how to interact with the layers of the WAP protocol stack to initiate a request, trigger a secure transaction, suspend and resume a session if
necessary, and so on.

A WAP microbrowser may have additional capabilities. For instance, it may
have a cache much like the cache in an HTML browser. If so, it needs to know
what's in the cache, when to retrieve a URL from the cache, and when to
remove an item from the cache. Unlike HTML, the Wireless Application Environment has variables that have a lifetime longer than individual documents,
simplifying applications development. The microbrowser needs to know their
names, their values, and how to substitute them in expressions when necessary.
The microbrowser may also have a history stack that contains the N most-
recently visited URLs.

The microbrowser needs to understand some of the HTTP 1.1 protocol, in its
binary tokenized form, although it's up to the WAP gateway to deal with the
bulk of the translation between WAP and HTTP protocols. When the microbrowser sends a request, it needs to know what headers to include with that
request so that the request makes sense to the WAP proxy server and, ulti-
mately, to the content server. It also needs to know how to interpret the headers that are included with every response.

Finally, the WAP microbrowser is supposed to work in the hardware environment the WAP Forum is targeting—limited RAM and ROM, small screens, limited input/output capabilities, and wireless network connections. For
something that's supposed to fit in such a limited environment, the microbrowser needs to know how to do a lot of things.

Wireless Markup Language

The Wireless Markup Language, which is explained in detail in Chapter 2, is a tag-based language like HTML, designed for hardware-constrained, narrowband wireless devices with limited input/output capabilities. WML documents use a card-and-deck metaphor, whereby a card is a single unit of user interaction and a deck is a related set of cards. Like an HTML page, a card typically contains some viewable content and perhaps some user choices for selecting an option, entering some data, or navigating to another card. Instructions in a card may invoke new static or dynamic decks from content servers.

The WML specification defines the intent of individual language tags, not how a particular user agent should implement those tags. Each WAP device vendor has a great deal of latitude, as you will see in Chapter 4, in deciding how to present WML tags to the user, the data entry mechanisms available, the size of the screen, and so on. WML is user-interface independent.

WML has the following general capabilities:

- **Support for text and images,** including presentation hints like line breaks, formatting, and other placement clues. WAP-compliant devices are not required to support images.

- **Support for user input,** including text entry, choice lists, and controls that invoke tasks. For instance, you can assign a URL to a specific device button such that, when the user presses that button, a GET request is sent to that URL's server.

- **A variety of navigation mechanisms,** based on the Internet-standard URL naming scheme, that lets you move between the cards in a deck or from deck to deck. Each WAP device may also incorporate a history mechanism for cards already visited, so that the user can revisit a previous card just by pressing a Back button, much like revisiting a previous page in a Web browser.

- **Support for multiple languages and dialects** through the use of the Unicode character set.

- **State and context management features,** most notably variables that can be passed from deck to deck, variable substitution capabilities, and user agent caching of variables and decks to maximize cache hits and minimize server requests.

WMLScript

WMLScript is a lightweight but extensible procedural scripting language designed to enhance WML, somewhat like JavaScript enhances HTML documents. WML handles input and output, content rendering, and event processing, but it has no serious computational capabilities. WMLScript fills that void. WMLScript lets you define functions that you can call from WML programs. Within these functions you have the full power of "if . . . then . . . else" statements, assignment statements, function calls, loop constructs, weakly typed basic data types such as Booleans and integers, and more. WMLScript also includes a full, robust set of assignment, logical, arithmetic, and comparison operators.

WMLScript is also an extensible language through the use of libraries. WMLScript 1.1, the version that corresponds to the WAP 1.1 specification, includes floating-point, string, URL, and dialog libraries, a library for basic language functions like type conversions and string parsing, and a library of functions for interacting with the WAP microbrowser.

Although WMLScript can be extended with new libraries, the WAP Forum has not provided an open set of APIs so that third parties can define WMLScript libraries.

Wireless Telephony Applications Interface

Since WAP devices are inherently telephones, but with a lot more smarts than your average telephone, it makes sense to integrate telephony capabilities with WAP. This is the goal of the Wireless Telephony Applications Interface (WTAI), that part of the Wireless Telephony Application specification that details the APIs. Almost all of the WTAI features are designed specifically for cellular network operators. It lets them quickly create advanced telephone features with a special set of APIs that can be accessed from WML and WMLScript.

Using the WAE to create telephony applications has some distinct advantages over the current method of writing device-specific applications that are burned into a handset's ROM. Most notably, a cellular carrier can easily upgrade a WTAI application just by using the WAP microbrowser to fetch the latest version of the program. Also, they can write WTAI applications that can work on all WAP-compliant devices and all WAP-supported networks.

Although WTAI applications can take full advantage of the document-centric programming model supported by WML and WMLScript, most of the WTAI APIs for carriers use an asynchronous event-driven model, which more closely models the real activity of a telephone network. For instance, an incoming call is an event that is triggered by an activity outside the scope of a WAP device. You have no idea when it might occur. WTAI applications have to be able to respond to these types of events.

Because WTAI is designed primarily for carriers, we ignore it throughout the rest of this book.

NOTE

If you have a WAP device that uses any of the WTAI functions, it will probably have a direct connection to a WTA server, a cellular carrier server designed specifically for supporting telephony functions. The interaction between the device and the WTA server is usually direct, with no WAP proxy server in the middle of the connection. The WTAI functions may, however, use one or more layers of the WAP protocol stack to implement communication with the server.

Content Formats

All content that moves back and forth from user agent to proxy server to content server and back has to be in specific WAP-compatible formats. As we've discussed, the message formats comply with HTTP 1.1 message specifications. Between the user agent and the proxy server, the HTTP formats are compressed. Between the proxy server and the content server, they are standard text-based HTTP.

What about the message bodies, the critical information that's included with each response? When a content server dynamically creates a WML document to send back to a WAP user agent, it creates source code, a poor choice for content that is sent over a wireless link because of its bulk. The WAE includes specifications for binary encoding of both WML and WMLScript programs (see [WAP] for details). Each proxy server is responsible for taking the WML and WMLScript source code and compiling it into its binary equivalent, which is passed back to the user agent for execution. The user agent contains bytecode interpreters for WML and WMLScript.

It's possible for a WAP-compatible content server to emit WML and WMLScript bytecodes directly, bypassing the encoding step and taking the proxy server out of the transaction. The problem with that approach is that not only does the content server have to contain the language encoders, it also has to have decoders to understand the WSP-encoded requests arriving from user agents. Most applications developers would probably rather not deal with the nuts and bolts of compilers and protocol converters, and, instead, would prefer to focus on their application.

In addition to encoded WML and WMLScript, WAE supports four other content formats: (Wireless Bitmap) WBMP, MIME multipart messages, vCard, and vCalendar.

WBMP. Although there are several widely accepted Internet graphics formats, most notably Graphics Interchange Format (GIF) and Joint Photographic Experts Group (JPEG), none are well suited to transmission over wireless networks. The WAP Forum has defined the Wireless Bitmap format. It is an extensible, compact, and scaleable format that is optimized for user agents with minimal processing power. Although WBMP is the de facto WAP graphics format, WAP devices may also support additional standard Internet graphics types such as GIF.

MIME multipart messages. MIME originated as a message format for Internet e-mail, but it has proliferated into a general-purpose set of message formats that are also used for HTTP request and response messages (refer to [RFC822] and [RFC2045] for detailed discussion of MIME formats). At its simplest level, a MIME message is a bunch of ASCII text. In our case, that might be a WML document returned from a content server to a WAP proxy server in response to a request for a document. Slightly more complex is the case where that ASCII program gets encoded into WML bytecode for transmission back to the user agent. MIME handles that quite easily as well.

Things get interesting when you want to send multiple messages as part of one larger message, something that is very useful in a wireless situation. For instance, let's say you request a static document from a content server. Normally, if that document contains a reference to a graphics file, the document is first fetched and parsed, and then the graphics file is fetched in a separate request. In a wireless network, this can add a lot of overhead to a simple transaction. If you know absolutely that you need the graphics file, why not send it at the same time you send the original document? This saves you from initiating and waiting for the second transaction. MIME multipart messages let you bundle multiple documents (or graphics, or binary files, or anything else that MIME understands) into a single message. We explain this in more detail in Chapter 6.

vCard and vCalendar. The vCard and vCalendar formats are international standards that define the formats of business cards and appointment messages (see [VCARD] and [VCAL] for details). Although they are currently officially part of the WAP specification, at this time they are not widely supported by the various WAP vendors. We don't discuss them any further in this book.

User Agents

So far, we've referred to a WAP device and all the software in it that requests information from content servers as a user agent. This term is clearly defined in the HTTP 1.1 specification, one of the key specs used to define WAP 1.1. An HTTP 1.1 user agent is "The client which originates a request. These are often browsers, editors, spiders (Web-traversing robots), or other end user tools."

The WAE specification makes it very clear that it defines a general framework, not a rigid set of specifications. This framework approach results in a certain degree of ambiguity over the use of the term user agent. At times, the WAP specs use the term in the same sense as the HTTP 1.1 specification—as the client that originates the request, implying that the microbrowser is a user agent.

The WAP specs also used the term user agent in a more specific sense. There may be a user agent that displays WML documents, or one that executes WMLScript programs. There might also be a user agent that provides Wireless Telephony Applications support. Future specifications may define additional user agents as well. The differentiation has nothing to do with the ability to make a request. Instead, it's based on a class of service.

The WAP specs also indicate that there is no guarantee that any of the user agents you might find in a WAP handset are in control of the device. There may be other processes that manage the overall coordination of what happens when a WAP device is turned on. There may also be additional applications, such as message editors or phone books, that demand hardware resources. All the spec does is try and define how WAP user agents behave—they are fundamental services and formats that are needed to ensure interoperability among implementations. This approach suggests that a user agent is an execution thread that has a life of its own separate from other user agents.

Regardless of how you dice and slice the terminology, the important question is what can you, as an application developer, expect to find in a WAP device that you can use to build applications? At this stage, the WAP Forum is still wrestling with the question of the required and optional parts of the WAE spec. It appears as though they will require the following in all WAP devices:

- WML and WMLScript interpreters
- WBMP graphics support, if the device supports graphics
- The public WTAI functions
- The entire WAP protocol stack, except for the Wireless Transport Layer Security, which is required only in devices that support secure transactions

The engine underlying all of these capabilities, and in some respects tying them all together by providing common services, is the microbrowser.

Throughout the rest of this book, we employ the term user agent in the collective sense to mean all the WAP user agents that are available in a WAP device. When necessary, we also use it to identify individual WAE services, as in the WML user agent. Just keep in mind that it's fuzzy terminology, but it shouldn't interfere with your understanding of WAP.

Regardless of what you call the various WAP components—user agents, services, or execution threads—they need to interact with each other. Here's a summary of how they do it:

- You can link to WMLScript functions from WML documents just by using a URL. The URL document name specifies the location of the WMLScript library; the URL fragment name identifies the function name within the library.

- You cannot call WML documents directly from WMLScript functions, but you can access microbrowser variables, which can affect subsequent WML execution. You can also specify in a WMLScript function what WML card you would like to go to once the WMLScript function finishes.

- You can call WTAI public functions from both WML documents and WMLScript functions. From WML, you use a specific URL that identifies the WTAI function you want to call. From a WMLScript program, you can access a WTAI public function just by calling it.

Building WAP Applications

In Chapter 2, we delve right into the details of building WAP applications using WML. Before we do, we want to prepare you a bit for what you're going to need to do before you can actually write and test WAP code.

Here's what you need to write and test WAP applications:

A WAP 1.1-compliant software developer's kit (SDK). There are a variety of SDKs available, many of them at no charge. Check the WAP Forum Web site for a current list. They typically run on Windows 95/98 or some variant of Unix. Of course, we strongly encourage you to use the Phone.com SDK.

A Web server. This can be on the same machine as your SDK or it can be a server that you can access from your SDK.

You need to set the server up to properly recognize and serve up valid WAP MIME types. As of this writing, those are:

MIME Type/Subtype	Extension	File Type
text/vnd.wap.wml	wml	WML source code
application/vnd.wap.wml-wbxml	wmlc	Compiled WML
text/vnd.wap.wmlscript	wmls	WMLScript source code
application/vnd.wap.wmlscriptc	wmlsc	Compiled WMLScript
image/vnd.wap.wmpb	wbmp	Wireless bitmap

Most of the SDKs use a simulator that looks and acts like a typical WAP device. Integrated into the simulator, however, are WML and WMLScript encoders. Using a standard text editor, you create WML and WMLScript source files and put them in the appropriate places on your Web server. You can then invoke a WML program from a command line on the simulator. It gets loaded into the simulator, parsed, and checked for errors. If there are none, it gets loaded by the simulator's bytecode interpreter and executed.

Most of the SDKs provide some additional features, such as tools for looking at the contents of the cache, the current source code deck being executed, variable names, the history stack, and so on. At this stage, WAP is relatively new technology. Like all new technologies, the development tools meet basic needs and will evolve as more application developers enter the market.

Once you reach the point where you want to create and test dynamic Web content, you first have to decide how you want to create that content. Most Web servers support Perl scripts and C programs for CGI content generation. Others support Java servlets, active server pages, and other mechanisms. Check your documentation to find out what's available and how you set it up. Usually it involves setting some configuration flags to activate the CGI capabilities and tell your server how to recognize CGI programs when they are listed in a URL. This is usually done by file extension or location within the server's directory structure.

Once you start generating dynamic content, you may want to delve into the details of how the WAP request/response cycle works at its lower levels. To do this, you need to be able to examine both the HTTP headers that are generated by the SDK simulators and included in the requests they send to the server, and the response headers that are sent back from the server. We discuss this in detail in Chapter 5, "Caching."

For the former, you need to enable detailed logging on the Web server so that it outputs all the headers to some sort of log file. Not all Web servers can give you that level of detail. If that's a problem, you can probably grab copies of those headers yourself within your CGI programs and write them to log files.

Some of the SDKs let you see everything that comes back from the server to the simulator; others hide that level of detail. If the SDK you are using doesn't let you see the response headers, use Telnet. We also describe how to do this in Chapter 5, "Caching."

Finally, you need to test your application in the real world. To do this, you need a WAP-compatible device, wireless network coverage for that device, a way for that device to access a WAP-compliant proxy server, and a way for the server to find your application. Many of the WAP vendors have gateways you can use if you join their developer program. You might need a publicly visible Web site that the gateway can access. For instance, if you join the Phone.com developer program, you can test your application using one of Phone.com's controlled access WAP proxy servers.

Now that you've got an idea of what WAP is all about, let's talk about developing WAP applications.

CHAPTER 2

Wireless Markup Language

W ireless Markup Language (WML) version 1.1 is designed for creating applications that run on small, mobile devices such as cellular telephones and personal digital assistants. WML's origins are closely tied to a variety of Internet standards. As a result, WML looks somewhat like Hyper Text Markup Language (HTML) [HTML4], the lingua franca of the vast majority of Internet-based World Wide Web (WWW) transactions. HTML is itself based on Standardized General Markup Language (SGML) [ISO8879].

WML Basics

WML inherits most of its syntactic constructs from Extensible Markup Language (XML) [XML], a restricted subset of SGML, and a World Wide Web standard for Internet markup languages. WML is a formally defined XML application.

Elements

If you know HTML, SGML, or XML, WML should look familiar. WML is defined by a set of elements. Each element has a unique lowercase source code tag that can be in one of two forms. The first form is identical to HTML:

```
<tag>
```

.

```
. tag contents
.
</tag>
```

The second form

```
<tag/>
```

is used when the element cannot contain any visible content, or when an element that can have content is empty. As an example, the WML line break tag cannot have any content. Its format is

```
<br/>
```

Since each WML element has a unique tag name, it's common to use the terms element and tag interchangeably.

Attributes

Each WML element has zero or more attributes that describe various aspects of the element. Attributes are declared by adding a list of lowercase keywords and their settings, in single or double quotation marks, to the starting tag. The attribute/value pairs appear after the opening tag label.

For example, the paragraph element has two optional attributes, align and mode. They describe the text alignment and word-wrapping characteristics of the text that follows the paragraph's <p> tag. Here's a sample paragraph element that specifies left-justified text that wraps from one display line to the next.

```
<p
  align="left"
  mode="wrap"
>
  .
  . paragraph content
  .
</p>
```

There is one optional attribute that can be used with all WML elements that can contain displayable content: xml:lang. This attribute defines the natural or formal language, roughly equivalent to a spoken or written dialect, used by that element's content. It gives the WML user agent a hint it may use to properly display the content. You can find a list of valid language tags in [RFC1766]. We discuss languages and language tags more fully in Chapter 7, "Internationalization (I18N)."

There are two other optional attributes that can be used with all WML elements: id and class. An element's id is a unique identifier for that element within a deck, the smallest unit of WML that can be transmitted to a WAP device. The class attribute affiliates an element, using its id, with one or more class names. All elements with the same class attribute, within a deck, are considered members of the same class.

The id attributes, with the exception of the <card> id attribute, and the class attribute, are used primarily for server-side operations, such as style sheet transformations, and are currently ignored by WML user agents. Eventually, WAP user agents will most likely support the Document Object Model (DOM). These attributes are necessary to support DOM.

In subsequent sections of this book, when the attributes for specific elements are defined, we usually exclude the id, class, and wml:lang attributes for brevity's sake. You can always assume that an element can have an id and class and that any element that can have content can also have the xml:lang attribute.

Syntax Presentation

Throughout the rest of this chapter, we informally describe WML elements and their attributes. We first present an element using a form similar to the paragraph element we just described. We state the element name, followed by a list of its attributes, followed by a list of things that may be included as part of the element's content:

```
<element>
  attribute list and their possible values
>
  things that can be included inside this element
</element>
```

The attribute list includes all possible attributes, except for xml:lang, class, and id (id is included for cards) and their values. If an attribute can take on one value from a discrete set of values, we list the choices on the same line, separated by vertical bars. The default value for an attribute is highlighted with bold text. Attributes that are required are also highlighted using bold text. For example, here's the complete syntax for the paragraph element:

```
<p>
  align="left | center | right"
  mode="wrap | nowrap"
>
  <a>, <anchor>, <br>, DENTRY, <do>, FMTTEXT, <img>, <table>, TEXT
</p>
```

There are different types of entities that may be included in the content of an element. The most common are other elements. For instance, as shown in the preceding example, you can include images (**<img>**), URLs (**<anchor>**, **<a>**), and tables (**<table>**) in a paragraph.

We have created a set of abbreviations, listed in Table 2.1, to summarize more commonly recurring groups of elements and other things that may be included in an element or attribute. The abbreviations have uppercase names so they are easy to identify. These abbreviations probably won't all make sense at this point unless you already have some experience with WML. As you read through this book they should become more familiar.

In the appendixes of this book, we have also included some WML syntax summaries. Appendix A is an alphabetical list of all WML elements, their attributes, and the things they can have for content. Appendix A is simply a summary of the individual element descriptions in this chapter.

Appendix B is a one-page cross-reference chart showing the elements that can be included in WML elements. It's designed for quickly figuring out, for instance, if you can include a **<refresh>** element in a paragraph.

Appendix C is a one-page cross-reference chart showing the attributes used by each element. It is designed for quickly figuring out, for instance, which element you have to use to specify text alignment.

Although we have spent a lot of time preparing these appendixes to make it easier for you to figure out the nuances of WML, there is only one authoritative source: the WML Document Type Definition (DTD). It is the formal WML

Table 2.1   WML Content Abbreviations

DENTRY	Data entry elements: ‹**input**›, ‹**select**›,and ‹**fieldset**›
DOCHOICES	Valid ‹**do**› choices: **accept, prev, help, reset, options, delete,** and **unknown**
FMTTEXT	Elements for formatting text: ‹**em**›, ‹**strong**›, ‹**b**›, ‹**i**›, ‹**u**›, ‹**big**›, and ‹**small**›
ID	An XML-compatible name that uniquely identifies an element within a document
IEVENTS	Card-level intrinsic events: **onenterforward, onenterbackward,** and **ontimer**
LENGTH	An integer to indicate length in pixels, or an integer plus a percent sign to indicate length as a percentage of the screen width
NAME	A valid XML name—letters, digits, and underscore character
NUMBER	A valid integer greater than or equal to zero
STRING	Single-line Unicode 2.0 text that is not parsed
TEXT	Multiline Unicode text that is not parsed
VDATA	A **STRING** with possible variable references
URL	An absolute or relative Uniform Resource Identifier (URI), URL, or Uniform Resource Name (URN), possibly containing variable references

description of WML. You can find it at www.wapforum.org/DTD/wml_1.1.xml. When in doubt, go to the source.

URLs

WML is a markup language for creating Web-based applications. It needs a mechanism for referring to content and programs on Web sites. The WAP forum chose to use existing Web standards to provide this mechanism.

WML uses absolute URLs to refer to content located at specific Web sites or Internet Protocol (IP) addresses. In addition, WML also uses relative URLs, where the base URL of a WML document is the Web location of that document. Refer to [RFC2396] for a definition of URLs and URL character sets.

WML also employs the concept of fragment anchors, as used by HTML, to point to locations within documents. A fragment anchor starts with a URL, followed by a hash mark ("#"), followed by the fragment name. For WML documents, a fragment name is the name of a specific card within the document. See the next section of this chapter for a detailed description of cards.

Context

At any point in time, a WML-compliant user agent has a context. The context includes all currently defined variables and their values, and a history stack of the URLs that the user agent has recently visited. (The depth of the history stack depends on the user agent implementation.) A WML user agent must include a user interface construct, much like the Back button on HTML browsers, for navigating backwards in the history stack.

As you will see, there are ways to set variables and substitute their values in expressions. There are also commands that let you pop the top element on the history stack and go to it, and go to a new URL, pushing the current URL onto the history stack. You can also clear all variables and the stack by creating a new context.

The user agent context is persistent. It remains in the device, between document renderings, network transactions, and other events. Although not required by the WAP specifications, a good user agent might maintain the context during power-down—it saves network cost for the user. It is also global—variables and the history stack are available to all program components.

Character Set

WML uses the XML character set, ISO/IEC-10646 [ISO10646], which is, for all practical purposes, currently identical to Unicode 2.0 [UNICODE]. You can use any proper Unicode subset such as US-ASCII or UTF-8. If you use a subset other than US-ASCII you have to explicitly declare the character set using HTTP headers, meta information, or in a deck's XML prologue declaration using the **encoding** attribute. The XML prologue is described in the next section of this chapter. See Chapter 7, "Internationalization (I18N)," for a more detailed discussion about WML character sets.

Like XML, WML supports numbered character entities to refer to specific characters in the Unicode character set. Numbered entities can be expressed in either decimal or hexadecimal format. The decimal format starts with an ampersand and a pound sign ("&#"). The hexadecimal format starts with an ampersand, a pound sign, and an upper or lowercase "x" ("&#x"). The following encodings for a space (" ") character are equivalent:

```
&#32;          &#x20  ;
```

Special Characters

WML reserves several punctuation characters for its own use. To include them in formatted text, you have to use special character representations shown in the following. The semicolon (";") is part of the character entity and must be included. If it's not, a WML user agent interprets the representation as a series of individual characters, not as a special character representation.

CHARACTER	CHARACTER ELEMENT
‹	< (less than)
›	> (greater than)
'	' (apostrophe)
"	" (double quote)
&	& (ampersand)
$	$$ (dollar sign)
Nonbreaking space	
Soft hyphen	&shy;

A nonbreaking space is a space that cannot be removed. Normally, a WAP user agent removes sequential, redundant white-space characters of all types.

A soft hyphen is a hyphen in a text string that is not displayed unless it falls at the logical end of a line as rendered by the user agent.

Text

WML elements, attributes, and enumerated attribute values must be lowercase. All other language constructs are case sensitive. For instance, the variables **Var1, var1,** and **VAR1** are all different.

WML white space includes the following characters: newline (decimal 10 in the Unicode character set), carriage return (decimal 13 in Unicode), space (decimal 32 in Unicode), and tab (decimal 9 in Unicode). Except where noted, WML treats multiple white-space characters as a single character. The code examples in this book use carriage returns and tabs to improve readability. They are not necessary and are treated as normal white space by WML compilers and user agents.

When specifying attributes, you have to separate individual attribute/value pairs with white space, but you cannot use white space between an attribute name, the equals sign ("="), and the attribute's value.

Comments

WML comments use the same format as HTML comments:

```
<!-- comment -->
```

They can be included anywhere that an element can occur. Comments cannot be put in the middle of an element definition.

Quotation Marks

WML treats single ("'") and double quote ("'"") characters equally when used to delimit attribute values. You can enclose attribute settings with either character. If you want to use one of the quote characters in a literal, you need to enclose it with the other type of quote character. The following two elements are equivalent:

```
<p align="right" mode="wrap" >
  A paragraph.
</p>

<p align='right' >
  A paragraph.
</p>
```

Decks

A deck is the smallest unit of WML that is transmitted to a WAP device. A deck is, conceptually, a page of information, much like a Web page with which a user interacts. Throughout this book, we use the terms deck and document interchangeably.

WAP is designed for mobile devices operating over modest-bandwidth (on the order of 1 kilobit per second) wireless networks. Because of the characteristics of wireless networks, it's worthwhile to try and keep deck sizes as small as possible, preferably under 1 kilobyte.

Some WAP servers have an upper limit on the size of a deck they can transmit in one transaction, forcing you to keep your decks small. If you find yourself designing a particularly complex application, you may need to break it up into multiple decks to circumvent these restrictions.

A properly formed WML deck starts with a prologue, followed by some optional header information, followed by a sequence of cards. A card is a single unit of user interaction, such as a choice menu or screen of text. Ideally, a card's visible content fits entirely on the small screen of a mobile device. The content may, however, be larger than the screen, requiring horizontal or vertical scrolling. If the content contains a group of data entry fields that don't all fit onto the screen, the user agent may choose to present each of them on its own separate screen.

Since WAP applications are XML programs, they must start out with a valid XML prologue containing the XML version and a pointer to the XML definition of the language being used. All the samples in this book, which are also included on the companion CD-ROM, use the following prologue:

```
<?xml version="1.0"?>
<!DOCTYPE <WML> PUBLIC "-//WAPFORUM//DTD <WML> 1.1//EN"
  "http://www.wapforum.org/DTD/wml_1.1.xml">
```

The prologue is used by WAP compilers and servers to manage the creation and execution of WAP programs. The devices executing WAP programs never see this information.

For brevity's sake, we don't include the prologue in the code listings in the book (with the exception of the next example), but they are included in the CD-ROM source code files.

A deck's prologue is followed by the actual deck, delimited by the **<wml>** tag. Here's the syntax of a deck. Notice that a deck has no attributes.

```
<wml>
  <head>
  <template>
  <card>
</wml>
```

There are three elements that are valid in a deck:

The **<head>** element contains optional information about the deck as a whole, including access control and meta information. We describe the **<head>** element shortly.

The **<template>** element contains optional information about deck-level event bindings. See "Deck-Level Events" in this chapter for more details about the **<template>** element.

Cards define the user interface and processing logic of the deck. A deck must have one or more cards in order to be a valid WAP program. We describe cards in more detail in the next section of this chapter.

Here is an example structure for a properly formed WAP 1.1-compliant deck:

```
<?xml version="1.0"?>
<!DOCTYPE WML PUBLIC "-//WAPFORUM//DTD WML 1.1//EN"
  "http://www.wapforum.org/DTD/wml_1.1.xml">
<wml>
  <head>
    .
    . head information
    .
  </head>
  <template>
    .
    . template definition
    .
  </template>
  <card>
    .
    . card definition
    .
  </card>
    .
    . optional additional cards
    .
</wml>
```

The **<head>** element has no attributes but can contain two other elements. Its syntax is:

```
<head>
  <access>, <meta>
</head>
```

The **<access>** element lets you specify access controls, in the form of a domain name and path, for a WML deck. Its syntax is

```
<access
  domain="STRING"
  path="STRING"
>
```

domain is a valid partial or full domain name. Its default value is the current deck's domain. **path** is a valid relative or absolute path name. Its default value is "/".

As the user agent navigates from deck to deck, when it encounters a deck with access controls, it compares the domain of the referring deck to the **domain** and

path attributes of the controlled deck. If the domain and path match, the new deck is loaded and executed. Matching is done against full domain and path components. For instance, the domain **forum.org** matches **wap.forum.org,** but not **www.wapforum.org.** Similarly, the path "/X/Y" matches "/X" but not "/XY".

Similar to the HTML **<META>** tag, the WML **<meta>** element is for transmitting generic meta information about a deck. Its syntax is:

```
<meta
  http-equiv="STRING"
  name="STRING"
  forua="true | false"
  content="STRING"
  scheme="STRING"
>
```

There are two types of meta information you can specify, but you can specify only one type of meta information per **<meta>** element.

The first, **http-equiv,** defines an HTTP header, where the **http-equiv** value is the header name and the **content** value is the header's setting. A WAP gateway should convert an **http-equiv <meta>** element to an HTTP response header before sending the deck on to the user agent. For more information about HTTP headers and WML, see Chapter 5, "Caching."

The second type of **<meta>** information is **name** information, indicating that the meta information specified by the **content** attribute is anything other than an HTTP equivalent header. **name <meta>** elements are ignored by WAP user agents.

The **forua** attribute, if set to **true,** indicates that the meta information should be delivered to the user agent if the user agent supports the **<meta>** element (it's not required to do so).

The **scheme** attribute specifies secondary information for interpreting the meta data.

For a more detailed discussion of meta information, you should take a look at [RFC2616] for details on HTTP headers, and [HTML4] for details on the HTML **<META>** tag.

Cards

The heart of a WAP program is in the cards, so to speak. Much like an HTML program, a card contains a mixture of formatting information, displayable content, and processing instructions. Each card in a deck must contain one or more elements. The information inside the elements falls into two basic categories: instructions and content.

WML lets you manage, at a fairly high level, typical runtime tasks such as data entry, navigation, and responding to device events like keystrokes. Content includes unformatted and formatted text, choice lists, and user prompts, among other things.

When a WAP-compatible device receives a deck (or executes a ROM- or RAM-based deck), it examines the deck-level elements, looks for the first card in the deck, examines its attributes and other settings, and then displays the content of the first card in the deck (unless instructed otherwise). Program execution continues in response to user input or other events, such as the expiration of a timer, that might occur. At some point, the current deck probably links to another deck, starting the cycle over again.

Here's the syntax for the **<card>** element:

```
<card
  id="ID"
  newcontext="true | false"
  onenterbackward="URL"
  onenterforward="URL"
  ontimer="URL"
  ordered="true | false"
  title=VDATA
>
  <onevent>, <do>, <p>, <timer>
</card>
```

Cards have several attributes, all of which are optional:

id. The card's name. It can be used as a fragment identifier in a URL.

newcontext. A Boolean attribute that instructs the device to remove all context-specific variables, clear the history stack, and reset the device to a well-known state.

oneventbackward. A URL to go to if this card is executed as the result of a **<prev>** task. See "Tasks and Events" in this chapter for more details.

oneventforward. A URL to go to if this card is executed as the result of a **<go>** task. See "Tasks and Events" in this chapter for more details.

ontimer. A URL to go to if a **<timer>** element expires. See "Timers" in this chapter for more details.

ordered. A Boolean attribute indicating that the card's content should be presented in a list format. See "Complex Data" in this chapter for more details on the list format.

title. The label used for the card if the user bookmarks it. The title may also be displayed by some user agents.

At first glance, it may seem as though you cannot do much with a card, considering the small number of elements that a card can contain. When looking at WML element definitions, however, you have to think in a nested fashion: A card can contain paragraphs (the **<p>** element). Paragraphs can contain all sorts of other elements. In fact, you cannot put any visible content in a card without enclosing it in a paragraph element. See the next section of this chapter or Appendix A for a complete list of the elements that can be included in a paragraph.

Here's a complete WAP document (minus the XML header), the ever popular Hello World, showing how simple a WAP deck can be [ex2-01.wml].

```
<wml>
  <card>
    <p>
      Hello World.
    </p>
  </card>
</wml>
```

Figure 2.1 shows what that deck looks like running on the Phone.com browser.

Each card in a deck must contain one or more elements that can be characterized as either content, event handling instructions, or data entry elements. The next three sections of this chapter discuss these three types of elements in detail.

Content

The most basic information you can include in a card is content—strings of characters that are displayed on the screen of a WAP-compliant device. WML also provides several options for formatting text on the screen. Like HTML, you can't specify the exact formatting you want. You can only give the user agent hints about the content's characteristics and your preferences. The user agent makes the final decision about how to display the content.

All content in a card must be wrapped in a paragraph element. Its syntax is:

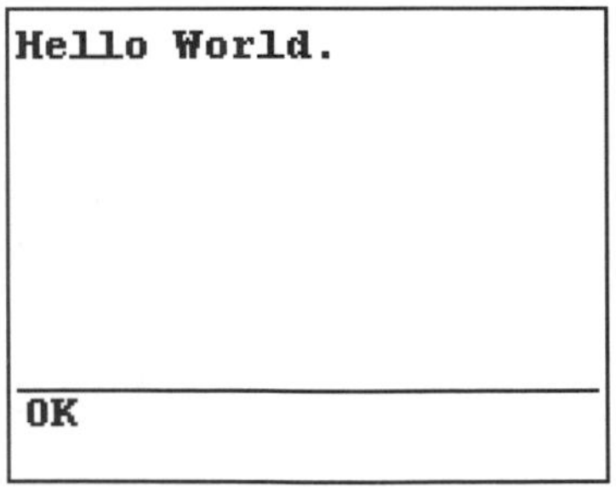

```
Hello World.




_____
OK
```

Figure 2.1   Hello World, WAP style.

```
<p
  align="left | center | right"
  mode="wrap | nowrap"
>
  <a>, <anchor>, <br>, DENTRY, <do>, FMTTEXT, <img>, <table>, TEXT
</p>
```

The **align** attribute aligns text to the left, right, or center of the display. The default value if no align attribute is specified is left.

The **mode** attribute controls whether or not the paragraph content wraps at the right edge of the display. If you specify **nowrap,** the user agent has to provide some mechanism for displaying the portion of each line in the paragraph that doesn't fit within the horizontal boundaries of the display.

We show an example of a paragraph using these two attributes in "Aligned Text." Refer to Table 2.1 or Appendix A for an explanation of **TEXT, FMT-TEXT,** and **DENTRY.**

Unformatted Text

A card can contain any text or special characters that are part of the language in effect at the time the card is displayed. When a WAP device encounters this text, it displays it on the screen in the sequence in which it appears in the card, or in a sequence specified by additional formatting instructions.

Like a Web browser, each WAP client device renders the content in a fashion most suitable for the device. For simple text, this typically means that extraneous white space is removed and text is wrapped at word boundaries. If the displayable rendering of the content cannot fit completely on the screen, the browser extends the card past the end of the page, and the user can scroll down the screen using a down-arrow key or scrollwheel perhaps.

Here's a simple text example. Figure 2.2 shows how this deck appears on the Phone.com browser [ex2-02.wml].

```
Let's write some WAP
apps! As you can see,
white space gets
removed, text gets
wrapped, & special
characters are
─────────────────────
OK
```

Figure 2.2   Simple text display.

```
<wml>
  <card>
    <p>
      Let's write some WAP apps!

      As you can see, white space gets removed, text gets wrapped,
      &amp; special characters are acknowledged.
    </p>
  </card>
</wml>
```

Aligned Text

WML includes two elements for aligning text. The first is the break element:

```
<br/>
```

which has the same effect as an HTML break—it starts a new line on the display. The break element has no attributes and contains no content.

WML also has a paragraph element, which we've already described. Here's an example of how you might use it [ex2-03.wml].

```
<wml>
  <card>
    <p align="left" mode="wrap">
      A long left-aligned wrapping line.
    </p>

    <p align="left" mode="nowrap">
      A long, left-aligned non-wrapping line.
    </p>
  </card>
</wml>
```

The user agent decides how to manage unwrapped text. The Phone.com browser lets the user scroll up and down, using the arrow keys, to each line of text that extends beyond the right-hand side of the screen (wrapped lines cannot be scrolled to). When you reach an unwrapped line, the left-hand part of the line appears with a marker (Figure 2.3), and after a brief pause, the formerly invisible remaining part of the line appears (Figure 2.4).

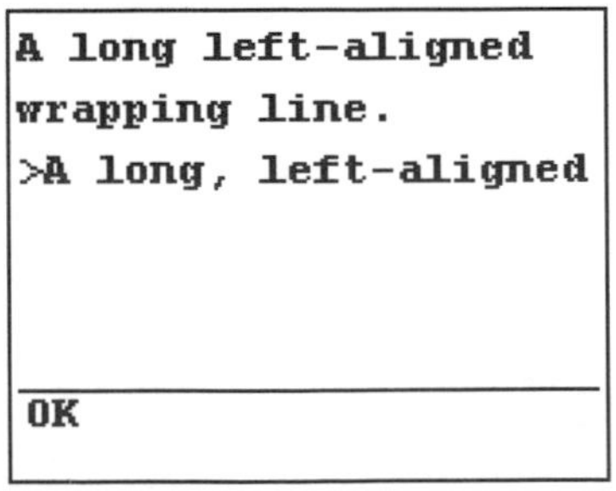

```
A long left-aligned
wrapping line.
>A long, left-aligned


────────────────────
OK
```

```
A long left-aligned
wrapping line.
non-wrapping line.


────────────────────
OK
```

Figure 2.3 The first part of a nonwrapping line.

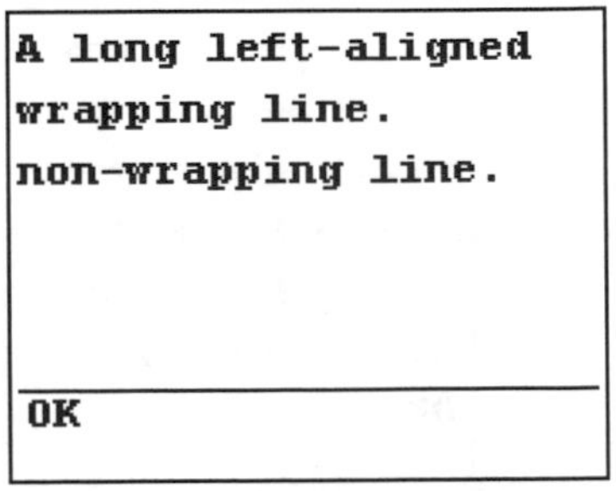

Figure 2.4 The second part of a nonwrapping line.

Styled Text

Like HTML, WML includes a variety of elements for formatting text. Like HTML, their interpretation is left up to the browser. Here's a table of WML text styling tags:

TAG	FONT CHARACTERISTIC
‹b›	Bold
‹big›	Large
‹em›	Emphasize
‹i›	Italic
‹small›	Small
‹strong›	Strong emphasis
‹u›	Underline

Because of their more general nature, the WML specification encourages developers to use the **<strong>** and **<em>** elements when possible. WAP user agents may ignore style tags and render the text unstyled.

Each of the styled text tags has the same basic syntax. They have no attributes, and they can contain the following entities:

```
<a>, <anchor>, <br>, FMTTEXT, <img>, <table>,TEXT
```

Here's a simple deck that uses the various styled text elements [ex2-04.wml].

```
<wml>
  <card>
    <p>
      <big>    Hello </big>  <br/>
      <em>     Hello </em>  <br/>
      <i>      Hello </i>  <br/>
      <small>  Hello </small>  <br/>
      <strong> Hello </strong>  <br/>
      <u>      Hello </u>  <br/>
    </p>
  </card>
</wml>
```

Figure 2.5 shows how this deck appears on the Phone.com browser. Notice that it supports only italic text styling.

Tables

In addition to the simple paragraph alignment attributes described in the previous section, WML has three other elements—table, table row, and table data—

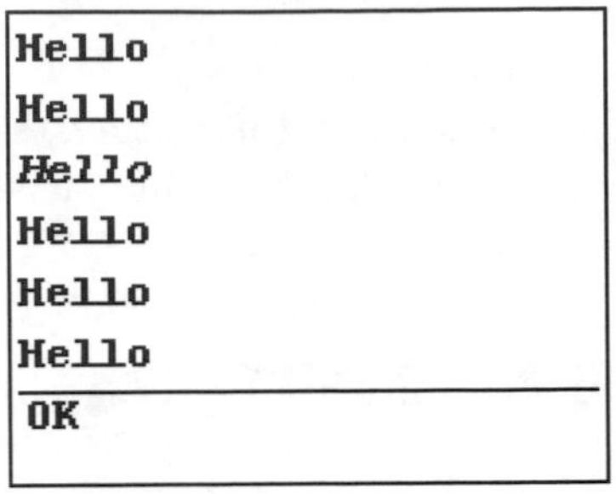

```
Hello
Hello
Hello
Hello
Hello
Hello
OK
```

Figure 2.5 WML formatting elements.

that let you define more complex columnar content. WML tables are similar to HTML tables but with fewer formatting options. For instance, you can control the relative alignment of the columns, but not the exact location of each column on the display.

When defining a table, you have to declare the number of columns, followed by some content. The content can include empty rows, columns, and cells. The device displaying the content does its best to compensate for the missing items.

Here's the table syntax:

```
<table
  align="STRING"
  columns="NUMBER"
  title="VDATA"
>
  <tr>
</table>
```

The **align** string is a list of alignment designators, one per column. Valid values are "L" (left), "C" (center), and "R" (right). The **columns** attribute, which is required, indicates the number of columns in the table; **title** is the name of the table. The user agent may use the title when displaying the table.

Like HTML tables, you define the table content by nesting one or more data declarations inside a row of declarations. Table data can be simple or formatted text, images, or anchors. The user agent fits the data into the table cells and displays the result.

A table row can only contain one or more table column elements, the number specified by the table's **columns** attribute. Here's the syntax for the table row element:

```
<tr>
  <td>
</tr>
```

The table data element is a bit more complex:

```
<td>
  <a>, <anchor>, <br>, FMTTEXT, <img>, <table>, TEXT
</td>
```

A table data element can include most types of content, including images, anchors, and other tables.

Here's a simple table example [ex2-05.wml].

```
<wml>
  <card>
    <p align="center">
      <i>Appointments</i>
    </p>
    <p>
      <small>
        <table columns="2">
          <tr> <td> Date </td> <td> Start/Stop </td> </tr>
          <tr> <td> 02/25 </td> <td> 9:30-10:45A</td> </tr>
          <tr> <td> 03/03</td> <td> 4:45-6:00P</td> </tr>
        </table>
      </small>
    </p>
  </card>
</wml>
```

Figure 2.6 shows what this table might look like on the Phone.com browser.

Images

In this age of graphics-intensive Web sites, it may seem strange to display images on a resource-constrained device such as a WAP-compliant device. Rich graphical user interfaces are possible, however, on small mobile devices. A picture is worth quite a few words and can take up much less display space.

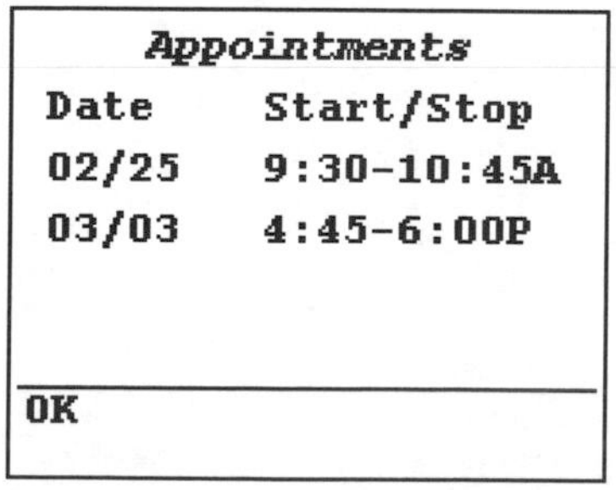

Figure 2.6 A simple WAP table.

WAP's designers have included an image element, which uses the **<img>** tag, for those situations where a picture is the best choice. Images are displayed within the context of the normal text flow. There are attributes that a device's user agent can use, if supported, that give you a certain amount of control over how the image might be displayed. If those hints are ignored, however, about the most you can control is putting the image on its own separate line.

Here's the syntax for the **<img>** tag:

```
<img
  align="top | middle | bottom"
  alt="VDATA"
  height="LENGTH"
  hspave="LENGTH"
  localsrc="VDATA"
  src="URL"
  vspace="LENGTH"
  width="LENGTH"
/>
```

The image element has several attributes, but only two are required: **alt** and **src**. **alt** are a string that can be displayed in place of the image. This is necessary for devices that don't support graphics or in a situation where the image cannot be fetched. The **src** attribute is the actual URL of the image. Just like an HTML browser, a WAP user agent normally first fetches the deck containing the **<img>** tag and, as a separate operation, requests the image located at the **src** URL.

The **localsrc** attribute specifies the name of a ROM- (or RAM-) based image that can be used instead of the image in the **src** URL. The WML 1.1 specification says that **localsrc** images have precedence over **src** images and should be used if they exist. This makes sense—local images load faster and avoid a separate data fetch operation. The Phone.com user agent includes an extensive list of ROM-based icons and images for this purpose.

Here's a simple deck that displays the weather report [ex2-06.wml].

```
<wml>
  <card>
    <p>
      Today's forecast:
      <br/>
        <img
          alt="Partly cloudy"
          src="./pics/pcloudy.wbmp"
          localsrc="partcloudy"
        />
      <br/>
    </p>
  </card>
</wml>
```

If the user agent doesn't support graphics, you would see the display shown in Figure 2.7. If the user agent doesn't have any internal images, you would see the monochrome bitmap stored in the URL "./pics/pcloudy.wbmp" instead of the string "Partly cloudy." If you use the Phone.com user agent, you would see the display shown in Figure 2.8.

NOTE

The WAP forum has defined its own image format, the Wireless Bitmap Format (WBMP), which is optimized for efficient transmission over low-bandwidth networks. All WAP-compatible gateways must recognize the WBMP format as a legitimate MIME type. Most WAP gateways, including the Phone.com gateway, automatically convert BMP files to WBMP files to simplify content development. For more details on this format, see Chapter 6, "Graphics and Multipart Responses."

The remaining **<img>** attributes are optional. **vspace** and **hspace** are white space that should be inserted above and below (**vspace**) and to the left and right (**hspace**) of the image. Both values can be expressed as an integer, indicating pixels, or as an integer followed by a percent sign ("%"), indicating a percentage of the available white space in the appropriate dimension.

The **align** attribute suggests image alignment relative to the current line of text: at the top, centered on the middle, or with the current baseline.

height and **width** give the user agent hints about the size of the image so that it can reserve space for it and continue rendering the current display while fetching the image. Like the **hspace** and **vspace** attributes, **height** and **width** can be in absolute pixels or a percentage of the display size. User agents can scale images to the height and width values if they want.

The optional attributes are merely hints to the user agent. They may be ignored. Also, they are open to interpretation. Don't expect two user agents with identical screen sizes to necessarily render the same images the same way.

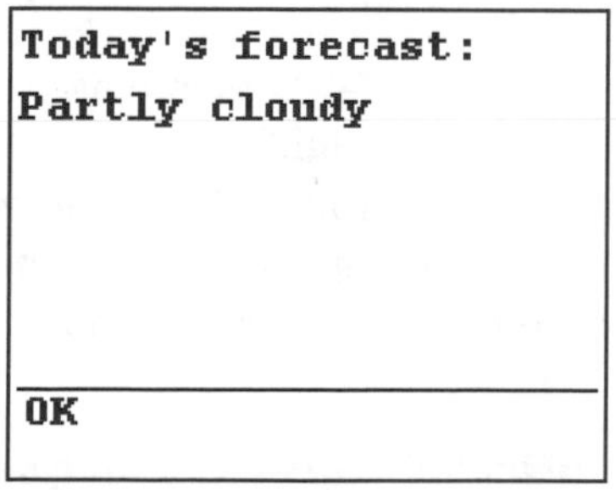

Figure 2.7 A user agent with no graphics support.

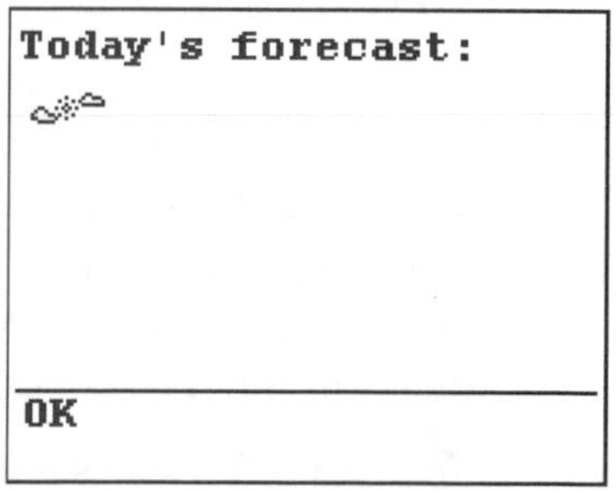

Figure 2.8 A graphic weather report.

Variables

Unlike HTML, you can define variables in WML decks, assign them values, display them on the screen, and use them in expressions. The greatest benefit variables give you as a programmer is that you can maintain state information between decks, making it easy to pass information from one deck to another.

WML variables are untyped. They are all strings with their value set to either a sequence of characters or a null value. Unassigned variables also have a null value. Like variables in Unix shell scripts and other macro-like programming and scripting languages, you can substitute variable values anyplace where text is allowed. This substitution has the highest parsing precedence of all WML operations at runtime, although it is done as late as possible to make sure that operations that set variables are done.

Variable names are case sensitive. They must start with either the underscore character ("_") or a US-ASCII letter, followed by one or more US-ASCII letters, digits, or underscores. The following are valid variable names:

```
URL_name     _Var1     A100200
```

The simplest way to set a variable's value is by using the **<setvar>** element.

```
<setvar
  name="VDATA"
  value="VDATA"
/>
```

<setvar> has two attributes: **name**, the variable's name, and **value**, the value you want to assign to the variable. **<setvar>** combines variable declaration and assignment in one step. For instance:

```
<setvar name="var1" value="some value" />
```

declares the variable **var1** and assigns it the value "some value." You can use **<setvar>** in **<go>**, **<prev>** , and **<refresh>** elements to initialize variables prior to a task's execution (see "Tasks" for more details).

You can also use the **<input>**, **<select>**, and **<postfield>** elements to declare and assign values to variables, and also to set the variables to default values. The **<input>** element is used for data entry (see "User Input" for more details). The **<select>** element lets users select one or more items from a set of choices (see "Choices" for more details). The **<postfield>** element is described in more detail in the next section of this chapter.

You can reference a variable in the content of any WML element, and also in the value of certain attributes. When you do this, the variable's value is substituted into the text of the deck.

There are three different ways you can reference variables. All start with a dollar sign character ("$"):

```
$varname
$(varname)
$(varname:conversion)
```

The first form is acceptable if there is no ambiguity about the variable's name in context. If there is ambiguity, you need to use the second form. The third form is explained shortly.

Because all variable references must start with "$," you need to use two dollar signs to represent a single dollar sign in a string or in text. In the following card, if the variable **amt** is set to "10.35," the string "Your current balance is $10.35" appears on the screen:

```
<card>
  <p>
    Your current balance is $$$amt.
  </p>
</card>
```

This card does the same thing:

```
<card>
  <p>
    Your current balance is $&#x24;$(amt).
  </p>
</card>
```

Variable values can be converted as they are substituted in WML programs. WML uses the URL-escaping rules defined in [RFC2396]. These rules provide a mechanism for embedding special characters, such as the colon character (":"), in a URL without having it interpreted as part of the URL. Although these rules were developed for URL references, you can apply these rules in any variable reference.

Escaped characters are preceded with a percent sign ("%"), followed by two hexadecimal characters that define the escaped character's octet code in the language currently in effect. For instance, the string

```
"Out #^?!~* spot!"
```

is converted to

```
"Out+%23^%3F!~*+spot!"
```

when escaped. The first form is not suitable for including in a URL as part of a variable setting. The second form is. Table 2.2 shows the URL escape characters from [RFC2396].

When a variable's string value is substituted in a WML deck, you can specify escaping, unescaping, or no escaping using the following syntax:

Table 2.2   URL Escape Characters

RESERVED		UNWISE		DELIMITERS	
;	%3b	{	%7b	<	%3c
/	%2f	}	%7d	>	%3e
?	%3f	|	%7c	#	%23
:	%3a	\	55c%		%25
@	%40	^	%5e		%22
&	%26	[	%5b		
=	%3d	]	%5d		
+	%2b	`	%27		
$	%24				
,	%2c				
space	%20				

US-ASCII 0x00-0x1F and 0x7F characters are also reserved.
They are converted to %00 - %1f and %7f, respectively.

```
$(var:e)       $(var:E)       $(var:escape)    <!-- escaping -->
$(var:u)       $(var:U)       $(var:unesc)     <!-- unescaping -->
$(var:n)       $(var:N)       $(var:noesc)     <!-- no escaping -->.
```

WML always applies escaping automatically when working with attributes that are normally set to URLs. Consequently, in almost all circumstances you can ignore variable escaping and assume that the WML user agent does the right thing.

Tasks

So far, we've only talked about content that can be included in WML documents. As any programmer knows, a program isn't really a program unless it contains instructions. There are several ways to define processing in a WML deck. The simplest place to start is with an explanation of tasks.

WAP 1.1 defines several different types of tasks. Tasks affect the execution order of WAP programs by defining actions that should be taken in response to events (see the next section of this chapter for a detailed discussion of events). When a task is executed, it typically causes some sort of branching, often changing the contents of the device's history stack in the process. There are four types of WML tasks: **<noop>**, **<prev>**, **<refresh>**, and **<go>**.

The simplest task is the **<noop>** element. Here's its syntax:

```
<noop/>
```

Just as you would expect, it does nothing. It is used to override (and disable) deck-level event definitions (see "Deck-Level Events" for more details).

You use the **<prev>** element to navigate to the previous card in the user agent's history stack:

```
<prev>
  <setvar>
</prev>
```

The current URL, the one containing the **<prev>** task, is popped from the history stack. If the **<prev>** task definition contains any **<setvar>** elements, they are processed before the transfer of control happens.

The **<refresh>** task initiates refreshing the user agent's visible contents:

```
<refresh>
  <setvar>
</refresh>
```

Prior to the redisplay, **<setvar>** elements in the task are processed, and if the current card contains a timer, it is started (see "Timers" for an explanation of timers).

The **<go>** element defines a navigation to a URL. That URL can point to a new WML deck residing on a server or, using a fragment, it can point to a different card in the current deck. The **<go>** element gives WML much of its power and flexibility.

The **<go>** element has the following syntax:

```
<go
  accept-charset="STRING"
  href="URL"
  method="post | get"
  sendreferer="true | false"
>
  <postfield>, <setvar>
</go>
```

href, which is required, is the URL of the next card or deck to fetch and display. If it is a valid absolute or relative URL, and can be fetched, the URL is pushed onto the history stack, and the first card of the new deck is displayed. If the URL is a fragment anchor to another card in the current deck, the history stack remains unchanged and the new card is displayed if it exists.

If **sendreferer** is true, the user agent must specify to the WAP gateway, using an HTTP "Referer" request header, the URL of the current deck, using the smallest possible relative URL. This attribute is designed to give servers some degree of access control over URLs based on which decks are referencing them. Its default setting is **false**.

method refers to the HTTP submission method used with this URL. The two valid choices are **get** and **post.** They generate, respectively, HTTP GET and POST server requests. The requests include any field declarations that are included in the body of the **<go>** element. The default **method** setting is **get**.

accept-charset is an exclusive-OR list of valid character set encoding names as specified in [RFC2045] and [RFC2616]. The server receiving the request generated by this **<go>** task must accept one of the encodings in the list. The default value for **accept-charset** is **unknown,** indicating to the user agent that it should use the same character set as the one used to transmit the deck to the device. For more details on this attribute, see Chapter 7, "Internationalization (I18N)."

Here is a simple **<go>** task definition:

```
<go href="./new-deck.wml" sendreferer="true" />
```

You use **<postfield>** elements to define name/value pairs that are passed to the HTTP server receiving the **<go>** request. Here's the postfield syntax:

```
<postfield
  name="VDATA"
  value="VDATA"
/>
```

When a task with <**postfield>** elements is executed, the user agent:

1. Identifies the name/value pairs and substitutes variables

2. Transcodes the name/value pairs to the correct character set

3. Escapes the name/value pairs according to the URL escape rules and assembles them into an application/x-www-form-urlencoded MIME content type

4. Completes the task based on the **method** attribute

How the values get passed to the server depends on what you specify for the **method** attribute.

If you specify a **get** method, the name/value pairs are appended to the query part of the HTTP request, and the request is sent to the specified URL. For instance, this **<go>** task might be used to request a list of all flights between San Francisco and Chicago on the upcoming Monday:

```
<go href="/flights.cgi" sendreferer="true" method="get" >
 <postfield name="day" value="Mon" >
 <postfield name="origin" value="SFO" >
 <postfield name="destination" value="ORD" >
</go>
```

It generates the following HTTP **GET** request:

```
GET /flights.cgi?day=Mon&origin=SFO&destination=ORD HTTP/1.1
.
. other HTTP headers
.
```

If you specify a **post** method, the same **<go>** task sends this HTTP **POST** request:

```
POST /flights.cgi HTTP/1.1
content-type="xxx-urlencoded"
.
. other HTTP headers
.
day=Mon&origin=SFO&destination=ORD"
```

See Chapter 5, "Caching," for a more detailed explanation of **GET** and **POST** requests and HTTP headers.

Events

Tasks don't operate in a vacuum. They have to be bound to an event in order to do anything useful. When the event happens, the task executes. There are three different elements you can use to bind a task to an event: the **<anchor>** element, the **<onevent>** element (see "Intrinsic Events" for a description of the **<onevent>** element), and the **<do>** element (see "User-Triggered Events").

Anchors

As in HTML, WML programs can include anchors, links to other program elements. An anchor has content that appears on the device display in such a way that the user knows there's an anchor there.

In HTML, anchors are usually underlined and displayed in a color different from that of normal content. WAP-compliant user agents have no hard-and-fast rules for displaying anchors. An agent just has to distinguish the anchor from the nonanchor content. For instance, the Phone.com browser encloses anchor text in square brackets.

Here's the syntax for the **<anchor>** element:

```
<anchor
  title="VDATA"
>
  <br>, <go>, <img>, <prev>, <refresh>, TEXT
</anchor>
```

Anchors have an optional **title** attribute. The manner in which the title is displayed is up to the user agent. The WML 1.1 specification mentions tool tips, dynamic button labels, and voice prompts as possible renderings. A user agent may also choose to ignore an **<anchor>** title. If titles are displayed, it's in addition to the textual contents of the anchor—the text must be displayed; the title may be displayed. The WML 1.1 specification suggests that **<anchor>** title attributes be six or fewer characters in length so that they work with a broad range of devices.

 In addition to some visible content, a valid **<anchor>** has to include a task definition that indicates to the user agent what to do if the user selects that anchor (how they select the anchor depends on the mechanics of the user agent). The task definition has to be a **<go>**, **<prev>** , or **<refresh>** element.

You can embed anchors anyplace in a WML program that text is acceptable, except in **<option>** elements (see "Choices" for a discussion of the **<option>** element).

There is also a short-form syntax for anchors.

```
<a
  href="URL"
  title="label"
>
  <br>, <img>, TEXT,
</a>
```

It uses the **<a>** tag instead of the **<anchor>** tag and can only be used to define (implied) **<go>** tasks that require a URL specification.

With just a basic introduction to tasks, events, and anchors, you can now create WML decks that have navigational capabilities [ex2-07.wml].

```
<wml>

<!-- the first card -->

  <card id="card1" >
    <onevent type="onenterforward">
      <refresh>
        <setvar name="origin" value="Card # one" />
      </refresh>
    </onevent>
    <onevent type="onenterbackward">
      <refresh>
```

```
          <setvar name="origin" value="Card # one" />
        </refresh>
      </onevent>

    <p>
      Select a destination:<br/>
      <a title="Card 2" href="#card2">
        Card # two
      </a>
      <br/>
      <a title="Display" href="#card3">
        Card # three
      </a>
    </p>
  </card>

<!-- the second card -->

  <card id="card2" >
    <onevent type="onenterforward">
      <refresh>
        <setvar name="origin" value="Card # two" />
      </refresh>
    </onevent>
    <onevent type="onenterbackward">
      <refresh>
        <setvar name="origin" value="Card # two" />
      </refresh>
    </onevent>
  <p>
      Select a destination: <br/><br/>
      <a title="Card 1" href="#card1">
        <img src="./pics/uparrow.bmp"
          alt="Card # one " localsrc="uparrow1"/>
      </a>
      <br/>
      <a title="Display" href="#card3">
        <img src="./pics/downarrow.bmp"
          alt="Card # three" localsrc="downarrow1" />
      </a>
    </p>
  </card>

<!-- the third card -->

  <card id="card3" >
    <p>
      You've just come from $origin <br/>
      Select a destination: <br/>
      <a title="Card 1" href="#card1">
        Card # one
      </a>
```

```
        <br/>
        <a title="Card 2" href="#card2">
        </a>
    </p>
  </card>
</wml>
```

This deck has three cards. When it's executed, the first card appears as shown in Figure 2.9. Notice how the Phone.com user agent highlights anchors with square brackets. If you select the anchor that takes you to **card2**, there are two possible outcomes. If the user agent has local icons with the names **uparrow1** and **down-arrow1**, you see a display similar to Figure 2.10. If the icons don't exist, you see the display shown in Figure 2.11. Finally, if you move to the third card, you see the display shown in Figure 2.12, including the name of the card you just came from.

Intrinsic Events

WML defines a set of intrinsic events, things that are triggered by the internal processing of the user agent. WML has four types of intrinsic events:

```
Select a destination:
>[ Card # two ]
 [ Card # three ]



_____
Card 0
```

Figure 2.9 The first card.

```
Select a destination:

>[ ⇧ ]
 [ ⇩ ]


_____
Card 1
```

Figure 2.10 The second card with icons.

```
Select a destination:

 [Card # one]
 [Card # three]


_____
OK
```

Figure 2.11 The second card with text anchors.

```
You've just come from
Card # two
Select a destination:
>[ Card # one ]
 [ Card # two ]

_____
Card 1
```

Figure 2.12 The third card.

oneventforward. Triggered when the user navigates to a card via a **<go>** task or any other mechanism, such as a scripting function, that has the same effect.

oneventbackward. Triggered when the user navigates to a card via a **<prev>** task or any other mechanism, such as invoking the **<prev>** mechanism of the device by pressing the **back** key, that has the same effect.

ontimer. Triggered when a program-defined **<timer>** expires. You define timers by using the **<timer>** element (see the next section of this chapter for a discussion of timers).

onpick. Triggered when the user selects or deselects an **<option>** item (see "Choices" for a discussion of **<option>** elements).

Just as with explicit events, you have to bind an intrinsic event to a task. You do this with the **<onevent>** element. The syntax of an **<onevent>** element is simple:

```
<onevent
  type="oneventforward | oneventbackward | ontimer | onpick"
>
  <go>, <noop>, <prev>, <refresh>
</onevent>
```

Here's a simple example using an intrinsic event [ex2-08.wml].

```
<wml>
  <card>
    <onevent type="oneventforward" >
      <refresh>
        <setvar name="var1" value="" />
        <setvar name="var2" value="" />
      </refresh>
    </onevent>
    <p>
      Now we're starting with a clean slate!
    </p>
  </card>
</wml>
```

Every time the card is entered, the variables **var1** and **var2** are reset to null values. The variables are not reset if the card is not navigated to using a **<prev>** task, the Back button on a WML-compatible device, or any action that gets the card's location by popping it off the history stack.

Timers

Timers provide a mechanism for invoking a task after a certain period of time. Any action that executes a card starts its timer. When the **<timer>** expires, its task is invoked. If the execution stream leaves the card before the **<timer>** expires, the **<timer>** stops. In effect, the scope of the **<timer>** is limited to the card where it is defined. A card can have only one timer, and a **<timer>** can have only one task.

The **<timer>** element has the following syntax:

```
<timer
  name="NAME"
  value="VDATA"
/>
```

The optional **name** attribute specifies the name of a variable that contains the timer's starting countdown value when the **<timer>** is activated and the time remaining on the **<timer>** when it is inactivated or expires. If **name** exists and is initialized to a nonnegative numeric value, it is used as the timer's starting value, overriding the **value** attribute.

The **value** attribute, which is required, contains the default setting, in tenths of a second, of the timer's starting value. This value is used if there is no **name** attribute or the variable specified in the **name** attribute is not initialized. It is ignored if the **name** attribute exists and is initialized.

The following program displays a series of images (see Figures 2.13 through 2.15). Timers are used to update the image every two seconds [ex2-09.wml].

```
<wml>

<!-- the automobile card -->

  <card id="card1">
    <onevent type="ontimer" >
      <go href="#card2"/>
    </onevent>
    <timer value="20"/>
    <p align="center">
      Forms of transportation:<br/><br/>
      <img src="./pics/car" alt="Automobiles" localsrc="car"/>
    </p>
  </card>

<!-- the airplane card -->

  <card id="card2">
    <onevent type="ontimer" >
      <go href="#card3"/>
    </onevent>
    <timer value="20"/>
    <p align="center">
      Forms of transportation: <br/><br/>
      <img src="./pics/airplane" alt="Airplanes" localsrc="plane"/>
    </p>
  </card>
```

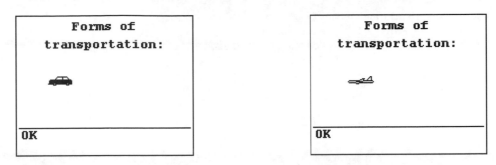

Figure 2.13 The automobile card.   **Figure 2.14** The airplane card.

Figure 2.15 The ship card.

```
<!-- the ship card -->

  <card id="card3">
    <onevent type="ontimer" >
      <go href="#card1"/>
    </onevent>
    <timer value="20"/>
    <p align="center">
      Forms of transportation: <br/><br/>
      <img src="./pics/ship" alt="Ships" localsrc="boat"/>
    </p>
  </card>
</wml>
```

You may remember from the section on card attributes the optional **ontimer** card attribute. It's equivalent to a **<go>** element. Here's the previous sample program using the short-form **ontimer** syntax [ex2-10.wml].

```
<wml>
<!-- the automobile card -->

  <card id="card1" ontimer="#card2">
    <timer value="20"/>
```

```
      <p align="center">
        Forms of transportation:
        <img src="./pics/car" alt="Automobiles" localsrc="car"/>
      </p>
   </card>

<!-- the airplane card -->

  <card id="card2" ontimer="#card3">
    <timer value="20"/>
    <p align="center">
      Forms of transportation:
      <img src="./pics/airplane" alt="Airplanes" localsrc="plane"/>
    </p>
 </card>

<!-- the ship card -->

  <card id="card3" ontimer="#card1">
    <timer value="20"/>
    <p align="center">
      Forms of transportation:
      <img src="./pics/ship" alt="Ships" localsrc="boat"/>
    </p>
 </card>
</wml>
```

User-Triggered Events

Every WAP-compatible device has a set of predefined user interface widgets that are available to the user. These widgets might be real buttons on a telephone, icons on a touch-sensitive screen, a voice-activated command, or any other readily identifiable interface component—their instantiation is left up to the device designers.

The WML 1.1 specification defines the following widgets that all WAP-compatible devices must support. Note that only one of these widgets, **prev**, has a predefined action. The rest are conceptually defined. It's up to application developers to define what actually happens when one of these widgets is activated.

accept. A positive acknowledgment

prev. Navigate backwards in the history stack

help. A (possible) context-sensitive help request

reset. Reset the device's context

options. A context-sensitive request for options or additional operations

delete. Delete the current item or choice

unknown. A generic **<do>** element

When a user activates one of these widgets, it creates an event that you can trap and respond to using the WML **<do>** element. Here's the **<do>** syntax:

```
<do
  type="accept | prev | help | reset | options | delete | unknown"
  label="VDATA"
  name="NAME"
  optional="true | false"
>
  <go> | <noop> | <prev> | refresh
</do>
```

The **label** attribute specifies a label that should be used by the UI widget, but may be ignored if it cannot be rendered by the user agent. The WML 1.1 specifications suggest that you restrict label names to six characters.

The **name** attribute uniquely identifies the event/task binding specified by the **<do>** element. Duplicate names are not allowed within a card. A card-level **<do>** element overrides a deck-level **<do>** element with the same name (see the next section for a discussion of deck-level **<do>**s). If no **name** is supplied, or if it is an empty string, **name** defaults to the value of the **type** attribute.

The **optional** attribute, if set to **true**, tells the user agent it can ignore this element.

Like other event/task bindings, the task definition for a **<do>** element must be a **<go>**, **<prev>** , **<noop>**, or **<refresh>** element.

Here's an example that shows how to use **<do>** elements [ex2-11.wml]. It lets you navigate through a series of cards, including an online help card, for an information service. This deck is shown in Figures 2.16 through 2.18.

```
<wml>
  <card id="card1" >

<!-- the welcome card -->

    <do type="accept" label="Go!" optional="false" >
      <go href="#startcard" />
    </do>
    <do type="help" label="Help" >
      <go href="#helpcard" />
    </do>
    <p>
      Welcome to WorldFAQ, your premier source for
      international reference information.
    </p>
  </card>

<!-- the start of the actual service -->

  <card id="startcard">
```

```
        <p>
          What do you want to find:<br/>
          <a href="phones.wml"> Phone codes </a><br/>
          <a href="times.wml"> Intl times </a><br/>
          <a href="weather.wml"> Weather </a>
        </p>
      </card>

  <!-- the help screen -->

    <card id="helpcard">
      <do type="accept" label="Go!" >
        <go href="#startcard" />
      </do>
      <p>
        Select <em>Go!</em> to pick a reference service.
        You can look up country dialing codes,
        international times, and average temperatures.
      </p>
    </card>
  </wml>
```

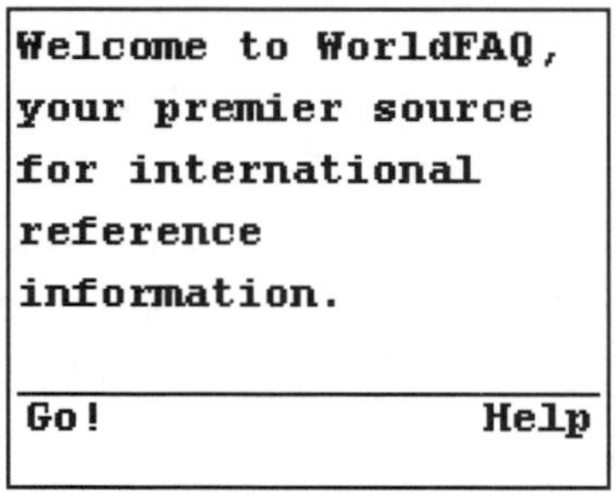

```
Welcome to WorldFAQ,
your premier source
for international
reference
information.
_____
Go!                        Help
```

Figure 2.16 A simple ‹do›
example.

```
What do you want to
find:
▶[ Phone codes ]
 [ Intl times ]
 [ Weather ]
_____
Link
```

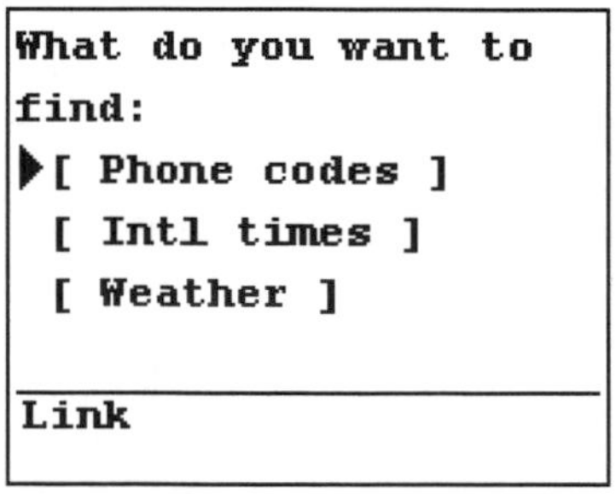

Figure 2.17 Picking a service.

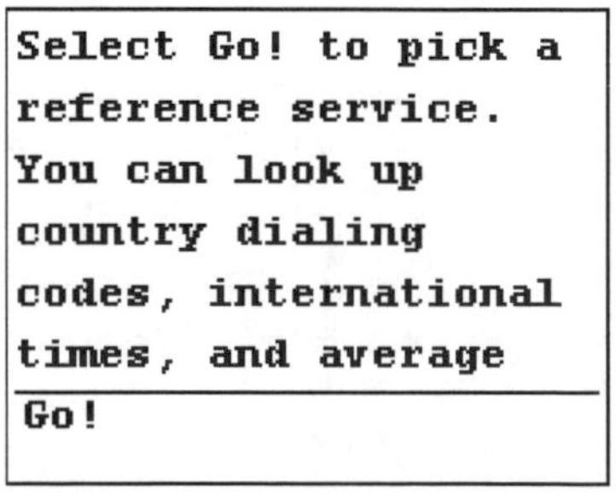

```
Select Go! to pick a
reference service.
You can look up
country dialing
codes, international
times, and average
_____
Go!
```

Figure 2.18 The help screen.

Deck-Level Events

Just as you can define **<onevent>** and **<do>** elements at the card level, you can also include **<onevent>** and **<do>** elements at the deck level. Because **<onpick>** events are not card-level events, but events triggered by **<option>** elements, you cannot define them at the deck level.

You define deck-level event/ask bindings using a **<template>** element. The **<template>** describes bindings that apply to all cards within the deck. You can then override deck-level bindings at the card level. If a card contains a **<do>** binding with the same name as a deck **<do>** binding, the card binding takes precedence. Similarly, intrinsic card-level bindings take precedence over intrinsic deck-level bindings for the same type of event.

Typically you use a **<template>** to avoid having to repeatedly redefine the same bindings for all the cards in a deck. It's often much easier to use a template and then override specific bindings for individual cards.

Here's the syntax for the **<template>** element:

```
<template
  oneventbackward="URL"
  oneventforward="URL"
  ontimer="URL"
>
  <do>, <onevent>
</template>
```

As with card attributes, the **oneventforward, oneventbackward,** and **ontimer** **<template>** attributes are short-form equivalents of full-length **<onevent>** definitions in the body of the **<template>**. You cannot use equivalent short- and long-form bindings in the same card or template.

Here's the previous deck with a **<template>**-based help card [ex2-12.wml].

```
<wml>
  <template>
      <do type="options" label="Help" >
        <go href="#helpcard" />
      </do>
  </template>

  <card id="card1" >

<!-- the welcome card -->

    <do type="accept" label="Go!" >
      <go href="#startcard" />
    </do>
    <p>
```

```
      Welcome to WorldFAQ, your premier source for
      international reference information.
    </p>
  </card>

<!-- the start of the actual service -->

  <card id="startcard">
    <p>
      What do you want to find:<br/>
      <a href="phones.wml"> Phone codes </a><br/>
      <a href="times.wml"> Intl times </a><br/>
      <a href="weather.wml"> Weather </a>
    </p>
  </card>

<!-- the help screen -->

  <card id="helpcard">
    <do type="accept" label="Go!" optional="false" >
      <go href="#startcard" />
    </do>
    <p>
      Select <em>Go!</em> to pick a reference service.
      You can look up country dialing codes,
      international times, and average temperatures.
    </p>
  </card>
</wml>
```

Data Entry

Programs are generally more use if a user can enter data, even if that data entry is as simple as selecting one item from a group. WML provides a variety of data entry mechanisms.

The problem of how to efficiently enter data on a small-screen, limited-capability device has not yet been solved by hardware or software designers. Telephone keypads are inadequate. Voice recognition works only for small command-and-control applications. Predictive methods that try to figure out what you want to enter before you finish entering it are limited by the data entry hardware. Handwriting recognition isn't suitable because it requires a display screen that is more expensive than a standard cell phone screen, and it's not clear that it makes sense to try and use a stylus with a cell phone. A lot of research is still needed in this area.

Until someone comes up with a great data entry mechanism for this type of device, you should try to limit the amount of data entry you require in your applications. The less the data entry, the more satisfied the user.

User Input

The simplest way that you can get data into a WML program is by using the **<input>** element. It lets users enter a string of characters, with optional formatting controls, into a variable. How users enter the text depends on the device. They may use a telephone keypad, a stylus and handwriting recognition, or voice recognition, for instance. You can then use that variable's value in decks and cards.

Here's the syntax for the **input** element:

```
<input
  emptyok="true | false"
  format="STRING"
  maxlength="NUMBER"
  name="NAME"
  size="NUMBER"
  tabindex="NUMBER"
  title="VDATA"
  type="text | password"
  value="VDATA"
/>
```

emptyok. A Boolean attribute that, when set to **true**, indicates that the user does not have to enter anything for this **input** element. Normally, input elements with **format** strings require that the user enter a properly formatted string. The default setting for **emptyok** is **false**.

format. A string that defines an input mask that can contain both mask control characters and static text that is displayed in the input area. See the next section of this chapter for a discussion of the valid format specifications.

NOTE Some input fields specify a formatting that cannot be empty—for example, four numbers followed by a dash followed by eight numbers, or an input field that contains literals. If the field is optional, you want it to be either empty or correctly formatted. By setting the **emptyok** attribute to **true**, you can specify an optional field that has strict formatting when the field is nonempty.

maxlength. The maximum number of characters that can be entered for this input element. The default is unlimited.

name. The name of the variable to which the input text is assigned. If this variable is already defined and it fits the format specification, its value is used as a default value for the **input** element. If **name** has a value that doesn't fit the format specification, the user agent instead tries to use the **value** attribute setting as the default value. **name** is a required attribute.

size. The width, in characters, of the text input area on the display screen.

title. A string that may be used, by the user agent, when presenting the **input** element to the user. The agent may display **title** as a label or a tool tip, for instance.

NOTE

Titles provide a user interface support function. Some user agents may go into a separate mode for input, and the title can be used to remind users of what they are entering. Another use for the title is in the case of aural browsers, which might use the title to indicate the current input focus.

type. An **input** element can echo entered characters back to the user in one of two ways. **text** echoing displays characters just as they are entered. **password** characters are displayed in an obscured or illegible manner such as by substituting asterisks ("*") for each input character.

value. A default value for the **input** element if one is not assigned from the preexisting variable **name**. **value** is used if it fits the format specification.

tabindex. The tab order of this element within the current card. WAP user agents are not required to implement the **tabindex** attribute.

When you use **input** elements, you normally precede each element with some text as a prompt for the user. Here's a simple data entry card [ex2-13.wml]. The Phone.com browser displays one field at a time. The first name, state, and password fields are shown in Figures 2.19 through 2.21.

```
<wml>
  <card>
    <p>
      First Name:
      <input name="fname"
        maxlength="15" /><br/>

      Last Name:
      <input name="lname"
        maxlength="15" tabindex="2" /><br/>

      State:
      <input name="state"
        maxlength="2" emptyok="true"
        value="CA" tabindex="3" /> <br/>

      Zipcode:
      <input name="zipcode"
        maxlength="9" tabindex="4" /> <br/>

      Password:
      <input name="password"
        maxlength="8" type="password" tabindex="5" /> <br/>
    </p>
  </card>
</wml>
```

```
First Name:
Steve|




OK                    ALPHA
```

Figure 2.19 A simple data entry field.

```
State:
CA|




OK                    ALPHA
```

Figure 2.20 A data entry field with a preset value.

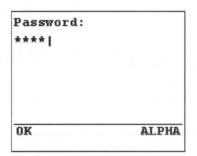

```
Password:
****|




OK                    ALPHA
```

Figure 2.21 A password data entry field.

Format Specifications

The **<input>** element's **format** attribute lets you define a control string to manage what a user can enter in a data entry field. It also lets you define static text, such as the dashes ("-") separating the parts of a social security number, that can be displayed as part of the data entry field. The valid format control characters are:

FORMAT	ALLOWABLE INPUT CHARACTERS
A	Uppercase alphabetic or punctuation
a	Lowercase alphabetic or punctuation
N	Numeric
X	Uppercase
x	Lowercase
M	Any character, but the user agent may prefer to show uppercase
m	Any character, but the user agent may prefer to show lowercase
\c	Display "c" as a single-character literal on the display

NOTE

For "M" and "m" format characters, the format is hinting that the character is most likely going to be uppercase or lowercase, respectively, even though any character can be entered. The use of an uppercase "M" would cause the user agent to start out in uppercase. For example, you might choose "M" for a last name and "m" for an e-mail address.

If you include literals, using the "\c" format specification, in a format string, the user agent includes the literals in the resulting text that is assigned to the input element's variable.

In addition, there are two multicharacter format specifications you can use. They can be used only once in a format string, at the end of the string:

FORMAT	ALLOWABLE INPUT CHARACTERS
*f	Enter any number of characters matching the **f** format specification.
nf	Enter from one to nine characters, as specified by **n**, of format f.

Here's the previous example with format strings [ex2-14.wml]. Figures 2.22 and 2.23 show how the zip code formatting appears on the Phone.com browser. As the user enters the fifth character of the code, the WAP user agent displays the hyphen and positions itself for entry of the first digit of the second portion of the code.

```
<wml>
  <card>
    <p>

<!-- One uppercase letter followed by up to 14
     lowercase or punctuation characters -->
```

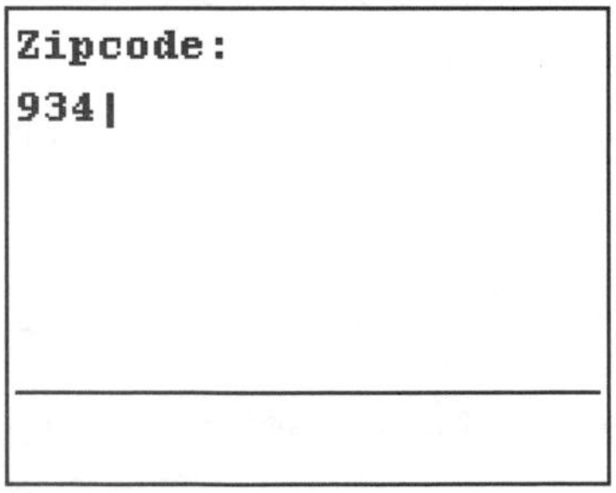

```
Zipcode:
934|
```

```
Zipcode:
93401-|



OK
```

Figure 2.22 The first part of a zip code.

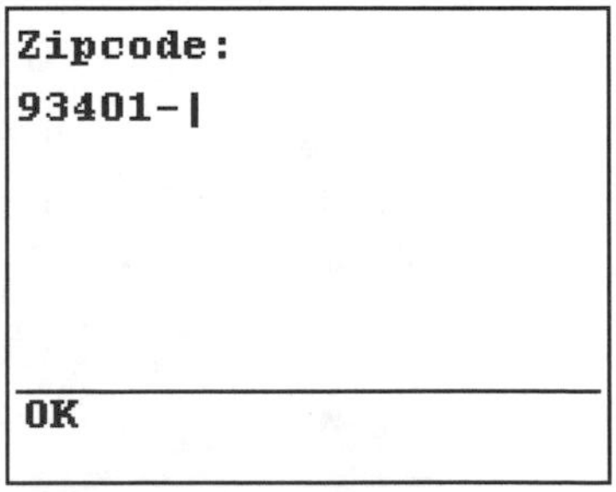

Figure 2.23 The second part of a zip code.

```
      First Name:
      <input name="fname"
        maxlength="15" format="X*M" /> <br/>

      Last Name:
      <input name="lname"
        maxlength="15" tabindex="2" format="X*M" /> <br/>

<!-- Two uppercase letters with a default value -->

      State:
      <input name="state"
        maxlength="2" emptyok="true"
        format="AA" value="CA" tabindex="3" /> <br/>

<!-- Five digits followed by up to four more digits -->

      Zipcode:
      <input name="zipcode"
        maxlength="10" tabindex="4" format="NNNNN\-*N"/> <br/>

<!-- Four to eight characters, obscured on the display -->

      Password:
      <input name="password"
        maxlength="8" type="password" tabindex="5"
        format="mmmm4m" /> <br/>
    </p>
  </card>
</wml>
```

Complex Data

It's not unusual for a card (such as in the preceding example) to contain several data entry elements. Small-screen devices may not be able to display all these input elements simultaneously. In these cases, the user agent must decide how to handle the user interface. For instance, should the elements be displayed as a scrolling list? Perhaps one item per display page would make more sense. Each user agent resolves these issues in its own way. There are two WML components that provide some hints to the user agent to help it render the content in the most optimal way.

The first hint available to the user agent is the Boolean **ordered <card>** attribute. By default, **ordered** is set to **true**. It indicates to the user agent that the content on the card is naturally organized as a linear sequence of field elements. A user agent may render a set of ordered input elements as a sequence of separate display pages, with one data entry field per page, and appropriate widgets that help the user easily navigate between the pages. In fact, this is what happens in the previous example.

The WML specification suggests that this attribute is suitable for short data entry forms where all fields are required. An example might be an e-mail message that requires an address, a subject, and a message.

If we take the preceding example and add the **ordered** attribute with a value of **false**, the Phone.com user agent puts all the fields on the same screen (see Figure 2.24).

```
<wml>
  <card ordered="false">
    .
    . the same code as in the preceding example
    .
  </card>
</wml>
```

For more complicated scenarios, there is one additional element, the **<fieldset>** element, that you can use to organize collections of text and fields. **<fieldset>** gives hints to the user agent about the relative placement and grouping of input elements and text so that it can optimize the user's navigation. This element is most useful for defining logical pages of visible content in cards that may span multiple display pages on small-screen devices.

Here's the **<fieldset>** syntax:

```
<fieldset
  title="VDATA"
>
  <a>, <anchor>, DENTRY, <do>, FMTTEXT, <img>, <table>, TEXT
</fieldset>
```

The user agent may use the **title** attribute to render the content.

Note two things. First, **<fieldset>** elements can be nested—you can organize data entry using a pages-within-pages metaphor. Second, a **<fieldset>**'s content is restricted to a limited number of other types of elements. This empha-

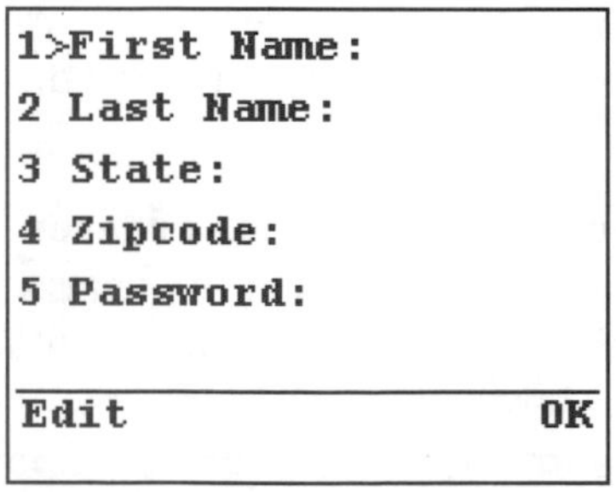

```
1>First Name:
2 Last Name:
3 State:
4 Zipcode:
5 Password:


Edit              OK
```

Figure 2.24 An unordered data entry card.

sizes its function as an element for organizing data entry function. (See the next section, "Choices" for a description of the **<select>** element.)

Here's a simple **<fieldset>** example that collects a person's contact information and submits it to a CGI script [ex2-15.wml]. In recognizing the **<fieldset>** element, where the card's **ordered** attribute is set to **true**, the Phone.com browser places the first **<input>** element of each **<fieldset>** on the first line of the display, by itself. It places each subsequent **<input>** element on the second line. When the user hits the OK button at the end of the last **<fieldset>**, the **<do>** task is executed.

```
<wml>
  <card ordered="false">

<!-- cgi parm structure -->

    <do type="accept">
      <go href="piminfo.cgi" method="post">
        <postfield name="fn" value="$fname"/>
        <postfield name="ln" value="$lname"/>
        <postfield name="a1" value="$addr1"/>
        <postfield name="a2" value="$addr2"/>
        <postfield name="ct" value="$city"/>
        <postfield name="st" value="$state"/>
        <postfield name="zp" value="$zipcode"/>
        <postfield name="cn" value="$country"/>
        <postfield name="ph" value="$phone"/>
        <postfield name="fx" value="$fax"/>
        <postfield name="em" value="$email"/>
      </go>
    </do>

<!-- name information -->

    <p>
      <fieldset title="Name" >
        First Name:
        <input name="fname" maxlength="15" emptyok="false" /> <br/>
        Last Name:
        <input name="lname" maxlength="15" emptyok="false" /> <br/>
      </fieldset>

<!-- address information -->

      <fieldset title="Address" >
        Address1:
        <input name="addr1" maxlength="25" emptyok="false" /> <br/>
        Address2:
        <input name="addr2" maxlength="25" /> <br/>
        City:
        <input name="city" maxlength="20" emptyok="false" /> <br/>
        State:
        <input name="state" maxlength="15" /> <br/>
```

```
        Post Code:
        <input name="zipcode" maxlength="10" /> <br/>
      </fieldset>

<!-- contact information -->

      <fieldset title="Contact Info">
        Phone:
        <input name="phone" maxlength="25" emptyok="false" /> <br/>
        Fax:
        <input name="fax" maxlength="25" /> <br/>
        Email:
        <input name="email" maxlength="20" emptyok="false" /> <br/>
      </fieldset>
    </p>
  </card>
</wml>
```

Choices

WML includes elements for defining choice lists where a user can select one or more items from a list of options. You can also nest choice lists, define default values, and execute tasks when a user selects a specific option.

The basic choice list element is the **<select>** element. It lets users select one or more options, where each option is defined by an **<option>** element. Here's the syntax of the **<select>** element:

```
<select
  iname="NAME"
  ivalue="VDATA"
  multiple= "true | false"
  name="NAME"
  tabindex="NUMBER"
  title="VDATA"
  value="VDATA"
>
  <optgroup>, <option>
</select>
```

The **<select>** element has the following attributes (none are required):

iname. The name of the variable to set to the index of the user's selection or selections.

ivalue. The index of the default option to select. **ivalue** has an affect only if the variable named by the **iname** attribute has no setting.

multiple. A Boolean that, if set to **true**, lets the user select more than one item from a group of **<option>** elements. The **<select>** execution assigns a semicolon-delimited list of choices to **name**. The default setting is **value**. In a similar fashion, **iname** is assigned a semicolon-delimited list of choice indices. The default is **ivalue**.

name. The name of the variable to set to the user's selection or selections.

tabindex. The relative tabbing order of this element within the context of the current WML card.

title. The element's title, which may be used when it is displayed.

value. The default value for the variable defined by the **name** attribute. This value is used only if the variable has no value when the element is first executed.

A **<select>** element must contain one or more **<option>** elements. Each **<option>** element is a single possible choice the user can make. **<option>** elements can have simple text content, which is displayed. Here's the syntax for the **<option>** element:

```
<option
  onpick="URL"
  title="VDATA"
  value="VDATA"
>
  TEXT, <onevent>
</option>
```

option elements have the following attributes:

onpick. A URL to execute if this **<option>** is selected or deselected. Single-option lists generate the **onpick** event only when an item is selected. Multiple-option lists generate **onpick** events when individual items are both selected and deselected.

title. The option's title, which may be used when it is displayed.

value. The value that is used when the user agent sets the **select**'s **name** variable.

The following example implements a survey form that lets users enter some personal information about themselves [ex2-16.wml]. The first card lets them **<select>** what portion of the survey they want to fill out and displays the choices they've already selected next to each section choice. Figures 2.25 through 2.29 show the program running on the Phone.com simulator.

```
<wml>
  <card id="card1">
    <do type="accept" >
      <go href="piminfo2.cgi" method="post" >
        <postfield name="sex" value="$sex" />
        <postfield name="income" value="$income"/>
        <postfield name="hobbies" value="$hobbies"/>
      </go>
    </do>
```

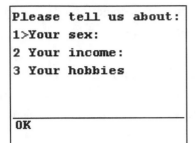

```
Please tell us about:
1>Your sex:
2 Your income:
3 Your hobbies




OK
```

Figure 2.25   A simple survey.

```
What is your sex?
1>Male
2 Female




OK
```

Figure 2.26   The sex card.

```
How much do you make?
1>$10-25K
2 $25-50K
3 $50-100K
4 Over $100K


OK
```

Figure 2.27   The income card.

```
Do you have hobbies?
1   Skiing
2* Reading
3*>Movies


OK                 Pick
```

Figure 2.28   The hobbies card.

```
Please tell us about:
1 Your sex: Female
2 Your income:
$50-100K
3>Your hobbies


OK
```

Figure 2.29   The final results.

```
<!-- starting card -->

    <p>
      Please tell us about:
      <select>
        <option onpick="#sexcard"> Your sex: $sex </option>
        <option onpick="#incomecard"> Your income: $income </option>
        <option onpick="#hobbiescard"> Your hobbies </option>
      </select>
```

```
      </p>
    </card>

  <!-- sex data entry -->

    <card id="sexcard" >
      <p>
        What is your sex?
        <select name="sex" >
          <option value="Male" > Male </option>
          <option value="Female" > Female </option>
        </select>
      </p>
    </card>

  <!-- income data entry -->

    <card id="incomecard" >
      <p>
        How much do you make?
        <select name="income" >
          <option value="$$10-50K" > $$10-25K </option>
          <option value="$$25-50K" > $$25-50K </option>
          <option value="$$50-100K" > $$50-100K </option>
          <option value="Over $$100K" > Over $$100K </option>
        </select>
      </p>
    </card>

  <!-- hobbies data entry -->

    <card id="hobbiescard">
      <p>
        Do you have hobbies?
        <select name="hobbies" multiple="true">
          <option value="ski" > Skiing </option>
          <option value="book" > Reading </option>
          <option value="film" > Movies </option>
        </select>
      </p>
    </card>
</wml>
```

Multilevel Choices

Just as the **<fieldset>** element lets you define hierarchical relationships between groups of data entry fields, the **optgroup** element lets you define hierarchical relationships between **<option>** elements. Its syntax is:

```
<optgroup
  title="VDATA"
>
  <optgroup>, <option>
</optgroup>
```

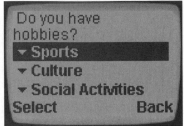

Figure 2.30 Some option groups.

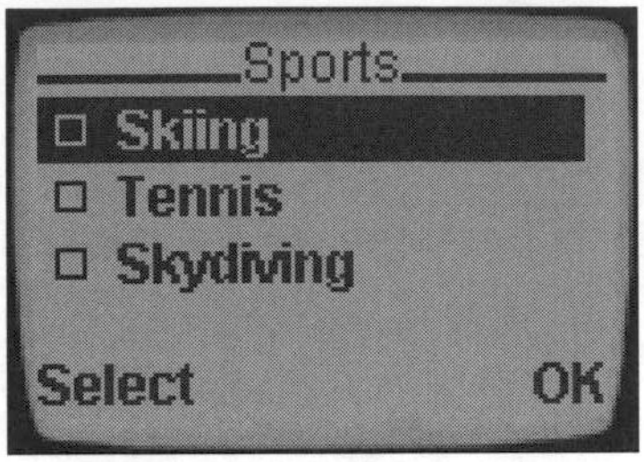

Figure 2.31 The Sports option group.

The **<optgroup>** element has only one attribute, **title**. The user agent may use the **title** when displaying an **<option>** group.

An **<option>** group can contain **<optgroup>** and **<option>** elements.

This example reworks the **hobbiescard** card of the previous example to include more hobbies divided into different groups [ex2-17.wml]. The sports subgroup is shown in Figures 2.30 and 2.31.

```
<card id="hobbiescard">
  <p>
    Do you have hobbies?
    <select name="hobbies" multiple="true">

      <optgroup title="Sports" >
        <option value="Skiing" >    Skiing </option>
        <option value="Tennis" >    Tennis </option>
        <option value="Skydiving" > Skydiving </option>
      </optgroup>

      <optgroup title="Culture" >
        <option value="Books" > Books </option>
        <option value="Plays" > Plays </option>
        <option value="Opera" > Opera </option>
        <option value="Films" > Films </option>
      </optgroup>

      <optgroup title="Social Activities" >
        <option value="Food/Wine" > Food/Wine </option>
        <option value="Dancing" >   Dancing </option>
        <option value="Traveling" > Traveling </option>
      </optgroup>
    </select>
  </p>
</card>
```

WMLScript

At some point in the WAP design life cycle, it became clear that WML could benefit from a way to include client-side procedural logic for doing simple things like checking user input and generating messages and dialogs locally. To solve this problem, the WAP Forum added a new component to the WAP application model: WMLScript [WAP]. Derived from ECMAScript [ECMA], which is itself derived from JavaScript [JAVASCRIPT] and Self [SELF], WMLScript is a lightweight scripting language that adds many capabilities to a WAP user agent. The WMLScript designers took all the best and most useful features of the language's ancestors, but removed all the features unnecessary or too complex for a wireless data environment.

The WMLScript execution model is function-oriented. There are no main programs. Instead, you create a set of functions and put the resulting text file on a server for access by WML and WMLScript programs. When a function is called, the WAP gateway automatically converts it into its compiled binary format and sends that optimized data over the wireless link. There are definite advantages to storing the source code on your content server. For instance, the WAP gateway can do inter-version adaptation for you—backward compatibility mapping if the language changes in the future.

To access the functions in a WMLScript compilation unit, you call them from a WML program using a URL, where the path points to the compilation unit and the fragment name is the function name. For example, here's a **<go>** element from the example we present at the end of this chapter:

```
<go href="bships.wmls#FireTorpedo ( $(gBoardWidth),
$(gBoardHeight) )"
```

The WAP gateway fetches the compilation unit source code, extracts the function **FireTorpedo,** and compiles it. The WMLScript bytecodes are downloaded to the user agent as part of the response and executed by the user agent. When the function is done, the interpreter returns control to the WML card that calls **FireTorpedo.**

Throughout the remainder of this chapter, we describe WMLScript and the WMLScript standard libraries. Because it is a fairly traditional procedural language like C and Java, and because we assume you already know how to program, we don't include a lot of short examples to demonstrate the language's obvious features. We do, however, include examples to explain some of the more complex features, and one larger example at the end of the chapter.

WML versus WMLScript

From a programmer's perspective, WML and WMLScript are different tools designed for different tasks. WML is a declarative markup language designed to express the characteristics of a user interface. WMLScript is an imperative scripting language designed to embody logic and functional programming constructs.

WML has one single, sequential execution thread that has an ongoing global context. There is no execution stack where parameters, instruction pointers, and local variables are stacked and unstacked. There is a history stack, but it contains locations—cards and URLs. WMLScript has functions, and you call one function from another. The execution is managed using a stack that contains parameters, the current instruction pointer, local variables, and so on. When you call a function, things get pushed on the stack. When you exit, they get popped and disappear.

All WML variables are global. In contrast, all WMLScript variables are local, lasting only as long as the function they reside in is executing. At compile time, WMLScript keeps track of three name spaces—variables, functions, and pragmas (compilation unit-level information).

WML has no procedural statements (although the event/task model does provide limited procedure-like capabilities). WMLScript has a useful set of traditional procedural language statements—an **if . . . else** statement, loops, and so on.

WML is content-focused, with elements for formatting output and entering data. WMLScript is procedure-focused. Other than one library function for letting a user enter a string, and another that lets you refresh the device's display, you cannot directly do any data entry or display manipulation with WMLScript.

WML has limited data handling capabilities. You can set variables, create choice lists, and create data-entry format masks. WMLScript, although a loosely typed language, has several internal data types, libraries for converting between types, strings (which you can use for simple array-like operations), and other more sophisticated data handling features.

WML is not extensible, except by revising the WML specification. WMLScript includes features for adding libraries of standardized functions. Currently, the WAP Forum does not provide tools or information for third-party developers to create their own libraries. Regardless, it's much easier to extend a language by adding a library than by overhauling a specification.

Even though WML and WMLScript are separate tools for separate tasks, you can use them together. You can call a WMLScript function from a WML deck, passing parameters to the function. In addition, WMLScript has library functions that let you read and write WML variables, create new contexts, and execute **<refresh>** tasks from a WMLScript program. You can also queue **<go>** and **<prev>** tasks for execution after the WMLScript interpreter finishes its current execution thread.

WMLScript Basics

Like all programming languages, WMLScript is a sequence of case-sensitive language tokens, words, and literals, separated by white space. Groups of tokens form statements, which are separated by semicolons.

You use identifiers to name variables, functions, and pragmas (compilation unit information). WMLScript uses the same rules for naming identifiers that WML uses for variable names:

- Identifiers are case sensitive.
- They can only include alphabetic and numeric characters and the underscore character ("_").
- They cannot start with a digit.

WMLScript has one additional rule for identifier names: They cannot be the same as a reserved word. Table 3.1 shows a list of the current WMLScript reserved words.

WMLScript tracks three separate name spaces—variables and function parameters, function names, and pragmas. You can use the same identifier in each of the name spaces so that you can, for instance, have a variable, a function, and a formal parameter with the same name.

Table 3.1 WMLScript Reserved Words

access	else	invalid	this
agent	enum	isvalid	throw
break	equiv	lib	true
case	export	meta	try
catch	extends	name	typeof
class	extern	new	url
const	false	null	use
continue	finally	path user	while
debugger	for	private var	with
default	function	public void	
delete	header	return	
div	http	sizeof	
div=	if	struct	
do	import	super	
domain	in	switch	

Source code comments come in two forms, both identical to C and C++:

```
//single line comments
```

```
/*
multiline
comments
*/
```

Data Types

WMLScript is a weakly typed language. You don't declare data types, but the compiler and runtime environment keep track of the current type of a variable, which is determined when a value is assigned to it. The language supports five data types:

Boolean   Valid values are **true** and **false**.

Integer   Valid range is −2,147,483,648 to 2,147,483,647. You specify hexadecimal and octal literals by preceding appropriate hex and octal digits with "0x" (or "0X") and "0" (zero), respectively.

Float   Valid range is ±1.17549435E-38 to ±3.402823476E+38. You can specify floating-point literal exponents with "e" or "E". Floating-point underflow results in the value 0.0. All other errors result in the value **invalid**.

String   Strings can be enclosed in single or double quotes. You include special characters in strings by preceding them with a backslash ("\"). Table 3.2 lists the special character sequences.

invalid   This literal denotes an **invalid** value. An invalid might occur, for instance, when a floating-point operation results in a number outside the allowable range for floating-point numbers. It is used any time there's a need to distinguish a data item's value from the other four data types.

Variables

Like all programming languages, WMLScript programs have variables. Variables are weakly typed—their data type changes based on their most recent assignment. They also have local scope, lasting only as long as the function in which they're declared is executing. Statement blocks delimited by curly brackets ("{" and "}") have no effect on variable scoping.

You must declare variables before using them in an expression; a declaration can be placed anywhere a WMLScript statement can occur. It consists of the reserved **var** followed by a case-sensitive variable name, which can include alphabetic characters, digits, and the underscore ("_") character. Variable names cannot begin with a digit.

Table 3.2 Special Character Sequences

SEQUENCE	INTERPRETATION
\'	Single quote
\"	Double quote
\\	Backslash
\/	Forward slash
\b	Backspace
\f	Form feed
\n	Newline
\r	Carriage return
\t	Horizontal tab
\xhh	The ISO8859-1 character encoded by the hexadecimal digits hh.
\ooo	The ISO8859-1 character encoded by the octal digits ooo.
\uhhhh	The Unicode character encoded by the hexadecimal digits hhhh.

A declaration can include an optional initial value. If there is one, the WMLScript compiler uses that value to determine the initial type of the variable.

Operators

Because WMLScript is designed to provide procedural logic, it contains a rich set of assignment, arithmetic, and logical operators. You combine variables and literals with operators to create expressions that are evaluated in a certain order. An expression's evaluation order depends on the precedence and associativity of its operators.

Table 3.3 lists the full set of WMLScript operators. It also shows:

- Default precedence when an operator is evaluated in an expression (you can override the default precedence using parentheses);

- Associativity, the order in which the operands are evaluated—left to right ("L") or right to left ("R");

- Valid operand types and the types of the resulting values;

- A brief description.

Here are some comments about the less-obvious operators, from top to bottom.

typeof returns an integer value that describes the internal type of its operand. Valid values range from zero to four, representing integer, floating point, string, Boolean, and **invalid**, respectively.

isvalid returns a Boolean value indicating the type validity of its operand. **false** indicates that the operand is not a valid expression. For instance, **isvalid** (**1/0**) is **false**.

The conditional operator is the only ternary WMLScript operator. It takes three operands. If the first operand evaluates to **true**, it returns the result of evaluating the second operand; otherwise, it returns the result of evaluating the third operand. Here's an example:

```
result = male ? "John" : "Mary";
```

If **male** evaluates to **true**, **result** is set to "John"; otherwise, it's set to "Mary."

The comma operator (","), the operator with the lowest precedence, lets you evaluate multiple expressions in place of one expression. You can use it, for instance, to initialize more than one variable in a **for** loop initialization clause. The comma operator returns the result of its last operand.

NOTE

Parameter lists in function calls are not separated by the comma operator, just plain old commas. If you want to use the comma operator as part of a parameter passed to a function, you have to enclose it in parentheses.

Type Conversions

WMLScript does whatever type conversions it can. If the conversion seems logical, it probably does it. See the WMLScript specification in [WAP] if you want to read the gory details of the conversion rules. There are a few explicit cases you need to know about:

- Boolean **true** is converted to the string "true." Non-zero integers and floating-point numbers are converted to Boolean **true**.

- Boolean **false** is converted to the string "false." Integer 0 and floating-point 0.0 are converted to Boolean **false**.

- The empty string (" ") is converted to the Boolean **false**. All other strings are converted to **true**.

- The empty string cannot be converted to an integer or floating-point number.

NOTE

Most WMLScript operators, those with the Result flagged with an asterisk ("*") in Table 3.3, return an **invalid** value if any of its implicit data conversions fail or if one of its operands is **invalid**.

Functions

In order to use WMLScript, you need to create a collection of functions and put them in a compilation unit, a separately-compiled source code file. The compilation unit has no global variables and no main program. It's roughly equivalent to a subroutine library.

Each function is declared with the keyword **function,** followed by an optional parameter list, followed by a block statement that contains the body of the function. There are a few rules you need to follow when defining functions:

- Function names must be unique within a compilation unit.
- Function declarations cannot be nested.
- All parameters are passed by value—they behave like local variables that have been initialized prior to execution of the function body.

Table 3.3 WMLScript Operators

OPERATOR	PRECEDENCE	ASSOCIATIVITY	OPERAND(S)	RESULT	OPERATION
++	1	R	number	number*	pre- or post-increment (unary)
--	1	R	number	number*	pre- or post-decrement (unary)
+	1	R	number	number*	unary plus (does nothing)
-	1	R	number	number*	unary minus (negation)
~	1	R	integer	integer*	bitwise NOT (unary)
!	1	R	Boolean	Boolean*	logical NOT (unary)
typeof	1	R	any	integer	return internal data type (unary)
isvalid	1	R	any	Boolean	check for validity (unary)
*	2	L	numbers	number*	multiplication
/	2	L	numbers	floating-point	division*
div	2	L	integers	integer*	integer division
%	2	L	integers	integer*	remainder
-	3	L	numbers	number*	subtraction
+	3	L	numbers	number	number
+	3	L	strings	string	string concatenation
<<	4	L	integers	integer*	bitwise left shift
>>	4	L	integers	integer*	bitwise right shift with sign extension
>>>	4	L	integers	integer*	bitwise right shift with zero fill
<	5	L	numbers or strings	Boolean*	less than
<=	5	L	numbers or strings	Boolean*	less than or equal
>	5	L	numbers or strings	Boolean*	greater than

Symbol	Precedence	Associativity	Operands	Result	Description
>=	5	L	numbers or strings	Boolean*	greater than or equal
==	6	L	numbers or strings	Boolean*	equal (identical values)
!=	6	L	numbers or strings	Boolean*	not equal (different values)
&	7	L	integers	integer*	bitwise AND
<	8	L	integers	integer*	bitwise XOR
|	9	L	integers	integer*	bitwise OR
&&	10	L	Booleans	Boolean*	logical AND
||	11	L	Booleans	Boolean*	logical OR
?:	12	R	Boolean, any, any	any*	conditional expression
=	13	R	variable, any	any	assignment
*=	13	R	variable, number	number*	assignment with multiplication
-=	13	R	variable, number	number*	assignment with subtraction
/=	13	R	variable, number	floating-point*	assignment with division
%=	13	R	variable, integer	integer*	assignment with remainder
div=	13	R	variable, integer	integer*	assignment with integer divide
+=	13	R	variable, number	number	assignment with addition
+=	13	R	variable, string	string	assignment with concatenation
<<=	13	R	variable, integer	integer*	assignment with bitwise left shift
>>=	13	R	variable, integer	integer*	assignment with bitwise right shift sign extend
>>>=	13	R	variable, integer	integer*	assignment with bitwise right shift, zero fill
&=	13	R	variable, integer	integer*	assignment with bitwise AND
^=	13	R	variable, integer	integer*	assignment with bitwise XOR
|=	13	R	variable, integer	integer*	assignment with bitwise OR
,	14	L	any	any	multiple evaluation

- Function calls must contain exactly the same number of parameters as the function declaration.

- Functions always return a value. The default is an empty string.

Here's the basic syntax of a function declaration (items in square brackets are optional):

```
[extern] function funcname ( [parameter list] )
{
//function body
};
```

You use the **extern** keyword to indicate a function that can be called from outside its compilation unit. parameter list is a comma-separated list of names.

There are three different ways that you call WMLScript functions from other functions, depending on the caller's location. The first method, which should be familiar, is for calling functions within the same compilation unit. You include the function name and its parameter list in an expression:

```
x = foo_function ( parm1, parm2 );
```

The second method is for calling functions in other compilation units. You start with a **use url** pragma statement (see "Compilation Units" for more details about WMLScript pragmas):

```
use url unitName unitUrl
```

such as

```
use url FooUnit "http://www.worldfaq.com/foo";
```

You then call the function much the way you refer to a WML deck, using a fragment anchor plus a parameter list:

```
x = FooUnit#foo_function (parm1, parm2 );
```

In order for this function call to work, you have to declare **foo_function** as **extern** in the **FooUnit** compilation unit, and it has to have exactly two parameters.

The third way to call a WMLScript function is for functions that are included in the WMLScript standard libraries (see "WMLScript Libraries" for details on the currently-defined libraries). All you do is precede the function name with the library name. For instance, to get the maximum allowable floating-point number, you use

```
var maxfloat = Float.Max ( );
```

Statements

WMLScript has a straightforward, utilitarian set of procedural statements you can use. They can be loosely categorized into simple statements, flow control statements, and flow break statements.

You've already seen examples of most of the WMLScript simple statements:

```
;                              // the empty statement
var maxfloat, minfloat;        // the var statement
maxfloat = Float.Max ( );      // the expression statement
{ };                           // the block statement
```

There are three flow control statements that are functionally equivalent to the same statements in C:

```
if ( expression ) statement [else statement]
while ( expression ) statement
for ( [expression]; [expression]; [expression] ) statement
```

For all the expressions that evaluate to a Boolean value, **invalid** is considered **false.**

Finally, there are three flow break statements that are also functionally equivalent to the same statements in C: **break, continue,** and **return. break** terminates the currently executing **while** or **for** loop. **continue** terminates the current loop cycle of a **while** or **for** loop, but does not terminate the loop execution. **return** exits the current function, possibly returning a value.

The sample program at the end of this chapter includes examples of most of these statements.

Compilation Units

The final WMLScript language construct you need to know about is the compilation unit. A compilation unit is a separately-compiled source code file that contains definitions for a group of related functions.

Compilation units can include pragmas—statements that specify compilation unit-level information. Pragmas, which all start with the keyword **use,** must appear at the beginning of the compilation unit, prior to any function declarations. WMLScript has three pragmas: **url, access,** and **meta.**

url Pragma

You've already seen the **url** pragma in an earlier example. You use it to reference functions in other compilation units:

```
use url FooUnit "http://www.foosite.com/foo";


function UseFoo ( ) {

  var x = FooUnit#foo_function ( 5, 6 );
}
```

If you have multiple **url** pragmas in a compilation unit, they all need to go at the top of the source file.

access Pragma

The second pragma is the **access** pragma. It defines some rules, using domain name and path settings, about who can access the functions in the compilation unit. Function callers must be calling from URLs that match the **domain** and **path** settings.

Matching is done against full components of both the domain and path names—there is no implicit wildcard matching. For example, "wapforum.org" matches the domain "org" but not the domain "forum.org." The default domain is the compilation unit's domain. The default path is "/."

Paths can be both relative and absolute. Relative paths are converted to absolute paths by the user agent before they are checked against a compilation unit's **access** pragma.

Here's the syntax for the **access** pragma. There are three forms, shown separated by a vertical bar ("|") as follows:

```
use access
   domain   domain_name |
   path     path_name |
   domain   domain_name path path_name;
```

A compilation unit can have only one **access** pragma. By default, access control is disabled. For the following access control:

```
use access domain "worldfaq.com" path "/stats";
```

the following URLs can access the **extern** functions in the compilation unit:

```
http://www.worldfaq.com/stats/run1
http://www1.worldfaq.com/stats/bin-cgi/example1
```

The following URLs cannot access any of the **extern** functions in the compilation unit:

```
http://www.wfaq.com/stats/run1
http://www1.worldfaq.com/bin-cgi/example1
```

meta Pragma

The final type of WMLScript pragma is the **meta** pragma. You use it to define information that may be useful to an entity in the WAP Application Environment.

You specify meta information with a property name followed by the property's value. In addition, some meta information may include a scheme name for interpreting the data. Here's the syntax of the **meta** pragma:

```
use meta
  name        propName "propvalue"; |
  http equiv propname "propValue"; |
  user agent propName "propValue";
```

There are three types of meta information: **name**, **http equiv**, and **user agent**. **name** meta information is intended for use by origin servers:

```
use meta name "copyright" "(c) Phone.com, 1999"
```

User agents should ignore it. Network servers should not emit WMLScript containing it.

http equiv meta information should be interpreted by a WAP server as HTTP headers (see [RFC2616] and Chapter 5, "Caching," for more details on HTTP headers):

```
use meta http equiv "Keywords" "Reference, Encyclopedia";
use meta http equiv "cache-control" "no-cache";
```

It should be converted to WSP or HTTP response headers by a WAP gateway if the compilation unit is compiled before it arrives at the user agent.

user agent meta information is intended for user agents.

```
use meta user agent "persistent_store" "X:234, Y:122, Z:672"
"Pairs"
```

It must be delivered to the user agent and not removed by any network intermediary. This feature is not currently used by any WAP-compliant user agents. It may be used by specific browsers to implement WAP extensions.

WMLScript Libraries

Designed to be a lean-and-mean language, WMLScript lacks many basic programming language features such as string handling, robust arithmetic functions, and a way to interface with WML 1.1 programs. Fortunately, WMLScript 1.1 has six standard libraries that add quite a bit of functionality to the language: the **Lang**, **Float**, **String**, **URL**, **WMLBrowser**, and **Dialogs** libraries.

The **Float**, **String**, and **URL** libraries contain functions for handling floating-point numbers, strings, and URLs, respectively. The **Dialogs** library provides you with functions for presenting dialogs to the user. The **Lang** library enhances WMLScript with additional arithmetic functions. The **URL** library lets you fetch URL components and manage URLs. The **WMLBrowser** library provides a simple interface for reading and writing WML variables and executing some WML tasks.

A WAP 1.1-compliant user agent must support all of these libraries except **Float**. For integer-only devices that have no **Float** library, there are a few caveats you need to be aware of:

- **Lang.float**, the function used for testing for the presence of floating-point support, returns **false** (see the next section for a description of this function).

- Library functions accept only Boolean, integer, string, and **invalid** arguments.

- All floating-point conversion rules are ignored.

- The **Lang.parseFloat** function returns **invalid** (see the next section for a description of this function).

- All **Float** functions return **invalid**.

The WMLScript libraries use simple error handling techniques. If any parameter is **invalid**, the function returns **invalid**. Also, if a parameter is not the type expected by a function and cannot be converted to the proper type, the function returns **invalid**.

In the following sections, each function name is listed, followed by its parameter list. Each parameter list indicates the data type expected for each parameter. The libraries use WMLScript's standard data type conversion rules to get the proper parameter types. Any exceptions to the default rules are noted in the parameter descriptions.

All function parameters are passed by value. When a function such as a string handling function returns a value, it is a new data entity. None of the original parameter values are changed.

Appendix D contains a summary of all the WMLScript functions, grouped in the same order in which they appear in the following sections.

Lang Library

The **Lang** library provides some core language capabilities. Its functions can be categorized as arithmetic, conversion, flow control, environment, and random number functions.

Arithmetic Functions

The **Lang** library has three of the most basic arithmetic functions. The **Float** library has more sophisticated arithmetic capabilities.

abs (*number*). Return the absolute value of *number*, returning the same type as *number*.

max (*number1*, *number2*). Return the maximum of *number1* and *number2*. The returned type is the same as the selected number. If the numbers are equal, *number1* is returned.

min (*number1*, *number2*). Return the minimum of *number1* and *number2*. The returned type is the same as the selected number. If the numbers are equal, *number1* is returned.

Conversion Functions

The **Lang** library conversion functions let you test for and convert strings into integer and floating-point numbers.

isFloat (*value*). Return **true** if *value* can be converted to a floating-point number using **parseFloat**; **false** otherwise.

```
var x - Lang.isFloat (" 135E-4, a real #");  // x - true
var x = Lang.isFloat ("+125E");     // x = false
```

isInt (*value*). Return **true** if *value* can be converted to a integer using **parseInt**; **false** otherwise.

```
var x = Lang.isInt ("135.25"); // x = true
var x = Lang.isInt ("temp");   // x = false
```

parseFloat (*string*). Return the floating-point equivalent of *string*. Parsing stops with the first character that is not part of a valid floating-point literal. **parseFloat** returns **invalid** if there is a parsing error or the device does not support floating-point numbers.

```
var x = Lang.parseFloat (" 135E-4, a real #");   // x = 0.0135
var x = Lang.parseFloat ("+125E"); // x = invalid
```

parseInt (*string*). Return the integer equivalent of *string*. Parsing stops with the first character that is not part of a valid integer literal. **parseInt** returns **invalid** if there is a parsing error.

```
var x = Lang.parseInt ("135.25");   // x = 135
var x = Lang.ParseInt ("temp");     // x = invalid
```

Environment Functions

The **Lang** environment functions let you query the user agent about its capabilities.

characterSet ( ). Return an integer that is the value assigned by the IANA identifying the character set supported by the WMLScript interpreter (see [IANA] for more information about the valid character set identifiers).

float ( ). Return true if floating-point numbers are supported; false otherwise.

maxInt ( ). Return the maximum integer value (currently 2,147,483,647).

minInt ( ). Return the minimum integer value (currently –2,147,483,648).

Flow Control Functions

The **Lang** flow control functions let you terminate the current WMLScript interpreter execution thread and return control to the calling entity.

abort (*string*). Terminate the current WMLScript bytecode interpretation abnormally, returning a *string* describing the error. This string is not accessible in a WML document.

exit (*value*). Terminate the current WMLScript bytecode interpretation normally, returning *value* to the caller. This string is not accessible in a WML document.

Random Number Functions

The **Lang** library contains an integer random number generator, plus a function to seed the generator.

random (*integer*). Return a randomly-chosen positive integer between zero and *integer*. **random** returns **invalid** if integer is less than zero.

seed (*integer*). Initialize the random number generator and return an empty string. If the seed value is a floating-point number, **seed** uses **Float.int**, if it's available, to first convert the seed value to an integer. If **Float.int** is not available, **seed** returns **invalid**.

Float Library

The **Float** library contains two environment functions and six arithmetic functions. If floating-point operations are not supported on a particular device, all **Float** library functions return **invalid**. You can call **Lang.float** to find out if floating-point operations are available.

Environment Functions

The **Float** environment functions let you find out the range of valid floating-point numbers.

maxFloat ( ). Return the maximum positive floating-point value (currently 3.40282347E+38).

minFloat ( ). Return the smallest positive floating-point value (currently 1.17549435E-38).

Arithmetic Functions

The **Float** arithmetic functions provide arithmetic capabilities above and beyond what's in the Lang library.

ceil (*number*). Return the smallest integer value that is not less than *number*.

```
var x = Float.ceil ( "2.5" );  // x = 3
var x = Float.ceil ( -2.5 );   // x = -2
```

floor (*number*). Return the greatest integer value that is not greater than *number*.

```
var x = Float.floor ( 2.5 );    // x = 2
var x = Float.floor ( "-2.5" ); // x = -3
```

int (*number*). Return the integer part of *number*.

pow (*number1, number2*). Return *number1* to the *number2* power. If *number1* is negative, *number2* must be an integer. If *number1* is zero and *number2* is less than zero, **pow** returns **invalid**.

```
var x = Float.pow ( 3, 2.0 ); // x = 9
var x = Float.pow ( -1, 2 );   // x = 1
var x = Float.pow ( -1, 1.5 ); // x = invalid
var x = Float.pow ( false, "-1.5" );    // x = invalid
```

round (*number*). Return the integer closest to *number*. If two integers are equally close to *number*, **round** returns the larger of the two.

```
var x = round ( 2.5 );    // x = 3
var x = round ( "-2.5" ); // x = -2
```

sqrt (*number*). Return the square root of *number*. **sqrt** returns **invalid** if *number* is less than zero.

String Library

WMLScript has a robust string handling library with functions that can be grouped into basic, substring, element, and conversion functions. The element functions divide a string into a group of substrings separated by a specific character and let you manipulate individual elements using zero-based indices. All string operations are case sensitive.

Basic Functions

The basic functions let you test string length, extract individual characters, and remove string white space.

charAt (*string*, *number*). Return a single-character string from *string* containing the character at location *number*. If *number* is a floating-point number, it is first converted to an integer if **Float.int** is available; otherwise, **invalid** is returned. If *number* is out of range, **charAt** returns an empty string. Characters are indexed starting at zero.

compare (*string1*, *string2*). Do a lexical comparison of *string1* and *string2* using the character codes in the user agent's native character set. **compare** returns minus one if *string1* is less than *string2*, zero if they are identical, and one if *string2* is less than *string1*. The native character set is the same as the one identified by **Lang.characterSet** (see [IANA] for details on the valid character sets).

isEmpty (*string*). Return **true** if *string*'s length is zero; **false** otherwise.

length (*string*). Return the integer length of *string*.

squeeze (*string*). Return a string that is the equivalent of *string* with all consecutive white space removed. White-space characters include horizontal and vertical tabs, form feeds, spaces, line feeds, and carriage returns.

trim (*string*). Return a string that is the equivalent of *string* with all leading and trailing white space removed. White-space characters include horizontal and vertical tabs, form feeds, spaces, line feeds, and carriage returns.

Substring Functions

The substring functions involve identifying or manipulating a string that is part of a larger string. Substring indices start at zero.

subString (string, startNumber, lengthNumber). Return the substring of string that starts at location startNumber and has length lengthNumber. If startNumber is less than zero, then zero is used for the starting location. If lengthNumber exceeds the number of characters in the string starting at startNumber, the remaining characters are returned. If startNumber is larger than the length of string, or lengthNumber is less than or equal to zero, **subString** returns an empty string.

```
var x =
 String.subString ( "Hello Dolly!", 0, 5 );  // x = "Hello"
```

```
var x =
 String.subString ( "Hello Dolly!", -1, 5 ); // x = "Hello"
var x =
 String.subString ( "Hello Dolly!", 6, 10 ); // x = "Dolly!"
var x =
 String.subString ( "Hello Dolly!", 15, 0 ); // x = ""
```

find (string, subString). Return the integer index of the first location in string
that matches subString. If there is no match, **find** returns -1. Matching
requires identical character representations.

```
var x = String.find ( "Hello Dolly!", "doll" ); // x = 6
var x = String.find ( "Hello Dolly!", "dog" ); // x = -1
```

replace (string, oldString, newString). Return a new string in which all occur-
rences of oldString are replaced with newString. Matching requires identical
character representations.

```
var x =
  String.replace ("Hello Dolly!", "doll", "dog" );  // x = "Hello Dolly!"
var x =
  String.replace ("Hello Dolly!", "Doll", "dogg" ); // x = "Hello doggy!"
```

Element Functions

The element functions scan a string for one or more elements—substrings separated by a recurring character. The empty string is considered a valid element.
Although you specify the separating character with a string that can have length
greater than one, only the first character is used for identifying elements. Elements are numbered starting with zero.

elementAt (string, number, sepString). Return the numberth element in
string, where an element is any substring of string, including the empty
string, that is delimited by the first character of sepString. Elements are
indexed starting at zero.

   If number is less than zero, the first element is returned. If it is larger than
the number of elements in string, the last element is returned. If string is the
empty string, the empty string is returned. If number is a floating-point number,
it is first converted to an integer if **Float.int** is available; otherwise, **invalid** is
returned. **elementAt** returns **invalid** if sepString is an empty string.

```
var x =
 String.elementAt ( "Hello Dolly! ", 0, " # " ); // x = "Hello"
var x =
 String.elementAt ( "Hello Dolly! ", 1, " ! " ); // x = "Dolly!"
var x =
 String.elementAt ( "Hello Dolly! ", 2, "  " ); // x = ""
```

```
var x =
 String.elementAt ( "Hello Dolly! ", 3, " # " ); // x = ""
var x =
 String.elementAt ( "Hello Dolly! ", 0, "" ); // x = invalid
```

elements (*string, sepString*). Return an integer count of the number of sub-strings in *string*, including empty strings, that are delimited by the first character of *sepString*. **elements** returns **invalid** if *sepString* is an empty string.

```
var x = String.elements ("Hello Dolly !", " " ); // x = 3
var x = String.elements (" Hello Dolly ! ", " ; " ); // x = 5
var x = String.elements ("Hello Dolly !", ";" ); // x = 0
var x = String.elements ("Hello Dolly!", "" ); // x = invalid
```

insertAt (string, elemString, number, sepString). Return a new string consisting of string plus elemstring (and sepstring if necessary) inserted as the numberth element. Element indexes start at zero.

If number is less than zero, elemstring is inserted as the first element. If it is larger than the number of elements in string, elemstring is inserted as the last element. If string is the empty string, a new string set to elemstring is returned. If number is a floating-point number, it is first converted to an integer if **Float.int** is available; otherwise, **invalid** is returned. **elementAt** returns **invalid** if sepstring is an empty string.

```
var x = String.insertAt
 ( "x=2,y=3,z=4", "t=16", 0, "," ); x = "t=16,x=2,y=3,z=4"
var x = String.insertAt
 ( "x=2,y=3,z=4", "t=16", 5, "," ); x = "x=2,y=3,z=4,t=16"
```

removeAt (string, number, sepString). Return a new string consisting of string with the numberth element removed where element is any substring of string delimited by the first character of sepString. Elements indexes start at zero.

If number is less than zero, the first element is removed. If it is larger than the number of elements in string, the last element is removed. If string is the empty string, the empty string is returned. If number is a floating-point number, it is first converted to an integer using **Float.int,** if it is available; otherwise **invalid** is returned. **elementAt** returns **invalid** if sepString is an empty string.

```
var x = String.removeAt
 ( "t=16,x=2,y=3,z=4", 0, "," ); // x = "x=2,y=3,z=4"
var x = String.removeAt
 ( "t=16,x=2,y=3,z=4", 5, "," ); // x = "t=16,x=2,y=3"
```

replaceAt (string, elemString, number, sepString). Return a new string consisting of string with the numberth element replaced by elemString. An element is any substring of string separated by the first character of sepstring. Elements indexes start at zero.

If number is less than zero, the first element is replaced. If it is larger than the number of elements in string, the last element is replaced. If string is the empty string, a new string set to elemString is returned. If number is a floating-point number, it is first converted to an integer if **Float.int** is available; otherwise, **invalid** is returned. **elementAt** returns **invalid** if sepString is an empty string.

```
var x = String.replaceAt
  ( "t=16,x=2,y=3,z=4", "v=12", 0, "," ); // x = "v=12,x=2,y=3,z=4"
var x = String.replaceAt
  ( "t=16,x=2,y=3,z=4", "v=11", 5, "," ); // x = "t=16,x=2,y=3,v=12"
```

Conversion Functions

The String library has two conversion functions. One is similar to a simplified, one-argument **sprintf** C function.

format (fmtString, value). Convert value to a string using the formatting string fmtString. fmString is an arbitrary string that should have at least one format specifier of the form

% [*width*] [. *precision*] *type*

where *type* is either "d" for integer, "f" for floating point, or "s" for string. To include a percent sign in a format string, use two consecutive percent signs ("%%").

width specifies the minimum number of characters to print. If the formatting results in fewer than *width* characters, the converted *value* is padded with blanks on the left until it is *width* wide. If the number of characters in *value* is greater than *width*, or *width* is not specified, all characters are printed.

precision specifies the precision of the result. Its interpretation depends on the *type* of the format specification:

d The minimum number of digits to format (the default value is one). The result is zero, filled on the left if necessary. If *precision* is zero and *value* is also zero, the result is the empty string.

f The number of digits to the right of the result's decimal point (the default value is six), rounded to the appropriate value. If *precision* is zero, or a period with no *precision* value appears in the format specifier, no decimal point is included in the result.

s The maximum number of characters to print (the default is all characters).

format returns **invalid** if it encounters an illegal format specifier in *fmtString*, or if it cannot convert *value* to the type indicated in the format specifier.

```
var x = String.format ( "%5d", 45 );      // x = "   45"
var x = String.format ( "%5.4d", -45 );   // x = " -045"
var x = String.format ( "%f", 3.14159 );  // x = "3.14159"
var x = String.format ( "%8.3f", 3.14159 );    // x = "   3.141"
```

toString (*value*). Convert *value* to a string and return the result. This function does exactly the same thing as the WLMScript automatic data type conversions, except that the value **invalid** is converted to the string "invalid."

URL Library

The URL library contains a group of functions for manipulating and verifying both relative and absolute URLs. The syntax for a URL, defined in detail in [RFC2396], is:

```
[scheme://] [host] [:port] [/]path [;parameters] [?query]
[#fragment]
```

For those functions that return a string containing a component of a URL, leading and trailing delimiters are not included in the returned result. The one exception is the path name. It includes leading right slashes. For instance, this URL

```
http://www.worldfaq.com:80/scripts/addcity.wml;3;2?loc=houston&g
mt=7#usa
```

has the following components:

Scheme	http
host	www.worldfaq.com
port80	
path	/scripts/addcity.wml
parameters	3;2
query	loc=houston,gmt=7
fragment	usa

The URL library functions can be grouped into three categories: functions for managing URLs, functions for extracting individual components from URLs, and a function for retrieving content from a URL.

Managing URLs

The URL library lets you validate, retrieve, create, and escape URLs.

escapeString (string). Return a string, equivalent to string, in which each special character identified in [RFC2396] is converted to its hexadecimal escape sequence, a percent sign followed by its two-digit hexadecimal encoding. If string contains characters that are not part of the US-ASCII character set, invalid is returned. Table 2.2 lists the URL escape characters from [RFC2396].

```
var x =
 URL.escapeString ( "?x=2,y=3,z=4" );
// x = "%3fx%3d2%2cy%3d3%2cz%3d4"
```

getBase ( ). Return a string containing the absolute URL, without the fragment, of the current WMLScript compilation unit.

getReferer ( ). Return a string containing the smallest URL, relative to the base URL of the current compilation unit, to the resource that called the current compilation unit. An empty string is returned if there is no referrer. For example, if a deck at www.worldfaq.com/calcs/timecalc.wml calls a WMLScript function at www.worldfaq.com/scripts/timescript.wmls that contains

```
var x = getReferer ( );
```

x is set to "calcs/timecalc.wml."

isValid (*string*). Return **true** if *string* is a valid relative or absolute URL; otherwise, return **false**.

resolve (*baseString, embeddedString*). Return a string containing an absolute URL that is the result of combining *baseString* and *embeddedString* according to the rules specified in [RFC2396]. If embeddedString contains an absolute URL, it is returned unchanged.

```
var root = "http://www.worldfaq.com";
var path = "calcs/timecalc.wml";
set var x = resolve ( root, path );
// x = " http://www.worldfaq.com/calcs/timecalc.wml"
```

unescapeString (*string*). Return a string, equivalent to *string*, in which the special characters identified in [RFC2396] are converted from their hexadecimal escape sequences to their US-ASCII equivalents. If *string* contains characters that are not part of the US-ASCII character set, invalid is returned. Table 2.2 lists the URL escape characters from [RFC2396].

```
var x = URL.unescapeString ("%3fx%3d2%2cy%3d3%2cz%3d4" );
// x = "?x=2,y=3,z=4"
```

Component Extraction Functions

The component extraction functions let you retrieve individual components from relative and absolute URLs. These functions first test for a valid URL, using **isValid** ( ), before extracting any components. If **isValid** is **false**, these functions return **invalid**.

getFragment (*string*). Return a string containing the fragment portion of the relative or absolute URL *string*.

getHost (*string*). Return a string containing the host's name from the relative or absolute URL *string*.

getPort (*string*). Return a string containing the server's port number from the relative or absolute URL *string*.

getParameters (*string*). Return a string containing the parameters from the relative or absolute URL *string*.

getPath (*string*). Return a string containing the path from the relative or absolute URL *string*.

getScheme (*string*). Return a string containing the Internet protocol scheme from the relative or absolute URL *string*.

getQuery (*string*). Return a string containing the query portion of the relative or absolute URL *string*.

Content Retrieval Functions

The lone content retrieval function in the URL library lets you assign the contents of a text file to a WMLScript variable.

loadString (urlString, contentTypeString). Return a string containing the content specified by urlString and contentTypeString. contentTypeString can contain only one content type of the form "text/subtype" with no leading or trailing white space. "subtype" can be any valid subtype. If the load is unsuccessful, or the returned content is the wrong content type, **loadString** returns an integer error code based on the URL scheme. HTTP error codes are used if the scheme is HTTP or WSP.

To get the source code of the body of the WMLScript function "teststrings" in the compilation unit "testlib," you might use the following:

```
var loc = "http://www.worldfaq.com/test/testlib#teststrings";
var x = URL.loadString ( loc, "text/wmlscript" );
```

WMLBrowser Library

The WMLBrowser library contains functions that let you access WML variables in the current user agent context. In addition, you can tell the WML user agent to execute a particular task when the WMLScript interpreter terminates its current execution thread. You can also retrieve the relative URL of the currently executing WML card.

All these functions return **invalid** if the user agent does not support WML or if the WMLScript interpreter cannot be invoked by the WML user agent.

Variable Functions

The variable functions let you read and write variables in the current WML user agent context.

getVar (*string*). Return a string containing the value of the variable *string* from the current WML user agent context. **getVar** returns an empty string if the variable does not exist and **invalid** if *string* does not contain a properly formatted variable name. *string* may be a literal or a variable name.

setVar (*string, value*). Set the variable *string* in the current context to *value* and return **true** if the operation is successful; **false** otherwise. **setVar** returns **invalid** if *string* does not contain a properly-formatted variable name. *string* may be a literal or a variable name.

Task Functions

go (*urlString*). Signal the WML browser that when control passes back from the WMLScript interpreter to the WML user agent, it should load the deck specified by *urlString* and execute that deck as part of the normal execution sequence. **go** returns **invalid** if *urlString* does not contain a proper URL. A fragment name is considered **invalid**—you need to provide a qualified URL name.

    WMLBrowser.go and **WMLBrowser.prev** (see the following) override each other—if either of them are called prior to control returning to the user agent, only the last task request is honored. If **go** ( ) or **prev** ( ) sets the next URL to an empty string, all requests are cancelled.

prev ( ). Signal the WML browser that when control passes back from the WMLScript interpreter to the WML user agent, it should execute a **prev** task. **WMLBrowser.prev** returns **invalid** if *urlString* does not contain a proper URL.

    WMLBrowser.go (see the preceding) and **WMLBrowser.prev** override each other—if either of them is called prior to control returning to the user agent, only the last task request is honored. If **go** or **prev** sets the next URL to an empty string, all requests are cancelled.

refresh ( ). Signal the WML user agent that it should update its context and refresh the device display. This function has the same effect as the WML **refresh** task. **WMLBrowser.refresh** returns an empty string.

newContext ( ). Clear the current WML user agent context and return an empty string. This function operates exactly the same as the WML card **new-context** attribute—the history stack is emptied, all context-specific variables are removed, and the device is reset to a well-known state.

NOTE
WMLBRowser.newContext can be a very destructive function. Use it with caution.

Query Functions

getCurrentCard ( ). Return a string containing the smallest possible URL, relative to the base of the current compilation unit, of the card currently being processed by the WML user agent, or invalid if there is no current card. getCurrentCard returns an absolute URL if the deck containing the current card has a base URL different from the current compilation unit.

As an example, if a deck at www.worldfaq.com/calcs/timecalc.wml#card1 calls a WMLScript function at www.worldfaq.com/scripts/timescript.wmls",

```
var x = getCurrentCard ( );
```

sets x to "calcs/timecalc.wml#card1."

Dialogs Library

The Dialogs library contains three user interface functions. All three display on the device screen a message in a format determined by the user agent, and wait for a user response.

prompt (string, defaultString). Displays string and prompts the user for input, using defaultString as the default input value. It returns the user's input string.

The following code might create the prompt shown in Figure 3.1:

Figure 3.1 A prompt.

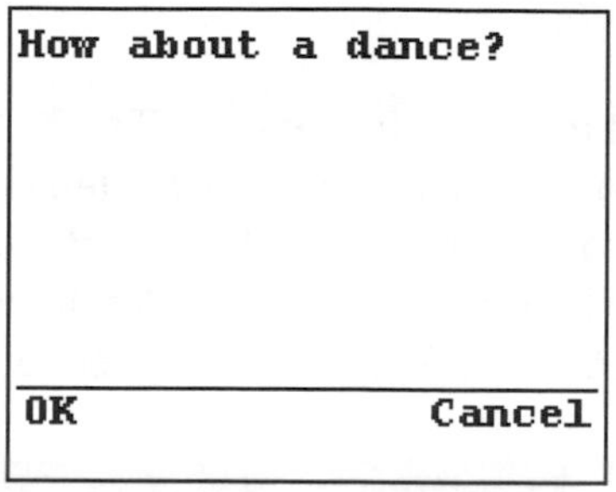

```
How about a dance?




OK                Cancel
```

Figure 3.2   A confirm dialog.

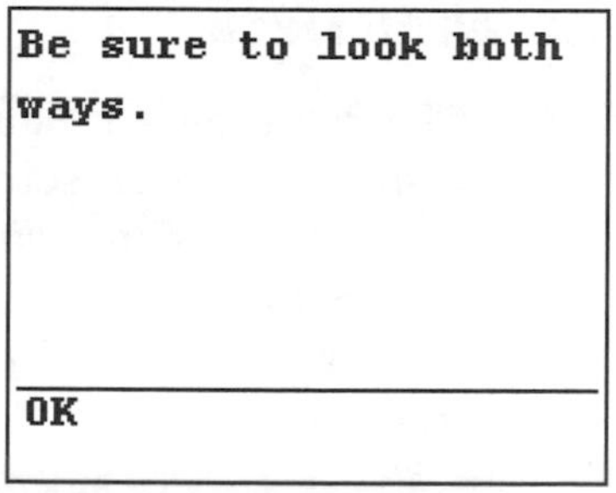

```
Be sure to look both
ways.




OK
```

Figure 3.3   An alert.

```
var ssno = "200.30.4000";
var ssno = Dialogs.prompt ("Social Security Number: ", ssno );
```

confirm (string, okString, cancelString). displays string and two choices for the user, OK, and Cancel, using okString and cancelString as the choice labels, and then waits for the user to select one of the choices. **confirm** returns **true** if the user selects OK, **false** if the user selects Cancel.

The following code might create the confirm dialog shown in Figure 3.2:

```
var OK="Sure";
var Cancel="No Way!"
var result = Dialogs.confirm ( "How about a dance?", OK, Cancel );
```

alert (*string*). displays *string*, waits for the user's confirmation, and returns the empty string. The following code might create the alert shown in Figure 3.3:

```
result = Dialogs.alert ("Be sure to look both ways.");
```

Battleships

Now that we've covered both WML and WMLScript, it's time for a fairly simple example—a game. We've developed a single-player version of the game Battleships.

Classic Battleships is a two-person game, where you set up your own board with multiple ships of different sizes, running both horizontally and vertically. Players then take turns firing torpedoes at each other. The first player to sink all the opponent's ships wins.

For this somewhat dumbed-down implementation, you first select a field playing size of up to 6 rows by 15 columns (the default size), and the device places a single coordinate ship on each row. You then select a series of coordinate destinations for torpedoes and keep firing until you hit all the ships.

The WML Deck

The Battleships deck is straightforward. It contains four cards. The first, **start**, displays a splash screen (see Figure 3.4) with two **<option>** elements in a **<select>** element: Play and Set Board Size. If you select Play, the deck calls a WMLScript function named **InitBoard,** which creates the display lines of the playing board, initializes some other variables, and returns to the second card, **display.**

display displays the game board (see Figure 3.5) and waits for the user to hit the Fire button, which is bound to an **accept** task. Individual firing locations are displayed with caret characters ("^") to simulate waves. When you Fire, the third card, **fire,** appears on the screen.

fire has two **<input>** elements for entering the row and column location that you want to fire upon (see Figure 3.6). Once you enter both values (they are required), and hit the OK button, the **fire** card calls the WMLScript function **FireTorpedo,** passing the firing location. **FireTorpedo** looks to see if you hit a ship at the firing location and updates the display accordingly. For each coordinate you shoot, if you hit a ship, the caret is replaced with a crosshatch ("#"); if you hit nothing, the wave is replaced with a hyphen ("-"; see Figure 3.7).

The final card, **bsize**, which is called from one of the **<option>**s on the **start** card, lets you enter the row and column dimensions of the game board you want to use. When both required values are entered, **bsize** calls **InitBoard**.

Here's the Battleships deck source code [bships.wml].

```
<?xml version="1.0"?>
<!DOCTYPE wml PUBLIC "-//WAPFORUM//DTD WML 1.1//EN"
  "http://www.wapforum.org/DTD/wml_1.1.xml">

<wml>
```

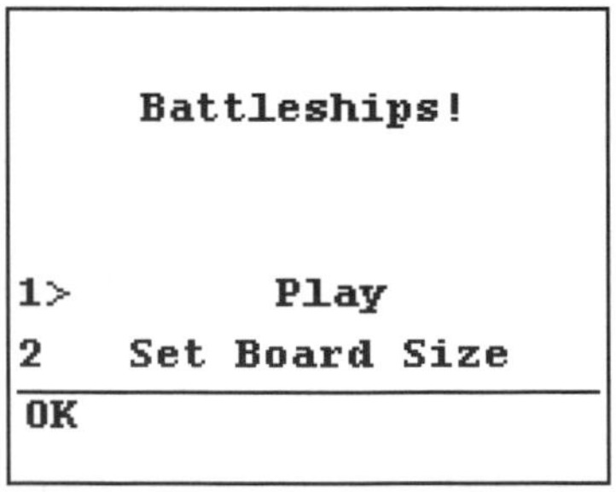

Figure 3.4 The Battleships splash screen.

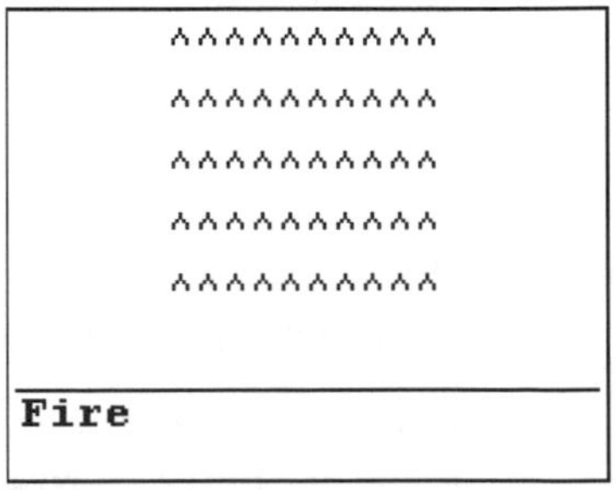

Figure 3.5 The playing field before firing.

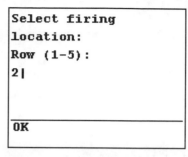

Figure 3.6 Entering a firing location.

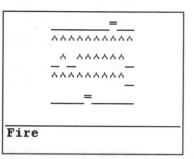

Figure 3.7 The playing field after firing.

```
<!-- Display the splash screen. The user can either
        start a game or reset the default board size -->

  <card id="start">

    <onevent type="onenterforward" >
      <refresh>
        <setvar name="iheight" value="5" />
        <setvar name="iwidth" value="10" />
      </refresh>
    </onevent>

    <p align="center" >
      <big>
      <br/> Battleships!<br/><br/>
      </big>
      <select>
        <option onpick="./bshipnew.wmls#InitBoard()">
          Play
        </option>
        <option onpick="#bsize">
          Set Board Size
        </option>
      </select>
    </p>
  </card>

<!-- Display the playing board and let the user fire a torpedo -->

  <card id="display" >
    <do type="accept" label="Fire" >
      <go href="#fire" />
    </do>

    <p align="center">
      <b>
```

```
          $gLine1
          <br/> $gLine2
          <br/> $gLine3
          <br/> $gLine4
          <br/> $gLine5
          <br/> $gLine6
          </b>
      </p>
    </card>

<!-- Get a pair of firing coordinates and fire a torpedo -->

  <card id="fire" >
    <do type="accept">
      <go href="./bshipnew.wmls#FireTorpedo($row,$col)" />
    </do>

    <p>
      Select firing location: <br/>
      Row (1-$(iheight)):
      <input name="row" format="1N" emptyok="false" maxlength="1" />
      Column (1-$(iwidth)):
      <input name="col" format="*N" emptyok="false" maxlength="2" />
    </p>
  </card>

<!-- Get the user's preferred board size -->

  <card id="bsize" >
    <do type="accept" >
      <go href="./bshipnew.wmls#InitBoard()" />
    </do>

    <p>
      Rows (1-5):
      <input name="iheight" value="5" format="1N"
        emptyok="false" maxlength="1"/>
      Columns (5-15):
      <input name="iwidth" value="15" format="*N"
        emptyok="false" maxlength="2" />
    </p>
  </card>

</wml>
```

Global Variables

There are four global variables that are stored in the user agent context so that they are accessible to all the WML cards and WMLScript functions in the application:

gBoardWidth	The horizontal dimension of the playing field, default (and maximum) 10
gBoardHeight	The vertical dimension of the playing field, default (and maximum) 6
gNumMoves	The number of moves taken so far this game, initialized to zero
gShipLocations	The locations of each of the ships for this game

There is also a set of variables for holding and displaying the current state of each line of the display, **gLine1–gLine6** (there can be at most six rows in a game). Although the globals are user agent variables, and are stored in the current device context, they are all initialized in the WMLScript function **Init-Board**.

Initialization

InitBoard is called from both the first and second cards of the Battleships deck. It first initializes the globals **gBoardWidth**, **gBoardHeight**, and **gNumMoves**. Next, it uses the **Lang** library random number generator to randomly place a ship on each line of the display, one ship per line, one coordinate pair per ship. It takes each ship's coordinates and converts them into single integers, using the function **MapCoords**, and adds them to a comma-separated list of ship locations. Finally, it initializes each display line to the proper length and goes to the **display** card in the WML deck so the user can see the initial playing board.

```
/**************************************************
  InitBoard
  Randomly position a single-cell ship on each board line.
  When done, set the global variable "gShipLocations" to a
  comma-delimited list of the ship positions, and
  return to the Firing card so the user can fire some torpedoes.
**************************************************/

extern function InitBoard () {

  var shiploc, shiplocs, x, y;

  var width    = WMLBrowser.getVar ( "iwidth" );
  var height   = WMLBrowser.getVar ( "iheight" );
  width            = Lang.parseInt ( width );
  height           = Lang.parseInt ( height );

// Initialize the global variables

    WMLBrowser.setVar ( "gNumMoves", 0 );
    WMLBrowser.setVar ( "gBoardWidth", width );
    WMLBrowser.setVar ( "gBoardHeight", height );

// Initialize one ship per board line, map zero-origin x & y
// coordinates into a single zero-origin integer index.
```

```
            for ( y = 0; y < height; y++ ) {
              x = Lang.random ( width - 1 );
              shiploc  = MapCoords ( width, x, y );
              shiplocs = shiplocs + shiploc + ",";
            }

            WMLBrowser.setVar ( "gShipLocations", shiplocs );

    // Set the length of each line of the playing board

            WMLBrowser.setVar ( "gLine1", SetLineLength ( 0 < height, width ) );
            WMLBrowser.setVar ( "gLine2", SetLineLength ( 1 < height, width ) );
            WMLBrowser.setVar ( "gLine3", SetLineLength ( 2 < height, width ) );
            WMLBrowser.setVar ( "gLine4", SetLineLength ( 3 < height, width ) );
            WMLBrowser.setVar ( "gLine5", SetLineLength ( 4 < height, width ) );
            WMLBrowser.setVar ( "gLine6", SetLineLength ( 5 < height, width ) );

    // Go display the game board.

            WMLBrowser.go ( "bships2.wml#display" );
            WMLBrowser.refresh();
    }


    /***************************************************
      MapCoords ( width, x, y )
      Convert a pair of zero-based coordinates in a space width x height
      into a single, zero-based index into a single string.
    ***************************************************/

    function MapCoords ( width, x, y ) {

      var index = ( y * width ) + x;
      return index;
    }
```

SetLineLength initializes each display line to its proper length.

```
    /***************************************************
      SetLineLength
      Initialize a game board line to lineWidth "^"s
      if it's not a NULL line.
    ***************************************************/

    function SetLineLength ( notEmptyLine, lineWidth ) {

      var defaultLine = "^^^^^^^^^^^^^^^^";

      if ( notEmptyLine ) {
        return ( String.subString ( defaultLine, 0, lineWidth ) );
      } else
        return "";
    }
```

Notice there are always six display lines. If the playing board has fewer than six rows, the rows outside the current dimensions are initialized to empty strings and subsequently ignored. You need to take this kind of approach, using a fixed set of globals, because WMLScript does not use any indirection when evaluating variables, and there is no such thing as a pointer.

Playing the Game

Once the game is set up, the user can start firing torpedoes. A firing is initiated using the **accept** button on the **display** card of the WML deck. If the user hits **accept**, control transfers to the **fire** card.

The **fire** card lets the user enter a pair of coordinates. When they hit the **accept** button on the fire card, the WMLScript function **FireTorpedo** is called. **FireTorpedo** first checks to see if the firing coordinates are valid. If so, it converts them to a single-integer ship location and looks for a matching location in **gShipLocations**. If it finds a ship, it sets **resultchar**, the character that gets displayed in the firing location to the ship marker, a crosshatch character. It then updates the display screen variables.

```
/***************************************************
  FireTorpedo
  Figure out if the user hit a ship.
  Alter the game board according to the result
  and return for another move.
***************************************************/

extern function FireTorpedo ( row, col ) {

  var resultChar = "_", move="", moves;

  var shiplocs = WMLBrowser.getVar ( "gShipLocations" );
  var width    = WMLBrowser.getVar ( "iwidth" );
  width = Lang.parseInt(width);
  var height   = WMLBrowser.getVar ( "iheight" );
  height = Lang.parseInt(height);

// Check for a valid firing location.

  if (( col >= 1 ) && ( col <= width ) &&
      ( row >= 1 ) && ( row <= height )) {

// Valid coordinates, increment the moves counter.

    moves = Lang.parseInt ( WMLBrowser.getVar ( "gNumMoves" )) + 1;
    WMLBrowser.setVar ( "gNumMoves", moves );

// Convert the location to a single zero-based
```

```
// coordinate and check for a ship there.

    var torpedoLoc = MapCoords ( width, col - 1, row - 1 );

    for ( var i = 0; i < String.elements ( shiplocs, "," ); i++ ) {
      if ( torpedoLoc == String.elementAt ( shiplocs, i, ",")) {
        resultChar = "=";
        shiplocs = String.removeAt ( shiplocs, i, "," );
        WMLBrowser.setVar ( "gShipLocations", shiplocs );
        break;
      } }

// Check to see if all ships have been obliterated. If so,
// tell the user they've won. Update the playing screen.

    if ( String.length ( shiplocs ) == 0 ) {
      Dialogs.alert ( "Congratulations! You've won after only " +
        WMLBrowser.getVar ( "gNumMoves" ) + " moves.");
    }
    UpdateDisplay ( col, row, resultChar );
  }

  WMLBrowser.go ( "bships2.wml#display" );
}
```

FireTorpedo keeps track of the number of moves that have been made. It also determines when the game is over. As each ship is torpedoed, its location is removed from **gShipLocations**. When **gShipLocations** is empty, the game is over and **FireTorpedo** congratulates the player (see Figure 3.8).

The final function in "bships.wmls" is the one that updates the display line that the player just fired upon. **FireTorpedo** sets **resultchar** to either a hyphen to indicate a miss or a crosshatch to indicate a hit. **UpdateDisplay** takes that character, inserts it into the proper display line variable, and resets the global variable for that line. If the user fires into a line with an already-discovered ship, nothing happens.

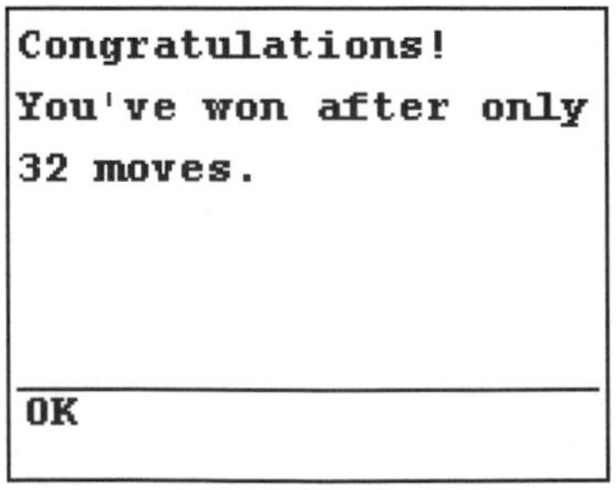

```
Congratulations!
You've won after only
32 moves.



OK
```

Figure 3.8 Winning Battleships.

```
/**************************************************
  UpdateDisplay ( x, y, char )
  Insert char in location x, y (one-based coordinates) and
  redisplay the playing board.
**************************************************/

function UpdateDisplay ( x, y, char ) {

  var part1, part2, len1, len2, line;

// Get the correct line to update

  if ( y == 1 ) {
    line = WMLBrowser.getVar ( "gLine1" );
  } else if ( y == 2 ) {
    line = WMLBrowser.getVar ( "gLine2" );
  } else if ( y == 3 ) {
    line = WMLBrowser.getVar ( "gLine3" );
  } else if ( y == 4 ) {
    line = WMLBrowser.getVar ( "gLine4" );
  } else if ( y == 5 ) {
    line = WMLBrowser.getVar ( "gLine5" );
  } else if ( y == 6 ) {
    line = WMLBrowser.getVar ( "gLine6" );
  }

// Check to see if the line has already been cleared. If so, do nothing.

  if ( String.find( line, "^" ) < 0 ) return;

// Split out its two parts--before and after the location to be marked--
// and insert resultchar at the firing location

  part1 = String.subString ( line, 0, x - 1 ) + char;
  part2 = String.subString ( line, x, String.length ( line ) - x );
  line  = part1 + part2;

// If it's a hit, clear the whole line except the ship location

  if ( char == "=" ) {
    line = String.replace ( line, "^", "_" );
  }

// Send the updated line back to the browser for redisplay

  if ( y == 1 ) {
    line = WMLBrowser.setVar ( "gLine1", line );
  } else if ( y == 2 ) {
    line = WMLBrowser.setVar ( "gLine2", line );
  } else if ( y == 3 ) {
```

```
      line = WMLBrowser.setVar ( "gLine3", line );
   } else if ( y == 4 ) {
      line = WMLBrowser.setVar ( "gLine4", line );
   } else if ( y == 5 ) {
      line = WMLBrowser.setVar ( "gLine5", line );
   } else if ( y == 6 ) {
      line = WMLBrowser.setVar ( "gLine6", line );
   }
}
```

Extending Battleships

This rendition of Battleships doesn't make for very challenging play, but it does demonstrate quite a few of the principles of basic WML and WMLScript programming. To make it more interesting, you could extend it into a two-person game initiated with a telephone call and played using messaging or notifications services, which are described in Chapter 8, "Beyond WAP 1.1." More graphics could spruce it up, too.

We hope that this example clearly demonstrates some of the basic principles of creating WAP applications: WML handles the user interface, WMLScript handles more complex processing, and the two complement each other quite nicely.

Our next chapter works through the development of a more complex example that focuses on content retrieval from a server.

WorldFAQ

A ll the WAP examples you've seen in this book so far use static content—decks and cards that never change. The real power of the Internet, however, lies in dynamic content that is assembled in response to a user's request for some special information. The same is true of WAP-delivered information. Its true power comes from dynamic content delivery.

In this chapter we show you the inner workings of a WAP application, World-FAQ, that delivers dynamic content. (WorldFAQ is a trademark of Creative Digital Publishing Inc.) Like any dynamic Web-based application, WorldFAQ requires a content server. This server receives a request from a WAP device for some content, assembles the content, and sends back a WML deck that includes the content. Like most WAP applications, there is a WAP gateway sitting in between the device and the content provider. The server's job is to forward the information request to the content provider, wait for a response, compile the response into WML bytecodes, and send it back to the WAP device for display.

Functional Requirement

There's a lot of information that can be useful to mobile computer and telephone users, particularly business users. For instance, let's say you want to call your new Paris office, but you have no idea what time it is there (the office may not be open) or the local area code. Or perhaps you're talking to an overseas supplier, and they quote you a price in francs. You need the current exchange rate in order for that number to make sense.

WorldFAQ is designed to provide you with a variety of global tidbits. You tell it the name of the city you need to know about, and it tells you any or all of the following: the current date and time, the time zone offset from Greenwich Mean Time (GMT), the current exchange rate and currency symbol, the population, the primary language spoken there, the telephone codes you need to dial into and out of the country, the area code for the city, and the symbol and name of the primary airport.

In case you don't know how to spell the name of the city for which you are searching, WorldFAQ does partial name lookups. It you want to find Bangalore, India, for instance, you can ask WorldFAQ to find all cities that start with the characters "Ba." The application returns a cities list so that you can select one and then request its details.

WorldFAQ has one other feature: It lets you tell it what information you want to retrieve. By default it returns everything in its database. It's possible that you don't really care about airports and languages and never want to request those items. By changing your profile preferences you can tell WorldFAQ to ignore airport and language information.

The Client Architecture

The WorldFAQ architecture is quite straightforward. There is a WML deck containing three cards. The first card, **startup**, lets you choose a function—either look up a name or change your profile. The second card, **lookup**, manages the name lookup. The third, **profile**, handles the profile editing.

The lookup card has an **<input>** element for getting the name (or partial name) you want to find. It also has an **accept** task that triggers the lookup by calling the content server, passing two parameters—the name to look for and the current profile, indicating the data the server should send back—in an HTTP POST request.

The profile card contains a **<select>** element with one **<option>** element for each profile setting that you can change. Once you customize your profile you have to navigate back to the **lookup** card to do a lookup. The lookup is done using this **<go>** element:

```
<go href="http://www.worldfaq.com/servlet/WFAQLookup1"
    method="post" >
  <postfield name="PROFILE" value="$PROFILE" />
```

```
    <postfield name="LOCATION" value="$LOCATION" />
</go>
```

The WAP browser parses the **\<go\>** element, substituting the current values for **PROFILE** and **LOCATION**, formats the **POST** request, sends it to **www .worldfaq.com/servlet/WFAQLookup1**, and waits for a response in the form of a valid, compiled WML deck.

There are four possible responses:

- If the string you enter matches nothing in the WorldFAQ database, it returns a message telling you that.

- If your string matches just one location in the WorldFAQ database, **WFAQLookup1** returns the location's details according to the profile settings.

- If your string matches between two and nine locations, **WFAQLookup1** returns a deck containing a **\<select\>** element listing those locations so that you can complete your search by selecting one of them.

- If your string matches more than nine locations, which we recommend as the reasonable upper limit for a **\<select\>** element, **WFAQLookup1** returns a message suggesting you enter a longer search string to narrow the choices.

Here's the static WML deck for the WorldFAQ client [wfaq1.wml]. There are also dynamically-created decks that we describe shortly.

```
<!-- *****************************************************
     WFAQ1.WML
***************************************************** -->

<wml>

<!-- *****************************************************
     CARD startup
     Init variables, display choices for user to select one.
     ***************************************************** -->

  <card id="startup">

<!-- initialize profile and location variables -->

    <onevent type="onenterforward">
      <refresh >
         <setvar name="LOCATION" value="" />
         <setvar name="PROFILE" value="G;T;C;H;A;P;L" />
      </refresh>
    </onevent>
```

```
<!-- display choices: edit profile, lookup a location -->

   <p>
     <b>WorldFAQ (tm) </b>
     <select>
       <option onpick="#lookup" > Lookup </option>
       <option onpick="#profile" > Profile </option>
     </select>
   </p>

 </card>

<!-- ******************************************************
    CARD lookup.
    Get a location name to lookup
    ****************************************************** -->

 <card id="lookup">
   <do type="accept" label="Lookup" >
     <go href="http://www.worldfaq.com/servlet/WFAQLookup1"
       method="post" >
        <postfield name="PROFILE" value="$PROFILE" />
        <postfield name="LOCATION" value="$LOCATION" />
     </go>
   </do>

   <p>
     Location Name:
     <input name="LOCATION" title="Location" emptyok="false"
       format="A*A" maxlength="10"/>
   </p>

 </card>

<!-- ******************************************************
    Card profile.
    Let the user select what information they want to see
    ****************************************************** -->

 <card id="profile" >

   <do type="accept" label="Done" >
     <go href="#startup" />
   </do>

   <p>
     <select title="WorldFAQ Profile"
       multiple="true" name="PROFILE">
       <option value="G"> GMT Offset </option>
       <option value="T"> Local Time </option>
       <option value="C"> Currency/Rate </option>
```

```
        <option value="H"> Phone Codes </option>
        <option value="A"> Airport </option>
        <option value="P"> Population </option>
        <option value="L"> Language </option>
      </select>
    </p>
  </card>
```

```
</wml>
```

The **startup** card initializes the **LOCATION** and **PROFILE** variables and waits for the user to select a function.

The **lookup** card requires that the user enter an alphabetic location (or partial location) name. When they hit the **accept** key **WFAQLookup1** is called.

The **profile** card contains a **<select>** element that lists all the information that WorldFAQ can return about a location. Each **<option>** element in the **<select>** is assigned a single letter identifier. As you change your profile, the variable's value changes. When **PROFILE** is sent to **WFAQLookup1,** the servlet returns information only for those data items for which it finds **PROFILE** identifiers.

Figure 4.1 shows the sequence of views presented to the user for both looking up a location and changing their profile.

The Content Server

The WorldFAQ content server is the heart of this application. It has to serve up various WML decks in response to different user requests. Traditionally, this type of interaction between a Web-enabled device and a Web server is done with **GET** and **POST** requests to Common Gateway Interface (CGI)—compatible programs written in Perl or C. Leveraging Web standards as much as possible, WAP 1.1 uses this approach as well.

We implement the WorldFAQ content server as a Java servlet. Java servlets are CGI-compatible Web server plug-ins. Servlets execute within the thread space of the Web server, one thread per servlet. This makes them more efficient and faster than many CGI implementations and also lets them interact with the server in ways that are not always possible with CGI scripts. Java servlets also have the full power of Java's core classes at their disposal, helping you create applications quickly and easily.

In this section of the book we don't provide a lot of details on either Java or Java servlets. There are a variety of books on those topics. [HUNTER] is particularly good. If you are even slightly familiar with object-oriented concepts and Java, the remainder of this chapter should be readily understandable.

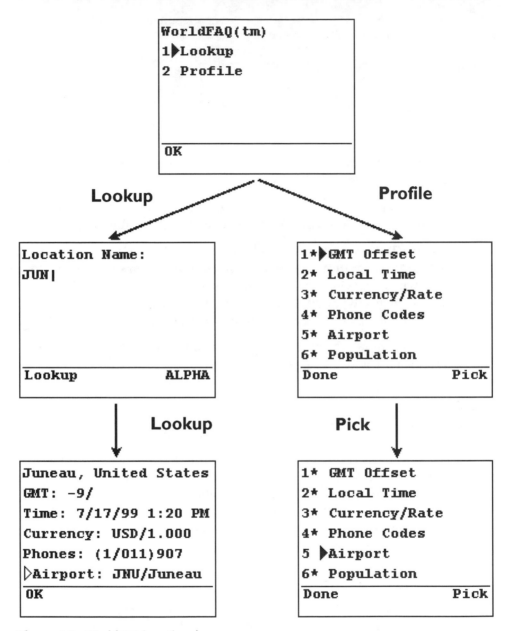

Figure 4.1 WorldFAQ in action.

WFAQLookup1 is a data retrieval program that sequentially searches a simple text file for records that start with the search string entered by the user. This text file contains one line per location. Each line contains a set of comma-delimited string fields:

- City name
- Country name

- Time zone hours offset from Greenwich Mean Time
- Time zone minutes offset from GMT
- Currency symbol
- Currency exchange rate (relative to $1 US)
- Country dialing codes (in and out)
- Area code
- Population in thousands
- Language

Null values are flagged by the string "—."

As the program searches, it builds a list of byte offsets in the WorldFAQ data file of the matching records. Once the whole file is searched, the servlet checks to see how many matches it found and builds an appropriate response deck.

Servlet Startup

Java servlets have an optional **init** method that is executed only once when they are first loaded by the Web server under which they are running. In our case, all we need to do is open the WorldFAQ data file as a read-only file, and save its object for subsequent POST processing. Here's the opening section of the **WFAQLookup1** [WFAQLookup1.java].

```
import java.io.*;
import java.util.*;
import java.text.*;
import java.lang.Math;
import javax.servlet.*;
import javax.servlet.http.*;

class WFAQLookupException
  extends ServletException {
  public WFAQLookupException () {}
  public WFAQLookupException ( String s ) { super ( s ); }
}

//********************************************************************
// WFAQLookup1
//
// A Java servlet that searches for a user-entered location in a
// database and returns a list of information about that location.
// If the user enters a partial string, WFAQLookup looks for as many
// matching locations as possible and returns a deck with a <select>
// element so the user can select one of the matches. If there are
// more than nine matches, a message is returned telling the user to
// refine their search criteria.
//********************************************************************
```

```
public class WFAQLookup1 extends HttpServlet {

// global variables

  final int        SERVER_GMTHRS    = -8; // server GMT offset
  final int        MAX_SCREEN_LINES = 9;
  static String    gDataFileName    =

"/local/home/worldfaq/public_html/wfaqdat.txt";
  RandomAccessFile gDataFile;
  static String    gSiteName        = "www.worldfaq.com";
  static String    EOL              = "\r\n";
  static String    WMLEOL           = "<br/>\r\n";

//*****************************************************************
// init
//
// Servlet initialization routine. Open the data file and
// save its object.
//*****************************************************************

  public void init
    (
     ServletConfig config
    )
    throws
    ServletException
    {

// Open the WorldFAQ data file.

    try {
      gDataFile = new RandomAccessFile ( gDataFileName, "r" );
    }

// Unavailable. Set file pointer to null, notify the server.

    catch ( IOException e ) {
      gDataFile = null;
      throw new ServletException ();
} } }
```

The first part of the servlet includes a definition of an exception class **WFAQLookupException**. We include this to provide a convenient way to bubble various possible exceptions up to the topmost application level so they can be handled in one place.

Notice that the global variables are all essentially static—they don't change after **init** finishes executing. Servlets are multithreaded—they can handle multiple user agent requests simultaneously. You have to make sure that values that change from request to request are stored in local variables (or segregated some other way) so that the thread states don't get improperly mixed.

HTTP Request Handling

The base class for our Java servlet is **javax.servlet.http**. This class is designed for handling HTTP requests, notably **GET** and **POST**. It has methods for readily retrieving request parameters and creating an HTTP response. The key method we need to override is

```
public void doPost
  (
  HttpServletRequest req,
  HttpServletResponse res
  );
```

req and **res** are the request and response streams, respectively. We use the request stream to retrieve the **POST** parameters sent from **wfaq1.wml**. We use the response stream to create our response deck.

NOTE
All the requests we send from **wfaq1.wml** are **POST** requests created by the method=**"post"** attribute of the **lookup** card. For debugging purposes, we would also like to be able to respond to **GET** requests from a Telnet connection (we describe this debugging technique in more detail in Chapter 5, "Caching"). To do this as simply as possible, we override the **javax.servlet.http doGet** method. All it does is call **doPost**.

Here's the **doGet** method.

```
//*************************************************************
// doGet
//
// Respond to the GET request. Just call doPost.
//*************************************************************

  public void doGet
    (
    HttpServletRequest req,
    HttpServletResponse res
    )
    throws
    ServletException,
    IOException
    {

    doPost (req, res );
  }
```

Here's **getPost**, the heart of **WFAQLookup1**.

```
//*****************************************************************
// doPost
//
// Respond to the POST request received from the WAP device.
//*****************************************************************
  public void doPost
    (
    HttpServletRequest req,
    HttpServletResponse res
    )
    throws
    ServletException,
    IOException,
    WFAQLookupException
    {

  // Build the first part of the output deck.

    ServletOutputStream out = res.getOutputStream ();
    res.setContentType ( "text/vnd.wap.wml" );
    WriteResponseHeaders ( res );
    WriteDeckHeader ( out );
  // Don't bother doing anything if the data file is unavailable.

      if ( gDataFile == null ) {
        out.println ( "<p>WorldFAQ data file unavailable." );
        throw new IOException ();
      }

      try {

  // Get the user-entered location name. Skip lookup if name is null.

        String locationName = req.getParameter ( "LOCATION" );
        if ( locationName != null ) {
          if ( locationName.length () > 0 ) {
            locationName = locationName.toUpperCase ();
            Vector locOffsets = new Vector ();

  // Check to see if the user returned the file offset of one location
  // from a previous <select>. If so, just output that location.

            if ( Character.isDigit ( locationName.charAt ( 0 )))
            locOffsets.addElement ( locationName );
          else
            LookupLocation ( locationName, locOffsets );

  // Check for matches, and build the output deck based on the result.
```

```
            if ( locOffsets.size () > MAX_SCREEN_LINES )
              out.println (
                "<p>" + EOL + locOffsets.size () +
                " matches. Please narrow your search criteria."
              );
            else {

              switch ( locOffsets.size ()) {

                case 0: // no matches
                  out.println ( "<p>" + EOL + "Nothing matching " +
                    locationName + " was found." );
                  break;

                case 1: // one match, go output it.
                  String locOffset =
                    ( String ) locOffsets.firstElement ();
                  OutputLocation ( locOffset, out, req );
                  break;

                default: // multiple matches, build SELECT element.
                  OutputLocations ( locOffsets, out );
              } }
            } else out.println ( "<p>" + EOL +
                "Please provide a lookup string." );
          } else out.println ( "<p>" + EOL +
              "Please provide a lookup string." );
        }

// Exception handling

    catch ( WFAQLookupException e ) {
      out.println ( e.getMessage () );
    }
    catch ( IOException e ) {
      out.println ( "IOException in WFAQLookup" );
    }

// Finish up the output deck and leave.
    finally {
      out.print ( "</p>" + EOL + "</card>" + EOL + "</wml>" );
  } }

//****************************************************************
// WriteResponseHeaders
//
// Output the HTTP headers for this response.
//****************************************************************
  public void WriteResponseHeaders
    (
```

```
        HttpServletResponse res
        )
        throws
        IOException
        {

// Output the cache control header first.

        res.setHeader ( "Cache-Control", "no-store" );

// Output the Date header.

        Date now      = new Date ();
        long nowTime = now.getTime ();
        res.setDateHeader ( "Date", nowTime );
}


//******************************************************************
// WriteDeckheader
//
// Output the beginning of a WML deck.
//******************************************************************
  public void WriteDeckHeader
    (
    ServletOutputStream out
    )
    throws
    IOException
    {
    out.println (
      "<?xml version=\"1.0\"?>" + EOL +
      "<!DOCTYPE wml PUBLIC \"-//WAPFORUM//DTD WML 1.1//EN\"" + EOL +
      "\"http://www.wapforum.org/DTD/DTD/wml_1.1.xml\">" + EOL +
      "<wml>" + EOL +
      "<card id=\"lookupresponse\" >"
    );
  }
```

The very first thing **WFAQLookup1** does is set the content type of the output stream and write the HTTP response headers in **WriteResponseHeaders**. We explain HTTP response headers in much more detail in Chapter 5, "Caching." Ignore for the moment what happens in **WriteResponseHeaders**.

Regardless of the results of the search, we have to respond with a full deck (so to speak), even if it only contains an error message. To that end, we next write the beginning of the response deck, including the WAP 1.1 XML deck prologue, in **WriteDeckHeader**.

If there is a data file and the **LOCATION** parameter is not **null**, we check to see if **LOCATION** starts with a digit. If so, this indicates that the user has responded to a **<select>** element from a previous lookup, returning the byte offset in the data file of that location's record (more about this shortly).

NOTE

Because we use **emptyok="false"** for the **LOCATION <input>** element in **wfaq1.wml,** we shouldn't have to check for a **null** or zero-length **LOCATION.** We include this extra checking because we can also submit requests via Telnet. See Chapter 5 for a discussion of this debugging technique.

If **LOCATION** doesn't start with a digit, that means it's a normal, first-time lookup. **doPost** calls **LookupLocation**, which fills the **Vector locOffsets** with the file offsets of all matching records. **doPost** then checks the number of items in **locOffsets** and uses a **case** statement to create the correct response deck.

Ignoring the lookup process for the moment, let's look at what happens if the user enters a lookup string like "ZZ" that matches nothing in the WorldFAQ data file. **doPost** creates the following response deck by adding the message "Nothing matching ZZ was found." to the output deck and then writing the end of the deck in the **finally** clause. Here's the result, formatted for readability:

```
<?xml version="1.0"?>
<!DOCTYPE wml PUBLIC "-//WAPFORUM//DTD WML 1.1//EN"
  "http://www.wapforum.org/DTD/DTD/wml_1.1.xml">
<wml>
  <card id="lookupresponse" >
    <p>
      Nothing matching ZZ was found.
    </p>
  </card>
</wml>
```

Location Searching

LookupLocation uses a Java class called a **StringTokenizer**. Similar to WMLScript's element functions in the String library, it views strings as a set of tokens separated by a delimiter character. Each data record that is examined for a match is a set of comma-delimited tokens. As **LookupLocation** matches place names, it adds their byte locations to the **locOffsets**.

```
//****************************************************************
// LookupLocation
//
// Search thru the WorldFAQ datafile for places whose names
// start with a specific string.
//****************************************************************
```

```
   public void LookupLocation
     (
     String location,
     Vector locOffsets
     )
     throws
     ServletException,
     IOException,
     WFAQLookupException
     {

     try {

// Initialize the local variables.

       gDataFile.seek ( 0 ); // reset data file pointer
       long    filePtr = 0;   // current position in data file

// Loop through the WorldFAQ database looking for name matches.

       while ( filePtr < gDataFile.length ()) {

// Read the next line (another location) of the data file.

         String line = gDataFile.readLine ();
         StringTokenizer parser = new StringTokenizer ( line, ",");

// Check the first token for a match.

         String token   = parser.nextToken ( ); // the current token
         String ucToken = token.toUpperCase (); // the uppercase token
         if ( ucToken.startsWith ( location )) {

// If there's a match, add the file byte offset
// to the vector of matching locations.

           locOffsets.addElement ( String.valueOf ( filePtr ));
         }

// Update the file pointer for the next loop iteration.

         filePtr = gDataFile.getFilePointer ();
     } }

     catch ( IOException e ) {
     throw new WFAQLookupException (
       "Error accessing the WorldFAQ database" );
} }
```

If the user requests all places starting with the characters "BA," for example, **LookupLocations** adds the numbers 733 and 799 to the **Vector locOffsets,** indicating that the Baku record starts at byte 733 and the Bangalore record starts at 799. Note that the data file search assumes that the data is in random order—it looks at every record for every search. In real life, if we actually did use a text file for this application, it would make sense to sort the entries and stop searching when the last location less than or equal to the search string is found.

Single-Match Response

LookupLocation returns the **locOffsets** vector back to **doPost,** which decides how to proceed. In the case of a single location match, **doPost** calls **OutputLocation. OutputLocation** adds to the already-started deck the detailed information for the single location, based on the user's profile.

It converts the location's record to a **StringTokenizer** so that it can split off the individual fields. **GetNextToken** grabs each successive field, converting null indicators ("—") to null strings (" "), and handling token exceptions. Each field that the user requests, based on their **PROFILE,** is added to the response deck. If they request the current time, **OutputLocation** calls **CalcTime,** which calculates the location's current time based on its GMT information.

```
//*****************************************************************
// OutputLocation
//
// Matched on a single location match. Add the city's details to the
// returned deck.
//*****************************************************************

  public void OutputLocation
    (
    String locOffset,
    ServletOutputStream out,
    HttpServletRequest req
    )
    throws
    IOException,
    WFAQLookupException
    {
    String name="",   country="",    GMTHrs="",     GMTMins="",
      currSymb="",    currRate="",   dialIn="",     dialOut="",
      areaCode="",    airportCode="", airportName="",
      population="", language="";

// Get the user's profile to figure out what information to return.

    String profile = req.getParameter ( "PROFILE" );

    try {
```

```
// Get the location's data for parsing.

        int recordLoc  = Integer.parseInt ( locOffset );
        gDataFile.seek ( recordLoc );
        String locData = gDataFile.readLine ();

// Add the ACCEPT task to the card, and set the
// display mode of the items to be returned.

        out.println (
          "<do type=\"accept\" >" + EOL +
          "<go href=\"http://" + gSiteName + "/ch4/wfaq1.wml\"/>" + EOL +
          "</do>" + EOL +
          "<p mode=\"nowrap\">"
        );

// Retrieve the location's data and parse it for individual data items.
// Only include in the returned deck those items requested according
// to the settings of the user's profile string.

        StringTokenizer parser = new StringTokenizer ( locData, "," );

// Location name and country

        name         = GetNextToken ( out, parser );
        country      = GetNextToken ( out, parser );
        out.print (
          name + ", "  + country + WMLEOL
        );

// GMT offset, profile code "G"

        GMTHrs       = GetNextToken ( out, parser );
        GMTMins      = GetNextToken ( out, parser );
        if ( profile.indexOf ( "G" ) >= 0)
          out.print (
            "GMT: " + GMTHrs + "/" + GMTMins + WMLEOL
          );

// Current time, profile code "T"

        if ( profile.indexOf ( "T" ) >= 0) {
          String timeStr = CalcTime ( out, GMTHrs, GMTMins );
          out.print (
            "Time: " + timeStr + WMLEOL
          );
        }

// Currency symbol and exchange rate, profile code "C"

        currSymb     = GetNextToken ( out, parser );
        currRate     = GetNextToken ( out, parser );
```

```
        if ( profile.indexOf ( "C" ) >= 0)
          out.print (
            "Currency: " + currSymb + "/" + currRate + WMLEOL
          );

// Telephone codes, profile code "H"

        dialIn     = GetNextToken ( out, parser );
        dialOut    = GetNextToken ( out, parser );
        areaCode   = GetNextToken ( out, parser );
        if ( profile.indexOf ( "H" ) >= 0 )
          out.print (
            "Phones: " + "(" + dialIn + "/" + dialOut + ")" +
              areaCode + WMLEOL
          );

// Airport symbol & name, profile code "A"

        airportCode = GetNextToken ( out, parser );
        airportName = GetNextToken ( out, parser );
        if ( profile.indexOf ( "A" ) >= 0 )
          out.print (
            "Airport: " + airportCode + "/" + airportName + WMLEOL
          );

// Population, profile code "P"

        population = GetNextToken ( out, parser );
        if ( profile.indexOf ( "P" ) >= 0 )
          out.print (
            "People: " + population + ",000" + WMLEOL
          );

// Primary language, profile code "L"

        language = GetNextToken ( out, parser );
        if ( profile.indexOf ( "L" ) >= 0 )
          out.print (
            "Language: " + language + WMLEOL
          );
      }

    catch ( IOException e ) {
      throw new WFAQLookupException ( "IOException in OutputLocation" );
  } }

//****************************************************************
// GetNextToken
//
// Get the next data token from the location's data record
//****************************************************************
```

```
public String GetNextToken
  (
  ServletOutputStream out,
  StringTokenizer parser
  )
  throws
  NoSuchElementException
  {
  String str="";
```

```
// Get the next token. Missing values are indicated in the data file by
// the string "---". A NULL string is returned for them.
```

```
  try {
    str = parser.nextToken ();
    if ( str.startsWith ( "---" )) str = "";
  }
```

```
  catch ( NoSuchElementException e ) {
    throw new WFAQLookupException ( "GetNextToken exception" );
  }
```

```
  finally {
    return ( str );
  } }
```

```
//****************************************************************
// CalcTime
// Calculate the current time of the location at GMTHrs/GMTMins.
//****************************************************************
```

```
  public String CalcTime
    (
    ServletOutputStream out,
    String GMTHrs,
    String GMTMins
    )
    throws
    NumberFormatException,
    WFAQLookupException
    {

    int hrsDiff  = 0;  // hours diff between location and server
    int minsDiff = 0;  // minutes diff between location and server
    int gmtHrs   = 0;  // location's GMT hours offset
    int gmtMins  = 0;  // location's GMT minutes offset
    String result = "";// the location's date and time
    try {
```

```
// Get the GMT hour and minute offsets if they're there.
```

```
        if ( GMTHrs.length () > 0 )
          gmtHrs = Integer.parseInt ( GMTHrs );
        if ( GMTMins.length () > 0 )
          gmtMins = Integer.parseInt ( GMTMins );


        hrsDiff = gmtHrs + Math.abs ( SERVER_GMTHRS );

// get the current date and time, and adjust for the new location.

        DateFormat df = DateFormat.getInstance ();
        Calendar cal = df.getCalendar ();
        int curHr = cal.get ( Calendar.HOUR_OF_DAY ) + hrsDiff;
        int curMin = cal.get ( Calendar.MINUTE ) - gmtMins;
        int curYr = cal.get ( Calendar.YEAR );

// Reset the calendar to reflect the new time.

        cal.set ( Calendar.HOUR_OF_DAY, curHr );
        cal.set ( Calendar.MINUTE, curMin );
        cal.set ( Calendar.YEAR, curYr + 80 );

// return a date/time formatted string.

        result = df.format ( cal.getTime ());
      }

    catch ( NumberFormatException e ) {
      result = "";
      throw new WFAQLookupException (
        "NumberFormatException in CalcTime" );
    }

    finally {
      return result;
  } }
```

NOTE

We append end-of-line strings (EOL and WMLEOL) in various places in the response deck. This is not really necessary—WAP eliminates redundant white space and ignores standard ASCII text formatting characters. We include these strings strictly to make the response decks more readable when viewed using a Telnet client.

Here's what the response deck looks like, formatted for readability, if the user requests information on Madrid. Figure 4.2 shows the response on the Phone.com browser.

```
<?xml version="1.0"?>
<!DOCTYPE wml PUBLIC "-//WAPFORUM//DTD WML 1.1//EN"
```

```
        "http://www.wapforum.org/DTD/DTD/wml_1.1.xml">
<wml>
  <card id="lookupresponse" >
    <do type="accept" >
      <go href="http://www.worldfaq.com/ch4/wfaq1.wml"/>
    </do>
    <p mode="nowrap">
      Madrid, Spain<br/>
      GMT: 1/<br/>
      Time: 7/16/99 7:38 PM<br/>
      Currency: ESP/141.910<br/>
      Phones: (34/00)91<br/>
      Airport: MAD/Barajas<br/>
      People: 2910,000<br/>
      Language: Spanish<br/>
    </p>
  </card>
</wml>
```

Multiple-Match Response

If **LookupLocation** finds more than 1 match, but less than 10, **doPost** calls **OutputLocations**, which completes the response deck by adding a **<select>** element containing all the matches, with their byte offsets as the **<option> value** attribute settings. The deck also includes an **accept** task definition that points right back to WFAQLookup.

```
//*****************************************************************
// OutputLocations
//
// The user-entered location string has matched more than one
// location in the database. Create a SELECT element so the user
// can select one of the matches.
//*****************************************************************
```

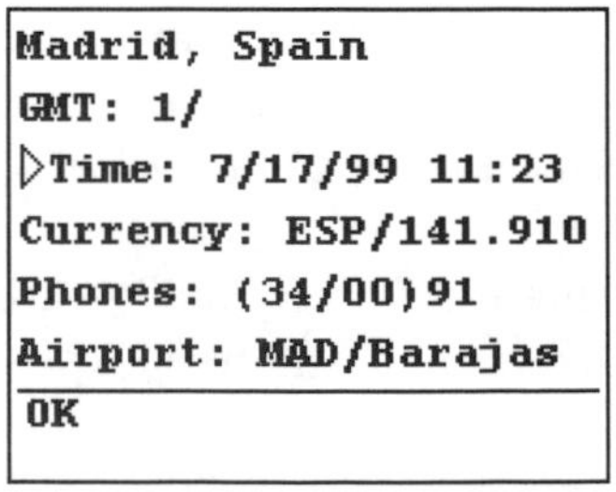

```
Madrid, Spain
GMT: 1/
▷Time: 7/17/99 11:23
Currency: ESP/141.910
Phones: (34/00)91
Airport: MAD/Barajas
OK
```

Figure 4.2 A single-location response.

```java
    public void OutputLocations
      (
      Vector locOffsets,
      ServletOutputStream out
      )
      throws
      IOException,
      WFAQLookupException
      {

      try {

// Output the DO method for the SELECT element and the SELECT element.

        out.println (
          "<do type=\"accept\" label=\"Lookup\" >" + EOL +
          "<go href=\"http://" + gSiteName +
            "/servlet/WFAQLookup1\" method=\"post\" >" + EOL +
          "<postfield name=\"PROFILE\" value=\"$(PROFILE)\" />" + EOL +
          "<postfield name=\"LOCATION\" value=\"$(LOCATION)\" />" + EOL +
          "</go>" + EOL +
          "</do>" + EOL +
          "<p>" + EOL +
          "<select title=\"Pick a location\" name=\"LOCATION\">"
        );

// Output each of the choices to the DECK.

        Enumeration lOffsets = locOffsets.elements ();
        while ( lOffsets.hasMoreElements () ) {
          String locOffset = ( String ) lOffsets.nextElement ();

// Get the data record to get the name.

          int recordLoc = Integer.parseInt ( locOffset );
          gDataFile.seek ( recordLoc );
          String locData = gDataFile.readLine ();
          StringTokenizer data = new StringTokenizer ( locData, "," );

// output the next OPTION element

          String locName = data.nextToken ();
          out.println (
            "<option value=\"" + locOffset + "\">" +
            locName + "</option>"
          );
      } }

      catch ( IOException e ) {
        throw new WFAQLookupException ( "Error in OutputLocations" );
      }

// Output the SELECT terminating tag.
```

```
      finally {
         out.println ( "</select>" + EOL );
} } }
```

Here's the response deck for a location string of "BA." Figure 4.3 shows this response on the Phone.com browser.

```
<?xml version="1.0"?>
<!DOCTYPE wml PUBLIC "-//WAPFORUM//DTD WML 1.1//EN"
  "http://www.wapforum.org/DTD/DTD/wml_1.1.xml">
<wml>
  <card id="lookupresponse" >
    <do type="accept" label="Lookup" >
      <go href="http://www.worldfaq.com/servlet/WFAQLookup1"
        method="post" >
        <postfield name="PROFILE"  value="$(PROFILE)" />
        <postfield name="LOCATION" value="$(LOCATION)" />
      </go>
    </do>
    <p>
      <select title="Pick a location" name="LOCATION">
        <option value="733">Baku</option>
        <option value="799">Bangalore</option>
      </select>
    </p>
  </card>
</wml>
```

If the user picks one of the **<select>** options, that location's data file byte offset gets sent back to **WFAQLookup1** in the **LOCATION** parameter. **doPost** realizes that it is being passed a data file offset, not a location name string, and calls **OutputLocation**.

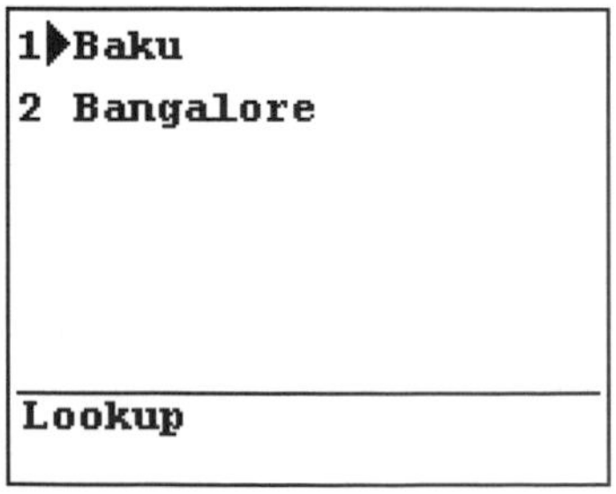

```
1▶Baku
2 Bangalore




────────────────────
Lookup
```

Figure 4.3 A multiple-location response.

Extending WorldFAQ

Although it's a good example to demonstrate delivering dynamic WAP content, WorldFAQ as presented here is obviously not ready for prime time as a serious commercial application. The data access methods are primitive and inefficient. For any sizeable number of records, sequentially searching a text file makes no sense. A relational or object database model is more appropriate. Also, the current algorithms should stop when more than nine locations are found, and the data file should be in sorted order so that the lookup can stop as soon as the first location with a name less than LOCATION is found.

The user profile handling is also a bare-bones implementation. You have to reset the profile from scratch every time you use the program if you want anything other than the default profile. That could get annoying very quickly. A persistent profile that doesn't change from session to session would be a useful addition. This could readily be done by using cookies. The Phone.com WAP gateway also provides persistent user profiles using subscriber ID numbers that you could use.

The WorldFAQ database is not a static data store. As time passes, more locations and more location data will most likely be added to it. It would be helpful to receive an alert whenever the data content changes so you can go and update your profile immediately. It might also be helpful to be able to fax a location map to a readily-accessible fax machine or initiate a phone call to a country using the country dialing and area code. In Chapter 8, "Beyond WAP 1.1," we briefly look at some Phone.com gateway technologies that you can use to add some of these types of features.

In the next chapter, we talk about HTTP headers and document caching, two concepts central to understanding how to write efficient WAP applications.

Caching

I n the previous chapters, we've looked at straightforward WAP applications that don't take advantage of some of the more advanced aspects of WAP 1.1. In this chapter we stretch a bit, showing you how to improve performance and minimize network traffic. Before getting into the specifics, however, we need to give you a brief introduction to HTTP 1.1 as described in [RFC2616]. If you are familiar with HTTP 1.1, particularly request and response headers, you can probably skip the first section of this chapter.

A Brief Introduction to HTTP 1.1

HTTP 1.1 is a predominantly text-based protocol that defines the interactions between Internet entities, whether they're user agents like WAP-compatible browsers, proxies like WAP gateways, or origin servers like the WorldFAQ Java servlet described in the last chapter. The interactions can be grouped into two categories: requests from clients to servers and responses from servers to clients. A single user agent/server interaction consists of a request from the agent to the server, followed by a response from the server back to the agent.

Both requests and responses use the generic Internet message format described in [RFC822]:

```
Message Definition
zero or more message headers
```

```
CRLF
optional message body
```

The **Message Definition** indicates the type of message being sent. Both requests and responses can include various message headers that further define and refine the user agent and server interaction. The **CRLF** part of the message delimits the message definition from its body.

Requests

The **Message Definition** for a request looks like this:

```
request-type URL HTTP/1.1
```

where **request-type** is one of the following:

OPTIONS. Return information about the communications options available between the requester and responder. This is useful for determining server capabilities.

GET. Retrieve the contents of the file, or the results of executing the program, identified by URL. The server, using file name suffixes, for instance, determines whether the target URL is a static file or a program.

HEAD. Retrieve the same information as you would for a **GET**, but don't return the message body of the response. This message is useful for testing links for validity, accessibility, and recent modification.

POST. Send the information in the message body to the URL for some further server-defined action. **POST** is most often used for submitting the contents of an HTML form for some data-processing action.

PUT. Send the information in the message body to URL for storage. Although similar to **POST**, **PUT** has a narrower definition, is used less often, and is supported less frequently by servers.

DELETE. Delete the resource identified by URL.

TRACE. Invoke a remote, application-layer loopback of the request message. The user agent that sends this message (normally) receives the same message back with additional information about the path the message took through the Internet.

The most often used requests, and the only ones we need to worry about when creating WAP applications, are **GET** and **POST**.

Here's a **GET** request for www.worldfaq.com/wml/wfaq.wml issued by the Phone.com desktop simulator, shown in Figure 5.1. The simulator has a command line where you can enter a URL for fetching and execution. When you enter

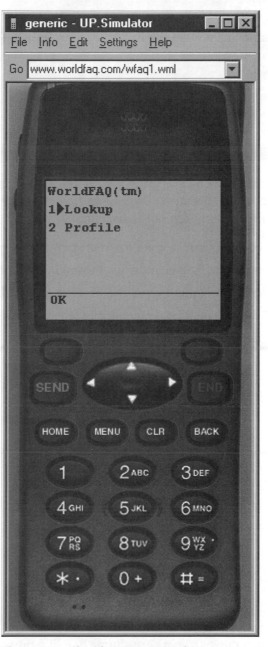

Figure 5.1   The Phone.com simulator.

```
www.worldfaq.com/wfaq1.wml
```

on this command line and hit the Enter key, here's the **GET** request that is sent to the worldfaq server:

```
GET www.worldfaq.com/wfaq1.wml HTTP/1.1
accept-charset: UTF-8
accept-language: en
accept: text/vnd.wap.wml, */*, image/bmp, text/html
user-agent: UP.Browser/3.1-UPG1 UP.Link/3.2
host: www.worldfaq.com
```

The HTTP headers are marked in bold. To keep this example short and manageable, we've removed some of the **accept** types and several proprietary headers. Here's a brief description of the headers:

accept-charset. The character set (or sets) that the user agent can display.

accept-language. The language the user agent is currently using.

Accept. The MIME document types the user agent can successfully receive.

user-agent. A vendor-defined designator for the user agent.

Host. The domain that the request is being posted.

We describe **accept-charset** and **accept-language** headers in more detail in Chapter 7, "Internationalization (I18N)."

Responses

The **message definition** for responses looks like this:

```
HTTP/1.1 Status-code Status-description
```

[RFC2616] defines almost 40 different status codes grouped into five sets. The most common are:

```
200   OK
401   Unauthorized
404   Not Found
```

You've probably all seen your Web browser display a 404 response at one time or another. It can range from a very simple one-line message to a more detailed response like the one shown in Figure 5.2.

We've already discussed HTTP responses, but in the previous examples we excluded any mention of the HTTP response message and headers. For instance, we said that the response to

```
GET www.worldfaq.com/wfaq1.wml HTTP/1.1
```

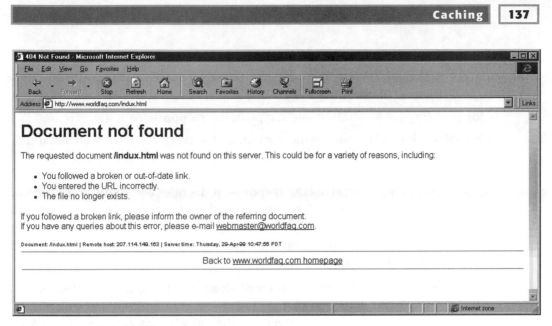

Figure 5.2 A typical 404 response.

was the deck stored in the file wfaq1.wml on the WorldFAQ server. In fact, the response really looks something like this:

```
HTTP/1.1 200 OK
Server: Zeus/3.1
Date: Tue, 20 Jul 1999 21:38:04 GMT
Connection: Keep-Alive
Content-Length: 3343
Content-Type: text/vnd.wap.wml
Last-Modified: Sat, 17 Jul 1999 21:19:02 GMT

<?xml version="1.0"?>
<!DOCTYPE wml PUBLIC "-//WAPFORUM//DTD WML 1.1//EN"
"http://www.wapforum.org/DTD/wml_1.1.xml">

.
. The rest of the deck stored in wfaq1.wml
.
```

It contains the response status, both the numerical code and the text message, followed by a set of headers, followed by a carriage return and line feed, followed by the message body. The message body in this case is the source code file located at www.worldfaq.com/wfaq1.wml.

Here's a brief description of the response headers:

Server. The Web server delivering the response.

Date. The date and time the response is being sent.

Connection. An indication to the user agent to keep this connection active.

Content-Length. The length of the response message, starting with the first "<" character of the WML deck.

Content-Type. The MIME content type of the response.

Last-Modified. The date the file containing the response deck was last modified.

When the user agent receives the response, it decodes the status and headers, and decides what to do with the message. With an OK response, the user agent normally takes the message body and displays it on the screen of the requesting device. For a desktop Web browser, the message body is (hopefully) in HTML; for a WAP browser, WML.

HTTP is an exceedingly verbose protocol. Even simple requests and responses, with practically no data, can end up being several hundred characters long. WAP addresses this problem by requiring that all WAP applications use a WAP gateway. Among its other duties, a WAP gateway converts HTTP 1.1 messages, both requests and responses, into Wireless Session Protocol (WSP) messages. WSP, which is a compact binary protocol, is HTTP 1.1 compatible. Take any one of the requests or responses you've seen so far, parse it, and convert it into the most compact set of bits you can imagine—that's what WSP does.

That's a very brief introduction to HTTP 1.1. It's obviously much more complex than we describe. [RFC2616] is a lengthy, detailed specification that defines how user agents and content servers interact. We don't plan on describing in detail all the HTTP 1.1 message formats and headers. In addition to the specification, there are other sources such as [WONG] for that information. We want you to leave this section remembering one key point: There's more being passed back and forth between a user agent and a content server than just **GET** and **POST** requests and static and dynamic content. There are also request and response headers, and they can have a significant impact on the performance and execution of WAP applications.

As you'll see shortly, understanding a few key HTTP headers is the secret to minimizing wireless network traffic in a WAP environment.

Caching

According to [RFC2616], a cache is a "program's local store of response messages and the subsystem that controls its message storage, retrieval, and deletion. A cache stores cacheable responses in order to reduce the response time and network bandwidth consumption on future, equivalent requests." [RFC2616] has quite a bit of detail about caching. Fortunately, we can ignore most of it.

Simply put, when writing WAP applications, you want to minimize message traffic as much as possible. The way to do this is to cache as much as possible, refetch from the cache as often as possible, and make this all transparent to the user. Fortunately, although not a requirement, most WAP devices have some degree of cache and, as a default, try to maximize caching. Unless directed otherwise, the responses to all URL fetches are cached.

When a WAP user agent caches a response, it caches pretty much the whole thing: the URL, the response text, headers relating to caching, and enough information to validate the response (see the next section, "Validation and the History Stack," for more details on that process). Each cached item is uniquely identified by its full set of URL components: domain name, path, protocol, parameters, port number, and so on.

There are two HTTP headers that you can use to control the caching of individual WML decks and WMLScript functions. The most important header for our purposes is **Cache-Control.** It is an explicit mechanism by which you can control all caching entities throughout the request/response chain. All cache mechanisms must obey these headers. **Cache-Control** headers typically override a device's default cache behavior. They must be passed through, untouched, by all proxies and gateways in the message chain.

- **Cache-Control: no-cache** indicates that the URL should never be cached by the user agent or any server sitting between the content server and the user agent

- **Cache-Control: max-age=<seconds>** lets you define the longest time that a URL should stay in a device's cache. Once the entity lives for **max-age** seconds, it should be removed.

- **Expires:<date>** lets you specify the date after which a URL should be removed from the cache. The date/time format for all HTTP headers is formally defined in [RFC1123]. A typical **Expires** header looks like this:

```
Expires: Thu, 29 Apr 1999 19:47:52 GMT
```

When writing WAP applications, you can assume that the user agent will do whatever it can to maximize caching and minimize refetching content from a content server. There are four different caching cases you might need to consider to explicitly override the default caching behavior for your application.

Caching a URL Forever

A WAP user agent typically keeps a URL in its cache for as long as possible, getting rid of it only when necessary. The Phone.com browser defines "as long as possible" as approximately 30 days, a very large window if you use your WAP device on a regular basis.

However, there may be cases where you want to cache something even longer. Let's say, for instance, that you use a small graphics file containing your corporate logo as a splash screen for a service. You know that your logo isn't going to change in the near future. What's the point of forcing the user agent to reload it every 30 days? Why not cache it for a year or even longer?

There are two easy ways to do that. The first way is to specify an **Expires** date far into the future:

```
Expires: Mon, 01 Jan 2001 00:00:00 GMT
```

The second is to specify a large **max-age** value on a **Cache-Control** header:

```
Cache-Control: max-age=31536000
```

With a maximum user agent integer value of 2,147,483,647, and 86,400 seconds per day, you can specify in excess of 24,000 days. That's probably longer than the lifetime of your WAP device.

Caching a URL for a Specific Time

Probably the most common case you'll encounter is caching a URL for a specific period of time. For instance, you may have a stock quote service that updates its numbers every 15 minutes. If the user requests a quote at one point, and then again 5 minutes later, you may or may not want to fetch a fresh number. It depends on whether there's one available.

If your server is fairly deterministic, you should be able to calculate the number of seconds between the current request and the arrival of the new numbers. You can put that information in a **Cache-Control: max-age=<seconds>** header. Then, if the user requests a new value for the same quote before **max-age** expires, the cached quote is fetched. Otherwise, the cached quote is removed from the cache and re-requested from the content server.

The other way you can use that information is by specifying, in an **Expires** header, the date and time at which the information expires. The user agent can use that information to figure out when to flush the URL from its cache and refetch a fresh quote.

For example, to cache a response for approximately five minutes, assuming the response is created at 10 A.M. GMT on January 10, 2000, you could use either of these **Cache-Control** headers:

```
Expires: Mon, 10 Jan 2000 10:05:00 GMT
Cache-Control: max-age=300
```

Disabling Caching for a URL

For very volatile and rapidly changing services, where you always need to refetch a document from a server, you have to disable caching completely. This might be necessary, for instance, for a real-time stock quote data stream that is updated constantly throughout the day. Another example is the **WFAQLookup1** from the previous chapter. When you fetch the detailed information for a location, it includes the current date and time. It always needs to be refetched.

You disable caching using the **Cache-Control: no-cache** header. You can also use **Cache-Control: max-age=0** or an **Expires:** header with a date that has already passed. The second and third alternatives are not your best choices, however. First, they actually require more work on the part of the user agent. Not only does it have to first look for the URL in the cache, but if it finds it, it has to calculate its age. Second, it obscures your true intention. Third, they actually use a few more message bytes. You can eliminate the extra computation and clearly state your purpose just by using **Cache-Control: no-cache**.

These three headers give you the same end result if used on January 10, 2000, at 10 A.M. GMT:

```
Cache-Control: no-cache
Cache-Control: max-age=0
Expires: Sun, 10 Jan 2000 09:00:00 GMT
```

Validation and the History Stack

In addition to caching, HTTP 1.1 also describes the notion validation. Validation is the process of determining the validity of a cache entry—determining whether it has expired or not. Validation complicates the WAP user agent model a bit because of the possible presence of a history stack.

The WAP standard encourages all device manufacturers to include a history stack of at least 10 items. Every time a URL is fetched using a **<go>** element or any other kind of programmatic forward reference, it is put on the stack. Every time a URL is fetched using a **<prev>** element or the built-in backwards mechanism of a WAP device, the URL is popped off the history stack. The user agent can use these URLs to look up cached responses and all their details.

To make sure that your application behaves properly, you have to understand how the stack and the cache interact. The basic rule is: all forward references are validated, no backward references are validated.

For forward references, the WAP user agent always first checks to see if the URL is in the cache. If not, it issues a request for it. When it receives the response, it caches it (if it is allowed to do so) and pushes its URL on the history stack. If the URL is already in the cache, the user agent checks to make sure it is still a valid URL with valid content. If it is valid, the cached item is used as the response.

If it is no longer valid because, for instance, it's past its expiration date, the user agent requests the URL from the server again. The old cache entry is removed, the new response is put in the cache (if the user agent has permission), the URL is put on the history stack, and the new response is handled by the user agent.

For backwards references, the normal user agent response is similar to what happens when you press the Back button on a desktop browser. A **<prev>** operation is a request for the most recent, historical response for a URL. What's already in the cache is what the user wants, so there's no point in checking to see if it's still valid. Validation doesn't take place.

There may be a case, however, where you want a <prev> operation to revalidate a response to make sure it's still fresh. Fortunately, there is a **Cache-Control** header setting that does that. Use

```
Cache-Control: must-revalidate
```

to force a WAP user agent to validate an entry on the history stack when doing a backwards fetch. Validating the entry doesn't mean that the URL gets refetched. It gets refetched only if it is no longer valid. If it's still valid, the cached response is used instead.

To always force a reload on a **<prev>**, you should use

```
Cache-Control: must-revalidate, no-cache
```

If you want to force a reload for every **<prev>** reference older than five minutes, you can use

```
Cache-Control: must-revalidate, max-age=300
```

To summarize, to control caching for backwards references, use **Cache-Control: must revalidate** plus whatever other headers you need to specify the expiration criteria.

There are a variety of validation methods beyond those we've discussed relating to cache aging. A detailed discussion of all the validation methods, beyond what we've already described, exceeds the scope of this book. For more details, consult [RFC2616].

HTTP Headers versus META Elements

You manage caching and validation using HTTP headers. The next logical question is: How do you control the HTTP headers that are included in the responses sent from your content server back to a WAP user agent?

When a server creates a response to a user agent request, it automatically puts whatever headers it thinks are appropriate at the beginning of the response. If you create a static deck that gets returned in the response body, you have no way of setting any of the HTTP header values. The same is true if you create dynamic content using a technique that provides no means for setting headers.

The WML **<meta> http-equiv** element is designed to circumvent this limitation so that you can set response header values from within both static and dynamic documents. When a server returns a WAP document in response to a request, the WAP gateway scans the message body looking for character sequences like the following:

```
<meta http-equiv="Cache-Control" content="no-cache" />
```

If it finds that type of sequence, it extracts the **http-equiv** content and converts it to the WSP equivalent of an HTTP **Cache-Control** header. This header than gets passed on to the user agent so that it knows not to cache the response. You end up with the same result as if you had created the header and put it directly in the header portion of the response.

Here are some of the headers we've already seen and their **<meta>** equivalents.

```
Expires: Mon, 10 Jan 2000 10:05:00 GMT
Cache-Control: max-age=300
Cache-Control: no-cache

<meta http-equiv="Expires" content=" Mon, 10 Jan 2000 10:05:00 GMT" />
<meta http-equiv="Cache-Control" content="max-age=300" />
<meta http-equiv="Cache-Control" content="no-cache" />
```

The **<meta>** element is indispensable if you have no way of directly controlling the headers in an HTTP response, but it does create some extra work. First of all, you have to make sure you add the **<meta>** element to your response deck. Second, it requires extra work on the part of the WAP gateway. Third, historically, not all user agents and servers honor **<meta>** elements. If at all possible, you should instead use HTTP headers to control user agent caching.

Fortunately, some content server technologies provide methods for directly creating HTTP response headers. This is the case with Java servlets: There are APIs specifically for writing response headers. In the WorldFAQ example in Chapter 4, we skipped over explaining the routine **WriteResponseHeaders**. Now it should be obvious what it does.

We need to accomplish two tasks with the WorldFAQ response headers. First, we want to make sure that the response sent back by **WFAQLookup1** is never cached. Second, we want to provide a **Date** header because RFC2616 says that all content servers should provide a **Date** header to help user agents calculate cache-related algorithms.

WriteResponseHeaders does both of those things. It sets the **Cache-Control** header using **setHeader** and the **Date** header using **setDateHeader**, a Java servlet function designed specifically for creating a **Date** response header.

```
public void WriteResponseHeaders
    (
    HttpServletResponse res
    )
    throws
    IOException
    {

// Output the cache control header first.

    res.setHeader ( "Cache-Control", "no-store" );

// Output the Date header.

    Date now     = new Date ();
    long nowTime = now.getTime ();
    res.setDateHeader ( "Date", nowTime );
}
```

Testing with Telnet

One technique you can use for interacting with Web servers and figuring out what happens when you execute server-based programs is to use Telnet. Most operating systems have free Telnet clients. Telnet is a standard Unix system command. You can also access a Telnet program as a command-line program in Windows. There are several freeware and shareware Telnet clients for the Macintosh OS as well.

The Telnet protocol, which we don't describe here, lets you create a raw TCP/IP connection to a Web server, typically on port 80, the default HTTP port. From there you can submit an HTTP command, with all its detail, including headers, to the server. The server executes the command and returns the response to you. The interesting part is that you get the whole response—status line, headers, and message body if there is one. This is an excellent way to figure out how HTTP works and what your Web server is doing.

There's one problem with this technique. As you type in your command, the Telnet client interprets a double carriage return as the end of your request and sends it to the server. This complicates using **POST** commands because the **POST** data is put at the end of the message, after a double return. You can circumvent this problem by using a **GET** request, instead of a **POST** request, at least for testing purposes.

In Chapter 4, "WorldFAQ," we briefly mentioned that we included a **doGet** routine in **WFAQLookup1** specifically for this purpose.

```
//****************************************************************
// doGet
//
// Respond to the GET request received from the WAP device.
// Just call doPost.
//****************************************************************

  public void doGet (

    HttpServletRequest req, HttpServletResponse res )
    throws ServletException, IOException {

    doPost (req, res );
  }
```

Like **doPost**, **doGet** is automatically called by the server in response to a **GET** request. If you don't provide a **doGet** method, and one is sent to your servlet, the server typically responds with a 501 status (not implemented) message.

With our **doGet** method, which just calls the **doPost**, we can now easily call **WFAQLookup1** to see what headers are returned. The characters we enter are in **bold**.

```
% telnet www.worldfaq.com 80
Trying 209.249.155.109...
Connected to worldfaq.com.
Escape character is '^]'.
GET
/servlet/WFAQLookup1?LOCATION=J&PROFILE=G;T;C;H;A;P;L HTTP/1.1

HTTP/1.1 200 OK
Server: Zeus/3.1
Date: Wed, 21 Jul 1999 18:13:46 GMT
Cache-Control: no-cache
Connection: close
Content-Type: text/vnd.wap.wml

<?xml version="1.0"?>
<!DOCTYPE wml PUBLIC "-//WAPFORUM//DTD WML 1.1//EN"
  "http://www.wapforum.org/DTD/DTD/wml_1.1.xml">
<wml>
  <card id="lookupresponse" >

    . . . The rest of the deck.

  </card>
</wml>
```

Other Cache Management Techniques

Although we've discussed quite a few ways that you can manage a WAP user-agent's cache, there are even more techniques at your disposal. In the next chapter we discuss techniques for downloading more than one deck to a device in a single network transaction. Then, in Chapter 8, "Beyond WAP 1.1," we discuss how you can use some special features of the Phone.com WAP gateway to send decks and update a device's cache asynchronously, without request messages.

Graphics and Multipart Responses

The old adage is true—a picture is worth a thousand words, especially when used to enhance the user interface of an application on a small screen. Take a look at the WorldFAQ detail screen in Figure 6.1. A lot of precious screen real estate is taken up by a title of three to eight characters at the beginning of each line.

Worse still, look at the Airport line at the bottom of the screen. The total line length exceeds the screen width. Since the display mode is set to nowrap, an extra character to signal that there is more text is inserted at the beginning of the line, pushing it over yet another character. Also, the display automatically shifts from that of Figure 6.1 to that of Figure 6.2, revealing the second part of the Airport line, about once per second, creating a distracting blinking user interface.

Fortunately, in this case there is a much better and simpler way to present the information. Instead of using text titles, we can place small icons at the beginning of each line. This solution has several benefits:

- It uses less screen real estate.

- The icons don't need to be changed if we decide to localize the application for a different language.

- It eliminates the blinking display created by the **nowrap** mode.

- If properly designed, the icons can actually convey more information, more accurately, than text labels.

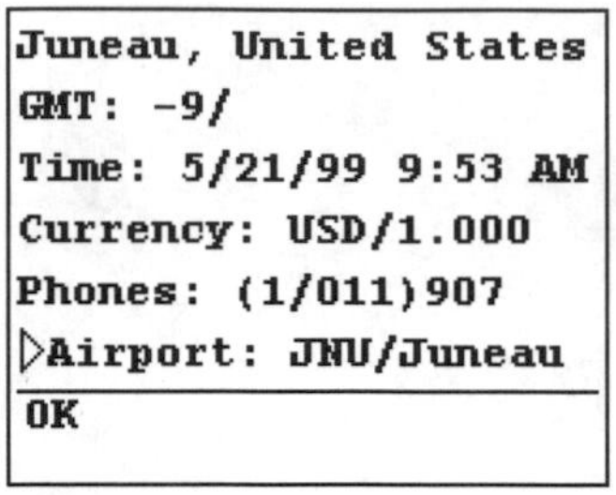

```
Juneau, United States
GMT: -9/
Time: 5/21/99 9:53 AM
Currency: USD/1.000
Phones: (1/011)907
▷Airport: JNU/Juneau
─────────────────────
OK
```

Figure 6.1 The WorldFAQ detail screen.

```
Juneau, United States
GMT: -9/
Time: 5/21/99 9:53 AM
Currency: USD/1.000
Phones: (1/011)907
Intl
─────────────────────
OK
```

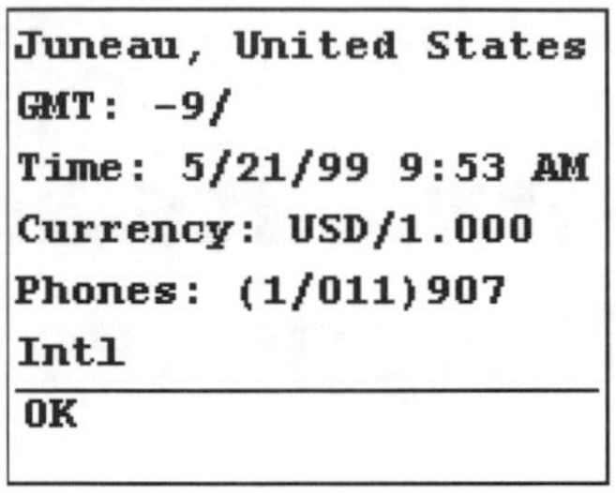

Figure 6.2 The WorldFAQ detail screen, part two.

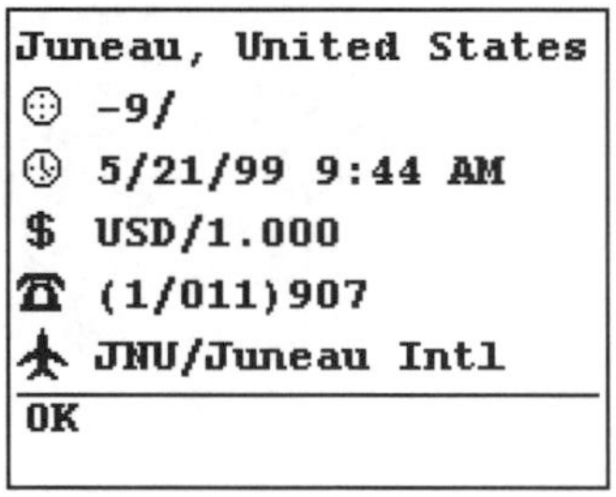

```
Juneau, United States
☺  -9/
🕐  5/21/99 9:44 AM
$  USD/1.000
☎  (1/011)907
✈  JNU/Juneau Intl
─────────────────────
OK
```

Figure 6.3 WorldFAQ detail with 15- × 15-bit icons.

Figure 6.3 shows the results of substituting 15- × 15-bit icons for each line title.

NOTE
Not all WAP user agents support images.

The first step in adding icons to an application is deciding where to add them and what to add. WorldFAQ is somewhat self-organizing in that respect. The content is very rigidly organized, with one separate piece of information per line. The logical thing to do is use one icon per line for labeling, adding an **<img>** element to each output line.

An **<img>** tag requires an **src** attribute that contains the URL of the image you want to use. It also requires an **alt** element that specifies a text alternative to the image in case the user agent doesn't support graphics.

Next, we need to decide what icons to use. You might remember, from Chapter 2, that the **<img>** element has an optional **localsrc** attribute that identifies a ROM-based icon. The Phone.com browser has a set of almost 200 icons available for **localsrc** access.

From an execution perspective, it makes a lot more sense to fetch a local ROM-based icon than to fetch a graphics file across a wireless network for each icon on the screen. For a full-profile WorldFAQ fetch, that would mean a total of eight separate requests just to display eight short lines of information. To take advantage of the local icons, let's include a **localsrc** attribute for each line.

Here's what each content line should look like in a full graphics version of WorldFAQ:

```
<img src="image URL" alt="text label" localsrc="icon name" /> content
```

The **src** and **alt** attributes are required, even if we also use **localsrc** elements. It would make sense to allow a combination of just **localsrc** and **alt** attributes, but WML 1.1 doesn't allow that.

Here's the deck that is returned by **WFAQLookup1** for any location starting with the character "J," requesting a full profile. Our WorldFAQ database has only one city starting with "J"—Juneau, Alaska.

```
<wml>
  <card id="lookupresponse" >
    <do type="accept">
      <go href="http://www.worldfaq.com/wml/wfaq.wml"/>
    </do>
    <p mode="nowrap">
      Juneau, United States<br/>
      GMT: -9/<br/>
      Time: 5/19/99 1:09 PM<br/>
      Currency: USD/1.000<br/>
      Phones: (1/011)907<br/>
      Airport: JNU/Juneau Intl<br/>
      Population: 27,000<br/>
      Language: English<br/>
    </p>
  </card>
</wml>
```

Here's what the deck looks like fully loaded for graphics, including some appropriate icons selected from the Phone.com **localsrc** ROM icons.

```
<wml>
  <card id="lookupresponse" >
    <do type="accept">
      <go href="http://www.worldfaq.com/wml/wfaq3.wml"/>
    </do>
    <p mode="nowrap">
      Juneau, United States<br/>
      <img src="../pics/gmt.bmp" alt="GMT:
        " localsrc="clock"/> -9/<br/>
      <img src="../pics/clock.bmp" alt="Time: "
        localsrc="wristwatch" />5/20/99 1:51 PM<br/>
```

```
    <img src="../pics/dollar.bmp" alt="Currency:
      " localsrc="dollarsign" />USD/1.000<br/>
    <img src="../pics/phone.bmp" alt="Phones: "
      localsrc="phone1" />(1/011)907<br/>
    <img src="../pics/airplane.bmp" alt="Airport: "
      localsrc="plane" />JNU/Juneau Intl<br/>
    <img src="../pics/person.bmp" alt="Population: "
      localsrc="smileyface" />27,000<br/>
    <img src="../pics/mouth.bmp" alt="Language: "
      localsrc="speaker" />English<br/>
  </p>
 </card>
</wml>
```

When we load this second deck into a WAP-compatible device that doesn't support images or graphics, we get the same display shown in Figures 6.1 and 6.2: plain text labels. With a device that supports graphics but not a **localsrc** set of icons, we get the display shown in Figure 6.3: vertically aligned 15 × 15 icons with the content to their right.

On the Phone.com browser that has **localsrc** icons, we get the display shown in Figure 6.4. The icons are all different widths, resulting in a skewed view. This display demonstrates a potential drawback of using **localsrc** icons: You have little or no control over their presentation.

According to the WAP 1.1 specification, **localsrc** attributes always take precedence over non-local graphics files. This makes sense; it's quicker and easier to retrieve an icon from a local graphics store than to fetch it across the network. **localsrc** images also take precedence over cached non-local images. Presumably, they are easier to fetch and display than cached images. Both **localsrc** and non-local images take precedence over the **alt** text. WAP 1.1 assumes that if you go to the trouble to specify images, you really want them, regardless of the cost to retrieve and display them.

Since **localsrc** images have the highest precedence, you should make sure that they give you the kind of presentation you want. There are other **<img>**

```
┌─────────────────────────┐
│ Juneau, United States   │
│ ◷ -9/                   │
│ ♨ 5/21/99 9:44 AM       │
│ $ USD/1.000             │
│ ☎ (1/011)907            │
│ ✈ JNU/Juneau Intl       │
├─────────────────────────┤
│ OK                      │
└─────────────────────────┘
```

Figure 6.4 WorldFAQ with localsrc icons.

attributes that you can use to specify white space (**vspace** and **hspace**), vertical alignment (**align**), and image size (**height** and **width**), but their interpretation can vary from device to device. If these attributes don't give you the results you want using **localsrc** images, the only way to guarantee that your graphics appear as you intend, at least in size and spacing, is to define them yourself.

NOTE
Not only are **localsrc** images optional in a WAP user agent, there is no uniformity of **localsrc** images between different user agents that support them. It's best to use **localsrc** images if you are deploying an application, perhaps a vertical or legacy application, on only one type of user agent. That way, you have guaranteed behavior every time.

Serving Up WorldFAQ Images

Now that we've discussed some of the ways we can get images into WorldFAQ, let's add the code to the WorldFAQ Java servlet to generate the proper deck when a single location match occurs. Instead of listing all the WorldFAQ source code, here's a summary of what we're changing.

NOTE
The source code for all the Java servlet changes described in this chapter can be found in the file WFAQLookup2.java on the accompanying CD-ROM. We have also created a renumbered version of wfaq1.wml to accompany this new servlet. You can find the new WML deck in the file wfaq2.wml.

First, we create a set of 15- × 15-bit icons and store them in the /pics directory of our content server. Then, we add the following global constants to **WFAQLookup2**:

```
static String  gPicsRelDir = "../pics/";
Hashtable      gProfileChunks;
```

gPicsRelDir is initialized to the directory, relative to the **WFAQLookup2** URL, that contains the graphics files. **gProfileChunks** is a hash table for storing information about each detail line. We add this for three reasons. First, the number of data items associated with each detail line is growing (we just added a graphics file name and a **localsrc** name to the text label). Second, putting them in a hash table lets us generalize the code that creates the output deck for displaying a location's details. Third, it lets us isolate all the hard-coded detail line strings in one place.

To that end, we modify the servlet's **init** routine to set up the hash table. Each hash table item is keyed by the profile's identifying character. It contains a semicolon-delimited list of the item's text label, its server-based graphics file name, and its **localsrc** name.

```
public void init
  (
    ServletConfig config
  )
    throws
    ServletException
  {

 // Open the WorldFAQ data file.

    try {
      gDataFile = new RandomAccessFile ( gDataFileName, "r" );

 // Initialize the profile data hash table.

      gProfileChunks = new Hashtable ();
      gProfileChunks.put ( "G", "GMT;gmt.bmp;clock" );
      gProfileChunks.put ( "T", "Time;clock.bmp;wristwatch" );
      gProfileChunks.put ( "C", "Currency;dollar.bmp;dollarsign" );
      gProfileChunks.put ( "H", "Phones;phone.bmp;phone1" );
      gProfileChunks.put ( "A", "Airport;airplane.bmp;plane" );
      gProfileChunks.put ( "P", "Population;person.bmp;smileyface" );
      gProfileChunks.put ( "L", "Language;mouth.bmp;speaker" );
    }

 // Database unavailable. Set file pointer to null and tell server.

    catch ( IOException e ) {
      gDataFile = null;
      throw new ServletException ();
  } }
```

With this code now in the **init** routine, we can easily add new profile items and individual detail lines in the future.

Next, we modify **outputLocation** in two straightforward ways. First, at the beginning of the function, we include the following code to check to see if the device looking up the location supports graphics. We do this because it makes no sense to generate all the graphics elements in the response deck if they are ignored.

```
boolean hasGraphics = false; // user agent supports graphics?

// Find out if the requesting device supports graphics
// by checking the user agent header.
```

```
device = req.getHeader ( "User-Agent" );
if ( device != null ) {
  if ( device.indexOf ( "UP.Browser" ) != -1 ) {
    hasGraphics = true;
} }
```

In this case, we check the "User-Agent" header for the value "UP.Browser," the Phone.com browser identifier. If this were production code, you would want to do this check a bit differently. First, there would most likely be more than one device that supports graphics. Second, it's a bad idea to hard-code user agent names (or any strings for that matter) in a program. Initializing a vector containing all the graphics-capable user agents would be a better approach. Finally, an even more elegant approach might be to store a series of device profiles in a separate database. These profiles might contain information such as screen size, a graphics support indicator, WML version in use, and whether the device includes WMLScript and floating-point support.

Our method is primitive, but it's an example of one way to check for graphics support. Also, it's an example of how to query the request headers in a Java servlet for some useful information.

Now that we know whether the requesting user agent can display graphics, we modify each of the individual profile output sections to include a call to a function called **addLineDetails.** For instance, here's the code section for outputting the GMT portion of the response deck:

```
// GMT offset, profile code "G".


    GMTHrs  = getNextToken ( parser );
    GMTMins = getNextToken ( parser );
    detail  = GMTHrs + "/" + GMTMins;
    if ( profile.indexOf ( "G" ) >= 0) {
      msg = msg + addLineDetails ( "G", hasGraphics, picNames, detail );
    }
```

This change handles all the line labeling and graphics support in a routine called **addLineDetails**. **addLineDetails** gets the hash table entry for this line item, pulls out the individual components using a **StringTokenizer**, and then returns a string containing either a simple text label, or a more complex line with the **img** URL, the **localsrc** attribute, and the **alt** element.

The last step to adding graphics support to **WFAQLookup2** is to add **addLineDetails**.

```
//****************************************************************
// addLineDetails
//
```

```
// Decide if the current output line should start with an icon
// or a text label. Return the result back for adding to the
// response message.
//****************************************************************

  public String addLineDetails
  (
    String  profHashval,
    boolean hasGraphics,
    Vector  picNames,
    String  detail
  )
  {

// Get the data for this profile item.

    String result = "";
    String hashContents = ( String ) gProfileChunks.get ( profHashval );

    if ( hashContents != null ) {

      StringTokenizer chunks = new StringTokenizer ( hashContents, ";" );

      String textLabel = chunks.nextToken ();
      String picName   = chunks.nextToken ();
      String lsrcName  = chunks.nextToken ();

// Return either a full-blown string with all the graphics
// information or just the text label.

      result = textLabel + ": ";

      if ( hasGraphics ) {
        picNames.addElement ( picName );
        result =
          "<img src=\""  + gPicsRelDir + picName + "\"" +
          " alt=\""      + textLabel   + ": " + "\"/>" + EOL;
    } }
    return result + detail + WMLEOL;
  }
```

These few changes give us the result we want, a response deck that is fully-loaded for graphics display.

Multipart Messages

Suppose you decide that you really must include some graphics in your application but the **localsrc** icons don't fit your needs very well. This means you have to create some graphics of your own, store them on your content server, and serve them up one by one in a series of individual requests. When the response deck comes back to the device, for each URL in that deck that points to an image, the user agent issues another request to the content server to retrieve that image.

This works fine in a standard Web situation with a desktop browser and a hard-wired, high-speed communications line. It doesn't, however, work with a wire-less network. For the Juneau, Alaska, lookup example earlier in this chapter, for a full profile, we would have to make eight separate requests to the content server just to display a location's detail information.

You can help minimize the delays that the user will certainly experience by making your graphics files as small as possible. That, unfortunately, probably won't help very much in this situation. Depending on server and network loads, the user could end up waiting as much as 15 or 20 seconds before the informa-tion is displayed. There is another technique, called *multipart messages*, that you can use to solve this problem.

MIME multipart messages, which are defined in [RFC2045], provide a mecha-nism for defining a single MIME-compatible message that contains several parts with differing formats. So far, most of the response messages we've dis-cussed are single-part messages with a specific content type:

```
Content-Type: text/vnd.wap.wml
```

This content type header indicates that the message body is coded in WML, Wireless Markup Language.

For MIME multipart messages, you specify a content type of

```
Content-Type: multipart/mixed;boundary="*****"
```

where **boundary** is any arbitrary string you care to use. This content type header tells the user agent receiving the response that it should expect to find a message body that has one or more parts. Each part has its own **Content-Type** header. The parts are separated by the boundary string preceded by two hyphens: "--." Here's the overall structure of a two-part message that uses the boundary string "*****":

```
--*****
Content-type: type1

message body 1
--*****
Content-type: type2

--*****
message body 2
--*****--
```

Note how the two message parts are separated by the boundary string, with the final part terminated by the boundary string plus an additional double hyphen. Also note how each message part includes its own **Content-Type** header followed by a double line-feed, carriage-return sequence, like all MIME messages, indicating the start of the message body. A MIME multi-part message is literally just a series of MIME messages, in which each message has its own individual message headers.

According to [RFC2616], most response headers, unless they are content headers, are ignored in a multipart message, even though each part of a multipart message can have any headers "which are significant to the meaning of the part." The preceding sample, containing just **Content-Type** headers, is all the information the receiving user agent needs to understand the message, identify the individual parts, and understand what to do with the message bodies.

The WAP 1.1 specification is a bit vague about the multipart message headers. [RFC2045] requires only **Content-Type** headers. However, individual WAP user agents may have more stringent requirements. For instance, in order for a user agent to know how to cache each part of a multipart message and easily resolve references between parts, it needs a URL for each part. Because of this, a user agent may require a **Content-Location** header that contains a relative URL, the location of the message part relative to the **Content-Location** URL from the message header. Absolute URLs are not used because of security concerns.

MIMEing WorldFAQ

Let's start with a simple case of an oxymoronically-named one-part, multipart message with no graphics references. For our previous Juneau, Alaska, lookup, with a full profile, we want the multipart response message to look something like this (the headers may vary depending on your content server). The important parts are highlighted with bold type.

```
HTTP/1.1 200 OK
Server: Zeus/3.1
Date: Sat, 22 May 1999 21:15:58 GMT
Cache-Control: no-cache
Connection: close
Content-Type: multipart/mixed;boundary="*****"
Content-Location:
http://www.worldfaq.com/servlet/WFAQLookup2
Expires: Sat, 22 May 1999 21:15:58 GMT

--*****
Content-type: text/vnd.wap.wml
```

```
<?xml version="1.0"?>
<!DOCTYPE wml PUBLIC "-//WAPFORUM//DTD WML 1.1//EN"
"http://www.wapforum.org/DTD/wml_1_1.xml">
<wml>
  <card id="lookupresponse" >
    <do type="accept">
      <go href="http://www.worldfaq.com/wfaq2.wml"/>
    </do>
    <p mode="nowrap">
      Juneau, United States<br/>
      GMT: -9/<br/>
      Time: 5/22/99 1:15 PM<br/>
      Currency: USD/1.000<br/>
      Phones: (1/011)907<br/>
      Airport: JNU/Juneau Intl<br/>
      Population: 27,000<br/>
      Language: English<br/>
    </p>
  </card>
</wml>
--*****--
```

This isn't a very interesting example by itself. It just shows a more complicated way of sending a single deck to a user agent. It lays the foundation, however, for adding more message parts to the **WFAQLookup2** servlet response. Here's how we change **WFAQLookup2** to get this result.

We start by adding the following global constant:

```
static String gMsgBoundary = "*****";
```

This defines the message boundary. It can be any string we want, and it can change from response to response if we like.

NOTE

Hard-coding of the boundary string can lead to failure if the message boundary string occurs in any of the documents included in the response. Because "***" is relatively rare, it's probably safe, but certainly not guaranteed to be so. For instance, if you put this string in a WML comment, you would have an erroneous multipart. A more appropriate solution would be to look for a unique string that does not exist in any part of the response.**

The bulk of the changes take place in the **doPost** function. Instead of just outputting the response deck to the output stream as we build it, we build it in a string variable named **resMsg** using the same code as before. Then, when all the processing is done, in the **doPost finally** clause, we output the whole response.

```
finally {

// Finish up results of the lookup first. One message part.

  resMsg = resMsg + "</card>" + EOL + "</wml>";
  resMsg = resMsg + EOL + "--" + gMsgBoundary;

// Start outputting the response headers, the MIME message type,
// and the message's starting delimiter.

  writeResponseHeaders ( res );
  res.setContentType ( "multipart/mixed;boundary=\"" + gMsgBoundary + "\"" );
  out.println ( "--" + gMsgBoundary );

// Now, add the location lookup response deck message part.
// Add an EOL to the header to indicate the message start.

  out.println ( "Content-type: text/vnd.wap.wml" + EOL );
  out.print ( resMsg );

// Output final boundary delimiter.

  out.println ( "--" );
  }
```

We also add a line to **writeResponseHeaders** to output the correct **Content-Location** header. This is in case the user agent requires relative URLs for the message parts (which we include)—it needs the absolute URL of the overall response in order for the relative URLs to be of any use.

```
res.setHeader ( "Content-location",
  "http://www.worldfaq.com/servlet/WFAQLookup2" );
```

These few changes give us a correctly formatted multipart response containing a single message part.

What we really want to do is add the graphics files to this same multipart message. Here's what the response should look like, with non-essential, repetitive, and binary parts removed:

```
Content-Type: multipart/mixed;boundary="*****"
Content-Location: http://www.worldfaq.com/servlet/WFAQLookup2

--*****
Content-type: text/vnd.wap.wml

<?xml version="1.0"?>
<!DOCTYPE wml PUBLIC "-//WAPFORUM//DTD WML 1.1//EN"
"http://www.wapforum.org/DTD/wml_1_1.xml">
<wml>
```

```
      <card id="lookupresponse" >
        <do type="accept">
          <go href="http://www.worldfaq.com/wml/wfaq3.wml"/>
        </do>
        <p mode="nowrap">
          Juneau, United States<br/>
          <img src="../pics/gmt.bmp" alt="GMT: " />
            -9/<br/>
              .
              .
              .
          <img src="../pics/mouth.bmp" alt="Language: " />
            English<br/>
        </p>
      </card>
    </wml>
    --*****
    Content-location: ../pics/gmt.bmp
    Content-type: image/bmp

    <contents of gmt.bmp>
    --*****
    .
    .
    .
    Content-location: ../pics/mouth.bmp
    Content-type: image/bmp

    <contents of mouth.bmp>
    --*****--
```

Notice that the **localsrc** attributes are gone. We're making the assumption that any device that supports **localsrc** icons also supports graphics files, and we'd rather use our own icons.

Since we've now put all the response-creation code in the **finally** clause, it's easy to add the graphics files. First, we need to keep track of which graphics files to include. If we add the vector data structure **picNames** to **doPost**, and add to it the correct graphics file names in **addLineDetails**, we can sequence through the vector back in **doPost** and output what we need.

Here's an updated copy of the **finally** clause from **doPost**. After outputting the response headers and the first part of the message, we just convert the vector **picNames** to an enumeration and sequence through it. On each pass, we output a **Content-Location** header with a relative URL, and a **Content-Type** header, followed by the file's contents.

```
finally {

    .
    .
    .

    // Output the graphics file parts of the message if there are any.
```

```
        String picName = "";
        Enumeration pNames = picNames.elements ();
        while ( pNames.hasMoreElements ()) {
          picName = ( String ) pNames.nextElement ();
          out.println ( EOL + "Content-location: " + gPicsRelDir + picName );
          out.println ( "Content-type: image/bmp" + EOL );
          addFileToResponse ( picName, out );
          out.print ( EOL + "--" + gMsgBoundary );
        }

// Output final boundary delimiter.

        out.println ( "--" );
  } }
```

addFileToResponse, called in the enumeration loop, adds the data from each file to the response stream.

```
//*****************************************************************
// addFileToResponse
//
// Add a file's contents to the response stream.
//*****************************************************************


  public static void addFileToResponse (

    String fileName,
    ServletOutputStream out )

    throws
    FileNotFoundException,
    IOException,
    WFAQLookupException {

    FileInputStream fis =
      new FileInputStream ( gPicsFullDir + fileName );

    try {

// Open the file with a 1024 buffer.

      byte [] buf = new byte [ 1024 ];
      int bytesRead;
// Write to response stream a buffer at a time.

      while (( bytesRead = fis.read ( buf )) != -1 ) {
        out.write ( buf, 0, bytesRead );
    } }
```

```
// Exception handling and finally clause.

   catch ( FileNotFoundException e ) {
     throw new WFAQLookupException (
       "Missing file: " + gPicsFullDir + fileName );
   }

   finally {
     if ( fis != null ) fis.close();
 } }
```

We also streamline **outputLocation** to modularize it a bit more, shift more of the details for handling each individual case into **addLineDetails**, and remove most of the location data local variables at the expense of making the code a bit more obscure. Here's a new version of **outputLocation** that incorporates all the changes we describe in this chapter.

```
public String outputLocation (

    String locOffset,
    HttpServletRequest req,
    Vector picNames )

    throws
    IOException,
    WFAQLookupException {

    String GMTHrs="", GMTMins="";

    String  msg = "";            // the response deck
    String  detail = "";         // detail data for one line
    String  device = "";         // the requesting user agent
    boolean hasGraphics = false; // user agent supports graphics?

// Find out if the requesting device supports graphics.

    try {

      device  = req.getHeader ( "User-Agent" );
      if ( device != null ) {
        if ( device.indexOf ( "UP.Browser" ) != -1 ) {
          hasGraphics = true;
      } }
// Get the user's profile so you can figure out what information to return.

        String profile = req.getParameter ( "PROFILE" );

// Get the location's data for parsing.
```

```
      int recordLoc = Integer.parseInt ( locOffset );
      gDataFile.seek ( recordLoc );
      String locData = gDataFile.readLine ();

// Add the ACCEPT task to the card, and set the
// display mode of the items to be returned.

      msg = msg +
        "<do type=\"accept\">" + EOL +
        "<go href=\"http://" + gSiteName + "/wml/wfaq3.wml\"/>" +  EOL +
        "</do>" + EOL +
        "<p mode=\"nowrap\">" + EOL;

// Retrieve the location's data and parse it for individual data items.
// Only include in the returned DECK those items requested according
// to the settings of the user's profile string.

      StringTokenizer parser = new StringTokenizer ( locData, "," );

// Location name and country.

      msg = msg + getNextToken ( parser ) + ", " +
            getNextToken ( parser ) + WMLEOL;

// GMT offset, profile code "G".

      GMTHrs  = getNextToken ( parser );
      GMTMins = getNextToken ( parser );
      detail  = GMTHrs + "/" + GMTMins;
      if ( profile.indexOf ( "G" ) >= 0) {
        msg = msg + addLineDetails (
           "G", hasGraphics, picNames, detail );
      }

// Current time, profile code "T".

      detail = calcTime ( GMTHrs, GMTMins );
      if ( profile.indexOf ( "T" ) >= 0) {
        msg = msg + addLineDetails (
           "T", hasGraphics, picNames, detail );
      }

// Currency symbol and exchange rate, profile code "C".
      detail = getNextToken ( parser ) + "/" + getNextToken ( parser );
      if ( profile.indexOf ( "C" ) >= 0) {
        msg = msg + addLineDetails (
           "C", hasGraphics, picNames, detail );
      }
```

```
// Telephone codes, profile code "H".

        detail = "(" + getNextToken ( parser ) + "/" +
                getNextToken ( parser ) + ")" +
                getNextToken ( parser );
        if ( profile.indexOf ( "H" ) >= 0 ) {
          msg = msg + addLineDetails (
            "H", hasGraphics, picNames, detail );
        }

// Airport symbol & name, profile code "A"

        detail = getNextToken ( parser ) + "/" + getNextToken ( parser );
        if ( profile.indexOf ( "A" ) >= 0 ) {
          msg = msg + addLineDetails (
            "A", hasGraphics, picNames, detail );
        }

// Population, profile code "P"

        detail = getNextToken ( parser ) + ",000";
        if ( profile.indexOf ( "P" ) >= 0 ) {
          msg = msg + addLineDetails (
            "P", hasGraphics, picNames, detail );
        }

// Primary language, profile code "L"

        detail = getNextToken ( parser );
        if ( profile.indexOf ( "L" ) >= 0 ) {
          msg = msg + addLineDetails (
            "L", hasGraphics, picNames, detail );
      } }

// Exception handling and finally clause.

    catch ( IOException e ) {
      msg = "";
      throw new WFAQLookupException ( "IOException in OutputLocation" );
    }

    finally {
      msg = msg + "</p>" + EOL;
      return ( msg );
  } }
```

Note that **addLineDetails** is now past the **picNames** graphics file vector, so that it can add the names of all the graphics files that need to be included in the multipart response. Also, it gets past part of the line content in the variable detail for adding to the response deck. Here's the final version of **addLineDetails**.

```
//******************************************************************
// addLineDetails
//
// Decide if the current output line should start with an icon
// or a text label. Return the result back for adding to the
// response message.
//******************************************************************

  public String addLineDetails (

     String  profHashval,
     boolean hasGraphics,
     Vector  picNames,
     String  detail ) {

// Get the data for this profile item.

     String result = "";
     String hashContents = ( String ) gProfileChunks.get ( profHashval );

     if ( hashContents != null ) {

        StringTokenizer chunks = new StringTokenizer ( hashContents, ";" );

        String textLabel = chunks.nextToken ();
        String picName   = chunks.nextToken ();
        String lsrcName  = chunks.nextToken ();

// Return either a full-blown string with all the graphics
// information or just the text label.

        result = textLabel + ": ";

        if ( hasGraphics ) {
          picNames.addElement ( picName );
          result =
            "<img src=\"" + gPicsRelDir + picName + "\"" +
            " alt=\""     + textLabel   + ": " + "\"/>" + EOL;
     } }
     return result + detail + WMLEOL;
  }
```

That's all we need to do to **WFAQLookup2** to generate multipart responses that include graphics. The full source code can be found on the accompanying CD-ROM in the file WFAQLookup2.java.

In Chapter 1, "Introducing WAP," we briefly described the graphics bitmap format that is part of the WAP specifications. If you take a look at the file names and their content type headers that we send as part of our multipart message, they are BMP, not WBMP files. This is where the WAP gateway comes into play. It recognizes BMP files and converts their contents into the proper WBMP data stream. It also transforms the content type headers into WBMP-compatible headers before sending them on to the user agent.

If you have tools for creating WBMP files, you can use those files in this situation just by changing the **Content-Type** header for each message part that contains a graphics file to read:

```
Content-type: image/vnd.wap.wbmp
```

and using the extension "wbmp" on the file names. This saves the WAP gateway the trouble of doing the conversion for you.

NOTE

If you do use WBMP files, you risk having your application code become incompatible in the future. WAP content standards change and devices change to adopt new standards. If the application sends BMP, it is much more likely that it will be correctly displayed—the WAP gateway will transform it to whatever format the device handles.

Multipart Caveats

The end result of all the work in this chapter is that **WFAQLookup2** is now capable of adding graphics to its response message, and appending the graphics files to a single multipart MIME message for transmission to the user agent. It does this only if the user agent supports graphics.

Using multipart messages in the way we describe in this chapter has both good and bad aspects. The good news is that everything you need for the response, including the graphics files, is included in one single transmission across the network. Network latency is minimized and the user response time is as quick as it can be.

The bad news is the same as the good news: Everything you need for the response is sent every time **WFAQLookup2** is called. The graphics files get cached in the user agent. Unfortunately, there's no way to programmatically check from a WML or WMLScript program to see if they are already in the cache and pass that information back to **WFAQLookup2,** telling it not to include one or more of the graphics files in a subsequent response. The icons are always sent, every time. We essentially trade off the quicker transmission time of a single message against a much longer wait for the first response, followed by a shorter wait on subsequent responses, which is what you would experience with a single-part message. Just how much sense this tactic makes depends almost entirely upon the cost, in both dollars and wait time, of sending the graphics. For a maximum of seven 128-byte files, the cost is not too bad.

NOTE

Even if there is a way to find out if the icons are in the cache, because we create a dynamic response message with the cache control header set to "no-cache," the icons, like the response deck, are marked the same way, and are refetched every time as well.

One way to circumvent this problem would be to set up a separate servlet that just delivers the full set of icons to any requesting user agent, just to get them in the cache. The response message would have **Cache-Control: max-age** set to a very large value, or an **Expires** header with an expiration date very far in the future. You could call this servlet when you first load the WorldFAQ WML deck, as part of the splash screen processing. The icons would load the first time you use the deck, but never again.

This example is meant to demonstrate multipart WAP messages, but because of the problems just described, it's not necessarily a good example of the best way to use multipart messages. Often, it makes more sense to send your graphics files as separate messages. Let the basic WAP programming model do what it's designed to do—fetch individual URLs one at a time, cache them, and then get them from the cache after that.

If you find yourself in a situation where multipart messages make sense, however, you're ready. A typical situation might be an application like Battleships, which we describe in Chapter 3. The WML and WMLScript components are both called for each execution of the program. They are a natural for a multipart message.

In this chapter, we've added our own multipart support to a Java servlet. Phone.com's WAP SDK includes multipart Perl and C libraries that you can use when building applications. If you're working with Perl or C, it certainly makes sense to take advantage of these libraries.

Internationalization (I18N)

For a standard like WAP, one designed to work throughout the world, internationalization (also called I18N by the World Wide Web Consortium) is an important topic. With desktop applications, localization is the term usually used to describe making software suitable for multiple countries. Localization is the process of modifying a program so that it can be used by people who understand a specific language. Internationalization, what we describe in this chapter, means adapting one program (or content server, in our case) to serve multiple nationalities simultaneously.

The WAP architecture is designed to support multiple character sets and languages. To that end, as in other areas, WAP borrows heavily from Internet standards to achieve that goal. For instance, it uses the IANA registry of character sets and codes that are also used in HTTP headers. It also mandates the use of Unicode, a universal character set that is rapidly becoming a de facto Web standard. WMLScript uses the Unicode collating sequence for string manipulations.

The WAP architecture makes the following assumptions about a WAP-compatible environment:

- User agents have a preferred language (either user or device defined), and can accept content in a set of well-known character sets.

- Content servers can emit content in one or more character sets, and preferably languages, and can accept input in one or more character sets.

- User agents and content servers can negotiate the encoding used in any transaction between them.

- All content and data types are transmitted using methods that support the declaration of language and character encoding.

Keeping these goals and assumptions in mind, we need to clarify some basic terminology before delving into the specifics of WAP I18N.

Character Sets

A character set, also called a character code, is a mapping that defines a one-to-one correspondence between a collection of character names or identifiers and a set of non-negative integers that may or may not be contiguous. A character set includes no information about how individual characters appear on a computer screen. It is an internal computer representation of a group of characters.

Over the years a variety of character sets have been defined by standards organizations and vendors. US-ASCII, one of the first used on the Internet, is still widely used. It is an eight-bit code that uses only seven bits. The most significant bit is always set to zero.

Currently, the most widely used character sets are the ISO Latin codes, ISO-8859-1 through ISO-8859-9. (For more information about the ISO character sets, visit www.iso.ch.) They are a series of eight-bit codes where the first 128 characters match the US-ASCII character set, and the second 128 codes are specifically defined for use with different groups of languages. [RFC2616] specifies ISO-8859-1 as the default character set for HTML documents, and user agents, as defined by Internet standards, are not required to support any character set other than ISO-8859-1.

Unicode, the official WAP character set, contains enough unique codes—over 65,000—to include virtually all the characters in all the spoken and written languages in the world. It is rapidly becoming the de facto standard for the Internet. In fact, since [RFC2070], Unicode (also denoted UCS, Universal Character Set) is used as a common reference when describing Internet character issues. In Unicode, the first 128 characters are the same as US-ASCII, and the first 256 codes are the same as ISO-8859-1.

The latest Unicode standard is Unicode 2.1. In an effort to provide one unified character set, the Unicode and ISO organizations have converged their efforts—Unicode 2.1 is for all practical purposes the same as ISO 10646-1:1993. Visit www.unicode.org to find out more about the Unicode standards.

There is a body that is responsible for maintaining a registry of character codes. The IANA Character Set registry [IANA] currently contains almost 200 recognized character sets and their multiple aliases. Table 7.1 contains a list of the character sets found most frequently on the Internet and some of the languages they can readily represent. Character set identifiers are case insensitive.

Transfer Encodings

A transfer encoding defines how each member of a character set is represented as bits, typically when being transported across a network. In theory, it makes sense to use the character code for the transfer encoding. The earlier character codes are still used that way: ISO-8859-1 is usually transmitted as the eight-bit codes defined by the ISO-8859-1 character set. However, there are networking systems that cannot readily transmit or receive eight-bit data values. In these

Table 7.1 Some Frequently Used Internet Character Sets and Their Languages

CODE	LANGUAGES		
iso-8859-1	Afrikaans	Albanian	Basque
windows-1252	Danish	Dutch	English
	Finnish	French	German
	Italian	Norwegian	Portuguese
	Scottish	Spanish	Swedish
iso-8859-2	Croatian	Czech	Hungarian
	Polish	Romanian	Slovak
	Slovenian		
iso-8859-5	Bulgarian	Byelorussian	Macedonian
	Serbian	Ukrainian	
iso-8859-6	Arabic		
iso-8859-7	Greek		
iso-8859-8	Hebrew		
iso-8859-9	Turkish		
windows-1254			
koi-8-r	Russian		
iso-8859-5			
shift_jis	Japanese		
iso-2022-jp			
euc-jp			

situations, a seven-bit encoding such as UUENCODE, a MIME-defined encoding technique, may be used instead.

The Unicode organization has defined two transfer encodings for Unicode 2.1, UTF-8 and UTF-16 (there is also a UTF-7 encoding, defined by ISO, for 7-bit transmissions). UTF-16 encodings are the same as the Unicode 2.1 character codes—each 16-bit Unicode code is represented by the same 16-bit UTF-16 value.

Unfortunately, character codes aren't always very space efficient. For instance, the first 256 Unicode character codes are used to represent the most frequently used letters on the Internet. It makes no sense to use two bytes to represent codes that can fit into one byte. The efficiency of that approach is only about 50 percent—for each two bytes, you have one empty (or null) byte.

To solve that problem, the Unicode organization defined UTF-8 encoding. UTF-8 uses from one to five bytes to represent all the Unicode character codes. As you might have guessed, the one-byte values are reserved for the first 128 characters of the US-ASCII character code. The remaining values try to use the fewest number of bytes for the most popular characters. Because of WAP emphasis on fitting as much information into as few bytes as possible for wireless transmission, the WAP Forum recommends and encourages the use of UTF-8 as the default transfer encoding.

UTF-8 can be used for all languages and is the recommended encoding on the Internet. Support for its use on the Internet is rapidly increasing.

NOTE

If you read the various standards documents and Requests for Comments (RFCs) that define Internet character sets and transfer encodings, you'll find that they can be quite confusing because there is no standardized terminology. One example is the IANA character registry. It contains an entry for Unicode, which is a character code, and UTF-8, which is a specific encoding of Unicode. It might be clearer if they used UTF-16 as an alias for Unicode, or as a replacement name, but they don't. Also, [RFC2616] uses the term *character set* to describe transfer encodings. This is probably because the HTTP **Charset** attribute, described later in this chapter, is used to specify encodings. Fortunately, because of Unicode, the number of character codes and encodings you need to know about is decreasing, not increasing.

As programmers, we need to know about character sets and encodings. WAP user agents are supposed to understand Unicode, the official WAP character code, but which encoding? The accepted default is UTF-8, because it's the most space efficient, but it's not required. WAP user agents can also use other encodings, too. An obvious choice is ISO-8859-1, the most common ISO Latin character set. We need to know how to figure the encoding a user agent prefers and use it if at all possible.

In addition to dealing with user agent character set issues, we can't usually choose the native character set or encoding for our origin servers. That decision is typically made at the operating system or programming language level. For instance, the Java servlets we described in earlier chapters generate Unicode, UTF-16 encoded strings. Some servers, however, may use US-ASCII or ISO-8859-1. WAP user agents are not required to understand those character sets. If they do, how can we manage the communication so that the user agent gets the right one?

Fortunately, as you will see later in this chapter, there are ways to manage these issues. On one level, you as a programmer can determine what type of encoding a user agent prefers, and deliver that encoding by generating content in the right encoding. An even simpler solution is to let the WAP gateway solve the problem. Most WAP gateways can monitor the communications between the user agent and content server, figure out the encodings each understands, and do the transfer encoding for you. That relieves you from having to deal with the issue. Just make sure that you know your server's capabilities.

Languages

Just as you need to be aware of the character set and encoding issues to make your WAP systems work properly, you also need to worry about the end users. You have to make sure that you deliver content that they can read and understand.

A language, which has nothing to do with computers or character sets, is a spoken dialect. Just coincidentally, for example, ISO-8859-5 is used to encode Russian. A language identifier, however, can be useful when rendering content on a computer display, to identify certain attributes of the language.

An obvious example is layout direction. Western languages are displayed and read from left to right. Japanese, on the other hand, is laid out and read from right to left. Also, a language may have special rules that define how to combine multiple character codes into visible entities on the screen. These attributes are properties of the language, not the character set or encoding.

HTTP defines a set of language tags that user agents and content servers can use to negotiate the most favorable language for a transaction. HTTP language tags consist of a list of two-character primary language abbreviations, from the [ISO639] standard, with optional two-character dialect abbreviations from the [ISO3166] standard. A typical language tag might look like this:

```
it, it-va, fr-fx, fr, en
```

This tag identifies the following languages from most to least important: Italian, Vatican Italian, Metropolitan French, French, and English. You can find a list of the primary language abbreviations in Appendix E, and the registered dialect abbreviations in Appendix F. You can also find more details on HTTP language tags in [RFC1766].

There is one final component of I18N that needs to be mentioned: rendering, the way that a character set appears on a device's display. Rendering is independent of character codes, transfer encodings, and languages (that's why the definition of a character set is a mapping between character names and unique integers, not character renderings). It involves fonts, style settings such as italic and bold, and the display capabilities of the device.

With typical Web-based applications, end users need to make sure they have the appropriate system setup to properly render specific character sets. There's no point in setting up your Web browser to request and accept Japanese documents if you don't have any Japanese fonts in your system, for instance.

With WAP-based applications, it's not usually a critical issue, just one you should be aware of. In WAP devices, the character set and rendering technologies are closely coupled. If a WAP user agent lets you set a device's default character set to Japanese (or if it sets it for you automatically), you can be relatively certain that it can display Japanese characters.

Multilingual Content Servers

If you want to implement a multi-lingual site, it's actually quite easy in WAP, using your knowledge of HTTP headers. There are two headers that are significant: **Accept-Language** and **Content-Language**. **Accept-Language** is a request header that is set by the WAP user agent in one of two ways: either it does it automatically because it can understand only one language, or it sets it in response to users indicating their language preferences. A typical **Accept-Language** header might look like the following:

```
Accept-Language: it, it-va, fr, en
```

indicating that the user (or perhaps the user agent) prefers Italian, then Vatican Italian, then French, then English. It's up to your content server to get this language tag, decode it, and return the most appropriate content.

If you're serving up static content, the method you use to retrieve the **Accept-Language** header value depends on your server. For instance, with the popular Apache Web server, it's possible to set up your directory structure so that users are automatically pointed to documents written in the correct language, based on the **Accept-Language** header value. The details of how to do that are beyond the scope of this book. Check your Web server documentation.

More typically, when serving up dynamic content, you can get the value of the **Accept-Language** header. For CGI programs, the **HTTP_ACCEPT_**

LANGUAGE environment variable is automatically set to the **Accept-Language** header value. For Java servlets, you can request the header setting using a statement similar to the following:

```
String language = req.getHeader ( "Accept-Language" );
```

Once you know what the user (or user agent) prefers, you need to generate that content and signal to the user agent receiving your response in the language used for the response. There are two ways to do that.

The first way, which is appropriate for both static decks and CGI programs where you can't set any header values, is to use the WML **<meta>** element. You might remember from Chapter 2 that the **<meta>** element, which can only be used in a deck's **<head>** element, lets you specify **http-equiv** tags. An **http-equiv** tag tells the WAP gateway that it should create an HTTP header for you and insert it into the response.

For instance, if you structure a static or dynamic WML deck in this fashion

```
<wml>
  <head>
    <meta http-equiv="Content-Language" content="EN"/>
  </head>
  .
  . rest of the deck
  .
</wml>
```

the gateway strips the **<meta>** element out of the deck before compiling it. After all, why send extraneous, redundant information across a bandwidth-constrained wireless connection? In its place, it tacks the following header onto the front of the deck:

```
Content-Language: EN
```

This tells the user agent the language of the response document so that it can properly deal with it.

If your dynamic content creation software gives you access to the response headers, like Java servlets do, you can skip the **<meta>** element and create the correct **Content-Language** header instead. This is the method preferred over using the **<meta>** element—it's faster, it uses less bandwidth, and not all gateways recognize the **<meta>** element.

Here's a simple international Hello World Java servlet that grabs the **Accept-Language** header from the request, figures out what language it should use, and returns the appropriate international response [IntlHello.java].

```
import java.io.*;
import javax.servlet.*;
```

```java
import javax.servlet.http.*;
import java.util.*;

public class IntlHello extends HttpServlet {

  static StringEOL = "\r\n";

  public void doGet (

    HttpServletRequest req,
    HttpServletResponse res)
    throws
    ServletException,
    IOException
  {

 // Figure out what language we have, default is English.

    String language = req.getHeader ( "Accept-Language" );
    String message  = "Hello World";
    String charset  = "ISO-8859-1";

    if ( language != null ) {

// If there is a language header with a value we can handle,
// change the message to reflect the proper dialect.

      language = language.toUpperCase ();

      if ( language.indexOf ( "FR" ) != -1 ) {
        message = "Bonjour monde!";
      }
      if ( language.indexOf ( "ES" ) != -1 ) {
        message = "Hola mundo!";
      }
       if ( language.indexOf ( "DE" ) != -1 ) {
        message = "Hallo welt!";
      }
    } else language = "EN";

// Set the language response header and content type,
// including the charset attribute.

    res.setHeader     ( "Content-location",
      "http://www.worldfaq.com/servlet/intlhello" );
    res.setHeader     ( "Content-language", language );
    res.setContentType ( "text/vnd.wap.wml; charset=" + charset );

// Output the Hello World deck.

    ServletOutputStream out = res.getOutputStream();
    out.println (
```

```
        "<?xml version=\"1.0\"?>" +
        "<!DOCTYPE wml PUBLIC \"-//WAPFORUM//DTD WML 1.1//EN\"" + EOL +
        "\"http://www.wapforum.org/DTD/wml_1_1.xml\">" + EOL +
        "<wml>" + EOL +
        "<head>" + EOL +
        "<meta http-equiv=\"Content-Language\" content=\"" +
        language + "\"" + "/>" + EOL +
        "</head>" + EOL +
        "<card id=\"multilingual\" >" + EOL +
        "<p>" + EOL +
        message + EOL +
        "</p>" + EOL +
        "</card>" + EOL +
        "</wml>"
    );

} }
```

Note that we don't take any chances. We use both a **<meta>** element and set a
Content-Language response header to make sure the user agent knows what
we're delivering.

When you execute this servlet using Telnet and an **Accept-Language** header
set to "fr"

```
GET /servlet/intlhello HTTP/1.1
accept-language: fr
```

you get the following response (we've inserted the indentation for readability):

```
HTTP/1.1 200 OK
Server: Zeus/3.1
Date: Thu, 03 Jun 1999 23:48:09 GMT
Connection: close
Content-Location: http://www.worldfaq.com/servlet/intlhello
Content-Type: text/vnd.wap.wml; charset=ISO-8859-1
Content-Language: FR

<?xml version="1.0"?><!DOCTYPE wml PUBLIC "-//WAPFORUM//DTD WML 1.1//EN"
"http://www.wapforum.org/DTD/wml_1_1.xml">
<wml>
  <head>
    <meta http-equiv="Content-Language" content="FR"/>
  </head>
  <card id="multilingual" >
    <p>
      Bonjour monde!
    </p>
  </card>
</wml>
```

NOTE

Our **Content-Type** header includes a second parameter, **charset,** that we have not yet discussed. We describe it in more detail in the next section of this chapter.

You can also specify a language preference for individual elements of a WML deck. This gives you much more flexibility if you are delivering multilingual content.

In Chapter 2, we briefly mentioned the **xml:lang** attribute, an attribute that can be used with those WML elements that can contain content. The **xml:lang** attribute tells the user agent to use its best efforts to properly render the content tagged with an **xml:lang** attribute.

Since WML has nested elements, you can also have nested **xml:lang** attributes. The WML 1.1-specification recommends that user agents use the following precedence (from highest to lowest) when identifying an element's language:

■ The element's **xml:lang** attribute

■ The closest parent's **xml:lang** tag

■ Any language information included in the response headers (a **Content-Language** header) and meta data

■ The user agent default preferences

The preceding response deck could be rewritten as follows:

```
<wml>
  <card id="multilingual" xml:lang="FR" >
    <p>
      Bonjour monde!
    </p>
  </card>
</wml>
```

Since the card **xml:lang** attribute takes precedence over any response attributes, we can remove the **<meta>** tag and **Content-Language** header.

Charset with Responses

Once you get a handle on language negotiation between the user agent and your content server, you may need to worry about the character sets involved. Like language negotiations between a user agent and a server, this works in two directions. First, when delivering documents, you need to make sure that you are sending a usable character set from your content server to the user agent.

Just as important, however, if the user agent sends you content, you need to make sure you understand it. You control the first of these mechanisms using the **charset** attribute of the **Content-Type** header. You control the second by understanding the **accept-charset** attributes sent to you by user agents.

When you deliver content to a user agent, you need to make sure that the user agent can understand and properly deal with the character set you plan on sending. Typically, all WAP user agents understand Unicode and expect to receive it in UTF-8 encoding. However, they should explicitly declare this capability by including an **Accept-Charset** request header that looks something like the following:

```
Accept-charset: UTF-8, utf-8, *
```

This tells the content server that the user agent can accept UTF-8 encoded responses. The single asterisk also explicitly says that the user agent will accept any encoding as a last resort. It may choke on it and display an error message, but it will try to deal with it in an orderly fashion before doing that.

Once you know that the user agent can handle UTF-8 encoding, you should be able to send back any mainstream encoding. The secret that makes this work is that the WAP gateway transcodes your content into UTF-8 before delivering it to the user agent. You just need to make sure that your gateway can handle all the transcodings you might need.

If the user agent doesn't handle UTF-8 encoding, it should send a more restricted character set header to you indicating what it likes. For instance, if the request includes the following header:

```
Accept-charset: ISO-8859-7
```

it probably means that the user agent is designed for the Greek market. You'd better respond with an ISO-8859-7 encoding in order for your content to appear properly on the device screen.

Once you know that the user agent prefers ISO-8859-7 encoding, you can generate the Greek content yourself using ISO-8859-7 character codes in your source documents and CGI programs. You can also make the WAP gateway do the work for you. First, generate Unicode (UTF-16) content using a Java servlet, for instance. Then, add a **Content-Type** header, like the following, to the response deck

```
Content-type: text/vnd.wap.wml; charset=ISO-8859-7
```

flagging the content as ISO-8859-7 content. (We haven't shown this form of the **Content-Type** header—one that includes an optional **charset** attribute—before.)

The gateway should transcode the Unicode into ISO-8859-7 character codes before sending it back to the user agent. Check the gateway's specifications to make sure it supports the transcodings you need.

As we've already discussed, how you get that **Content-Type** header into your response depends on your content server. With static decks, you might be able to configure the server to automatically insert the correct **Content-Type** header based on the document's name or directory location. For both static and dynamic decks, you can always use a **<meta>** tag in the deck header. For instance, the **<meta>** element

```
<deck>
  <head>
    <meta http-equiv="Content-type"
      content="text/vnd.wap.wml; charset=ISO-8859-7"
    </>
  </head>
```

tells the WAP gateway the same information as the preceding **Content-Type** header. The gateway should recognize the **<meta>** element and do any required transcoding.

Finally, for some CGI mechanisms such as Java servlets, you can create and modify the response headers in your servlets. As we've stated before, this is the method preferred over using the **<meta>** element.

NOTE

When talking about content delivery and encodings, it's important to realize that the encodings don't apply to the whole response message, but just to the message body. The message headers are all delivered in US-ASCII as mandated by the HTTP 1.1 specification. This rightfully suggests, that if you respond to a request with a multi-part MIME message, you can specify different encodings for each part of the message in the **Content-Type** headers.

To demonstrate some of the concepts in this chapter, we put together a sample application, called **ShowCharSet**, that includes a static WML deck and a Java servlet. The deck lets the user request a display of some sample characters in any of the ISO-Latin character sets. The response is a small table of some characters in the upper 128 character codes of each character set to show off some of their differences.

Figure 7.1 shows the primary screen for the WML desk ShowCharSet.wml. Figure 7.2 shows what appears if you select the ISO-8859-5 character set. Figure 7.3 shows what happens if you select the ISO-8859-7 character set.

Here's the WML deck for **ShowCharSet** [ShowCharSet.wml].

```
<wml>
  <card id="charsetselect" >
    <p>
      Select a char set:
```

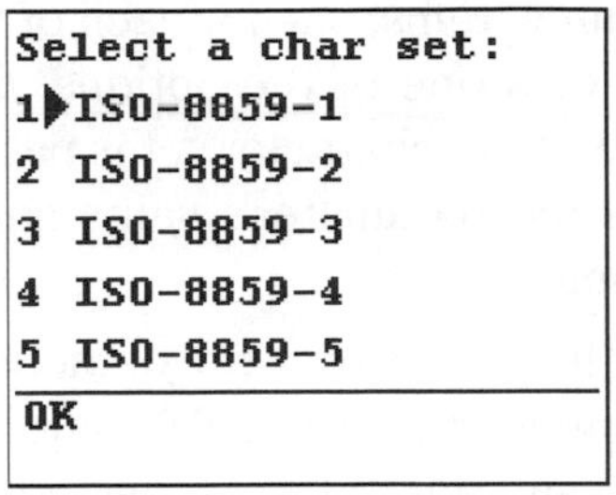

```
Select a char set:
1▶ISO-8859-1
2  ISO-8859-2
3  ISO-8859-3
4  ISO-8859-4
5  ISO-8859-5
OK
```

Figure 7.1 The ShowCharSet main screen.

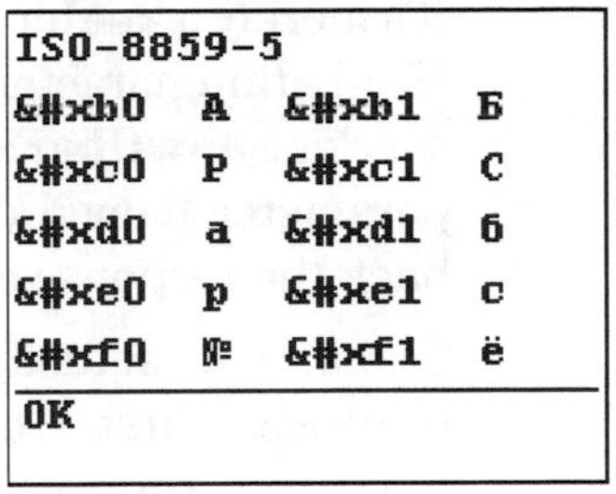

```
ISO-8859-5
&#xb0   A    &#xb1   Б
&#xc0   P    &#xc1   C
&#xd0   a    &#xd1   б
&#xe0   p    &#xe1   c
&#xf0   №    &#xf1   ё
OK
```

Figure 7.2 A sample of the ISO-8859-5 character set.

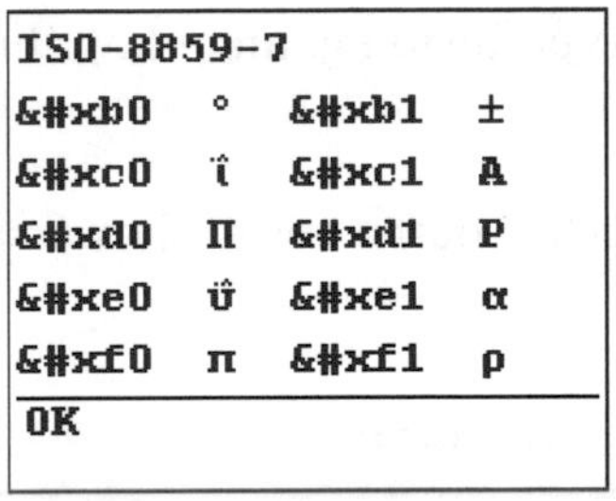

```
ISO-8859-7
&#xb0   °    &#xb1   ±
&#xc0   ΐ    &#xc1   A
&#xd0   Π    &#xd1   P
&#xe0   ΰ    &#xe1   α
&#xf0   π    &#xf1   ρ
OK
```

Figure 7.3 A sample of the ISO-8859-7 character set.

```
<select>
  <option onpick="../servlet/showcharset?charset=ISO-8859-1">
    ISO-8859-1 </option>
  <option onpick="../servlet/showcharset?charset=ISO-8859-2">
    ISO-8859-2 </option>
  <option onpick="../servlet/showcharset?charset=ISO-8859-3">
    ISO-8859-3 </option>
  <option onpick="../servlet/showcharset?charset=ISO-8859-4">
    ISO-8859-4 </option>
  <option onpick="../servlet/showcharset?charset=ISO-8859-5">
    ISO-8859-5 </option>
  <option onpick="../servlet/showcharset?charset=ISO-8859-6">
    ISO-8859-6 </option>
  <option onpick="../servlet/showcharset?charset=ISO-8859-7">
    ISO-8859-7 </option>
  <option onpick="../servlet/showcharset?charset=ISO-8859-8">
    ISO-8859-8 </option>
  <option onpick="../servlet/showcharset?charset=ISO-8859-9">
    ISO-8859-9 </option>
</select>
    </p>
  </card>
</wml>
```

It's merely a **<select>** element that includes nine items, one for each of the nine ISO Latin character sets. When the user selects one of the options, the Java servlet **ShowCharSet** is called and the name of the character set is passed in a parameter named **charset.** The servlet gets the parameter's value and sends back the response containing the sample display.

The servlet actually does a bit more than that, primarily for demonstration purposes. First, it checks to see if the user agent supports UTF-8 encoding. If not, it returns an error message instead of a sample of the requested character set. It also checks to make sure there is a **charset** parameter, which should always be true if the WML portion of the application is correctly coded. If there is no **charset** parameter, it returns error message. If the servlet makes it past those two error checks, it sends back a deck with the proper **Content-Type** heading, including the **charset** attribute that was sent to it.

Here's the Java Servlet source code [ShowCharSet.java].

```java
import java.io.*;
import javax.servlet.*;
import javax.servlet.http.*;
import java.util.*;

public class ShowCharSet extends HttpServlet {

  static StringEOL = "\r\n";

  public void doGet (

    HttpServletRequest req,
    HttpServletResponse res)
    throws
    ServletException,
    IOException
  {

// Make sure the user agent understands UTF-8. That means it can
// handle all character sets. Look for the Accept-Charset header
// with a UTF-8 setting.

    String charSets = req.getHeader ( "Accept-Charset" );
    boolean foundUTF8 = false;

    if ( charSets != null ) {
      StringTokenizer parser = new StringTokenizer ( charSets, "," );
      String token;
      while ( parser.hasMoreTokens () && ( !foundUTF8 )) {
        token = parser.nextToken ();
        token = token.toUpperCase ();
```

```
        if ( token.indexOf ( "UTF-8" ) != -1 ) foundUTF8 = true;
    } }

// Get the user-requested character set from the GET charset
// variable and output the response headers.

    String respCharSet = req.getParameter ( "charset" );
    if ( respCharSet == null )
      res.setContentType ( "text/vnd.wap.wml" );
    else
      res.setContentType ( "text/vnd.wap.wml; charset=" + respCharSet );

    res.setHeader ( "Cache-Control", "no-cache" );
    res.setHeader ( "Content-location",
      "http://www.worldfaq.com/servlet/showcharset" );

 // Output the beginning of the response message deck.

    ServletOutputStream out = res.getOutputStream();
    out.println (

      "<?xml version=\"1.0\"?>" +
      "<!DOCTYPE wml PUBLIC \"-//WAPFORUM//DTD WML 1.1//EN\"" + EOL +
      "\"http://www.wapforum.org/DTD/wml_1_1.xml\">" + EOL +
      "<wml>" + EOL +
      "<head>" + EOL +
      "<card id=\"showcharset\" >" + EOL +
      "<p>"
    );

// If there's no Accept-Charset=UTF-8 request header, error.

    if ( ! foundUTF8 ) {
      out.println (
        "This device does not accept UTF-8 encoding. "
      );
    }

// If there's not user-requested character set parameter
// (which shouldn't happen), error.

    else if ( respCharSet == null ) {
      out.println (
        "Sorry, no response character set was specified."
      );
    }

// No errors, return a sample of the requested character set.
// These codes will be transcoded by the gateway into UTF-8.

    else {
```

```
        out.println (

            respCharSet + "<br/>" + EOL +
            "<table columns=\"4\">" + EOL +

            "<tr>" + EOL +
              "<td>&amp;#xb0 </td>" + EOL +
              "<td>&#xb0; </td>" + EOL +
              "<td>&amp;#xb1 </td>" + EOL +
              "<td>&#xb1; </td>" + EOL +
            "</tr>" + EOL +

            "<tr>" + EOL +
              "<td>&amp;#xc0 </td>" + EOL +
              "<td>&#xc0; </td>" + EOL +
              "<td>&amp;#xc1 </td>" + EOL +
              "<td>&#xc1; </td>" + EOL +
            "</tr>" + EOL +

            "<tr>" + EOL +
              "<td>&amp;#xd0 </td>" + EOL +
              "<td>&#xd0; </td>" + EOL +
              "<td>&amp;#xd1 </td>" + EOL +
              "<td>&#xd1; </td>" + EOL +
            "</tr>" + EOL +

            "<tr>" + EOL +
              "<td>&amp;#xe0 </td>" + EOL +
              "<td>&#xe0; </td>" + EOL +
              "<td>&amp;#xe1 </td>" + EOL +
              "<td>&#xe1; </td>" + EOL +
            "</tr>" + EOL +

            "<tr>" + EOL +
              "<td>&amp;#xf0 </td>" + EOL +
              "<td>&#xf0; </td>" + EOL +
              "<td>&amp;#xf1 </td>" + EOL +
              "<td>&#xf1; </td>" + EOL +
            "</tr>" + EOL +
            "</table>"
        );
    }

// Finish up the response deck.

    out.println (
      "</p>" + EOL +
      "</card>" + EOL +
      "</wml>"
    );
} }
```

Charset with Requests

Normally, **charset** settings are used by a user agent to indicate the character set it prefers to receive in a response from a content server. An interesting side effect of the **Accept-Charset** request header is that any **POST** data that is included as part of the request is transcoded into the **Accept-Charset** character set before being sent to the content server.

NOTE
GET data, which is coded inline in the HTTP request, does not get transcoded based on the Accept-Charset header before being sent.

There may be times, however, when you don't want the **POST** data to be converted to the user agent's preferred character set. Instead, you want to specify a different character set.

Fortunately, the WML **<go>** element has an optional **accept-charset** attribute that lets you specify the character set to which you want the **POST** data transcoded. That attribute is sent on to the WAP gateway, which actually does the transcoding, passing the resulting data on to the content server as **POST** data. It's up to the content server to figure out what to do at that point.

NOTE
The accept-charset attribute setting of the WML <go> element takes precedence over any value the user agent might assign to the Accept-Charset request header.

It's important that the content server know that it's receiving data in an (perhaps) unexpected character set. To alert it, the WAP gateway adds the new character set setting to the outgoing **Content-Type** request header. The header should look something like this:

```
Content-type: application/x-www-forum-urlencoded; charset=ISO-8859-5
```

The gateway may also possibly change the **Accept-Charset** request header to reflect the outgoing data's character set.

Here's a simple WML/Java servlet application called **TransMsg** that lets you select one of three character sets, enter a message, and then send that message in a **POST** variable with the **accept-charset** attribute set to your character set choice. There's nothing particularly interesting about this function. What it does do, however, is give you an opportunity to look at the request headers and parameters to see what happens as a result of the **accept-charset** attribute. Here's the WML portion of the application [TransMsg.wml].

```
<wml>

<!-- select a character set -->

  <card id="charset" >
    <do type="accept" >
      <go href="#message" />
    </do>
    <p>

      Select a char set:
      <select name="charset" value="ISO-8859-1" >
        <option value="ISO-8859-1">ISO-8859-1 </option>
        <option value="ISO-8859-7">ISO-8859-5 </option>
        <option value="ISO-8859-7">ISO-8859-7 </option>
      </select>

    </p>
  </card>

<!-- get the message and send it off -->

  <card id="message" >
    <do type="accept" >
      <go href="http://www.worldfaq.com/servlet/transMsg"
         method="post" accept-charset="$(charset)" >
        <postfield name="message" value="$(message)" />
        <postfield name="charset" value="$(charset)" />
      </go>
    </do>
    <p>

    Enter a message:
    <input name="message" />

    </p>
  </card>

</wml>
```

Note that, in addition to sending the message, we also send the character set option in the variable **charset**. We check this variable and send the message back to the user agent, using the requested character set. This lets us see the resulting transcoded message. We use the **charset** variable just to make our life easier. It saves us from writing a bunch of code to decode the **Content-Type** and **Accept-Charset** headers for the character set.

As an example, assume that the user agent's native character set is ISO-8859-1, but it can display ISO-8859-5 and ISO-8859-7. When **TransMsg** is run, the entered message is stored internally in ISO-8859-1, the native character set. If the user selects ISO-8859-5 for the outgoing character set, however, the message gets transcoded on the way to the **TransMsg** Java servlet. The servlet receives the message in ISO-8859-5, and sends it back in the same character set, where it appears on the display as ISO-8859-5 characters.

Here's the Java portion of the application [TransMsg.java]. We not only figure out what character set to use for the response message body, but we also send back the settings for the **Accept-Charset** and **Content-Type** headers, and the **message** and **charset** variables, just so we can see what's going on.

```java
import java.io.*;
import javax.servlet.*;
import javax.servlet.http.*;
import java.util.*;

public class TransMsg extends HttpServlet {

  static StringEOL = "\r\n";

// Receive a text message that's coming in as a POST
// variable named "message", and send it back to the user
// agent in the character set identified by the
// variable "charset".

  public void doPost (

    HttpServletRequest req,
    HttpServletResponse res)

    throws
    ServletException,
    IOException {

// Get various headers and variables.

    String contType = req.getContentType ();
    String charSets = req.getHeader     ( "Accept-Charset" );
    String charset  = req.getParameter ( "charset" );
    String message  = req.getParameter ( "message" );

// Set the Content-type response header to reflect the
// desired outgoing message's character set.

    if ( charset == null )
      res.setContentType ( "application/vnd.wap.wml" );
    else
      res.setContentType ( "application/vnd.wap.wml; charset=" + charset );

// Output the other appropriate response headers.
```

```
        res.setHeader ( "Cache-Control", "no-cache" );
        res.setHeader ( "Content-location",
          "http://www.worldfaq.com/servlet/transMsg" );

// Write the output deck, which shows all the
// interesting incoming headers and variables.

        ServletOutputStream out = res.getOutputStream();
        out.println (

          "<?xml version=\"1.0\"?>" +
          "<!DOCTYPE wml PUBLIC \"-//WAPFORUM//DTD WML 1.1//EN\"" + EOL +
          "\"http://www.wapforum.org/DTD/wml_1_1.xml\">" + EOL +

          "<wml>" + EOL +
          "<card id=\"getContType\" >" + EOL +
          "<p>" + EOL +
          "AcceptCharsets: " + charSets + "<br/>" + EOL +
          "Content-type: " + contType + "<br/>" + EOL +
          "Charset: " + charset + "<br/>" + EOL +
          "Message: " + message + EOL +
          "</p>" + EOL +
          "</card>" + EOL +
          "</wml>"
        );

} }
```

There is one final way you can indicate character encoding in a response message, using the XML **encoding** attribute in a deck's prologue. For example:

```
<?xml version="1.0" encoding="ISO-8859-1" ?>
```

Because this isn't a book about WML, that's all we say about this technique. For more details, take a look at the XML specification [XML].

Conclusion

Much like caching, you can more easily understand WAP I18N issues if you also have some understanding of HTTP headers. To properly manage language issues, you need to understand the **Accept-Language** and **Content-Language** headers. To properly manage character sets, you need to understand the **Accept-Charset** header and **Content-Type: charset** attribute. Armed with this knowledge, you should easily be able to set up a multilingual, internationally-useful WAP application.

CHAPTER 8

Beyond WAP 1.1

A lthough WAP 1.1. is a formally approved standard, the WAP specifications process is not static. In addition, the current specifications have a certain amount of flexibility regarding what user agents and WAP gateways must include and ways in which they can enhance their offerings to differentiate them in the marketplace.

These two forces are shaping the next generation of WAP technologies. WAP vendors are enhancing their WAP 1.1-compatible products. As these enhancements mature they are being considered for inclusion in future WAP specifications.

This chapter focuses on two specific technologies—notifications and nested contexts—that make it possible for application developers to create whole new classes of applications. We describe the Phone.com notification APIs and tools. Nested contexts are in the early stages of development. We describe the underlying concepts and suggested enhancements to WML to accommodate nested contexts.

NOTE
Both of these technologies are Phone.com extensions to WAP. They are presented here as examples of vendor-specific WAP extensions that may, at some point, be incorporated into WAP. It's unclear whether notifications or nested contexts will formally be part of WAP. If they are, they may or may not be as described in this chapter.

Notifications

As we've repeatedly described in earlier chapters, the standard application model is a two-way communications model, where a user agent and content server engage in a series of request/response transactions. The user agent sends a request; the content server responds with a document.

Most wireless networks also provide for another type of communication that is best exemplified by paging. In this model, a content server originates a document for delivery to one or more user agents. The user agent probably knows nothing about the transaction until it arrives, asynchronously. This communication model has several different well-known names—*content push, asynchronous message delivery*, and *mobile and active channels* are a few. The term we use to describe the delivery of an asynchronous message to a user agent is *notification*.

Notifications are useful for many different things. Their primary purpose is to accommodate the delivery of highly-volatile information such as stock prices and hazardous weather warnings, and timely information such as sports scores. You can also use them to upload information, in the background, to a user agent. This is useful if you need to, for example, replace an obsolete deck in a user agent's cache. You can also use notifications to deliver unsolicited, untimely documents, such as advertisements, to a user agent.

The WAP WSP (Wireless Session Protocol) supports notification delivery. Unlike simple document delivery using the two-way WAP programming model, however, notifications also require the active participation of the gateway. The gateway is responsible for queuing notifications, attempting to deliver them, and removing them from the queue when delivered or timed out. You're responsible for deciding what to send, whom to send it to, and when to initiate delivery.

In order to do all these things in an orderly, organized fashion on a regular basis, you probably need to create a notification application that interacts with the Phone.com gateway. If you just need to occasionally send a notification to one or two users, however, Phone.com provides stand-alone utilities for Windows and Unix systems as part of their WAP SDK.

The WAP Forum is working on a full-blown push architecture similar to the one described here. It will consist primarily of protocol enhancements, and content-type definitions, with no specific APIs. It will be left up to each WAP gateway vendor to create tools that utilize that architecture. For that reason, we don't delve into the HTTP-level plumbing underlying the Phone.com architecture—it will probably change, but the APIs, at least for Phone.com push capabilities, will probably remain the same.

What to Send

There are three types of entities you can push to a Phone.com-compatible user agent: alerts, cache operations, and normal content, including multi-part messages that may include alerts and cache operations.

An alert is simply a message and an associated URL. When delivered to the user agent, the alert message is put into the user's inbox and the user is notified by a sound, a pop-up message, or an alert icon, unless the user has disabled all alert mechanisms. When the message is retrieved from the inbox, the URL is executed, delivering some content to the user agent.

A cache operation is a message that contains instructions for the user agent's cache. You can either invalidate a single URL or all URLs for your service. This is a great way to guarantee, for instance, that a user always fetches the most recent version of your application. Let's say you have an application that has a frequently-used static deck. When the user executes that deck, chances are good that the user agent retrieves it from its cache. If you rewrite the deck, you can force a device's user agent to refetch it by sending a cache operation invalidating that URL in the cache.

The third type of entity you can send using a notification is standard WAP content—WML decks, WMLScript functions, WBMP graphics, and so on, either as individual documents or using a multipart message. You can also add alerts and cache operations to a multipart message whether you deliver it using a notification or as part of a standard WAP request/response transaction. We do not include any discussion of alerts or cache operations in our chapter on multipart messages because they are not currently part of the WAP specification.

Sending a Notification

Because of the varying nature of wireless networks, there are actually two different types of notification delivery mechanisms described in the Phone.com SDK: push and pull.

Push is what you might expect: You send a notification to a WAP user agent, identified by a unique subscriber ID, via the Phone.com gateway. The gateway immediately tries to deliver the message, and periodically keeps trying until it's successful or the message delivery period expires. Once delivered or expired, the notification is removed from the notification queue.

If the notification is an alert, users are notified, unless they've disabled all notification mechanisms. When they are ready, they acknowledge the alert, triggering the fetching of the alert's URL, and, in essence, initiating a normal WAP transaction from that point on.

If it is a cache operation, the operation just happens, silently, with no warning to the user, unless the cache operation is part of a multipart message that includes an alert.

Pull is a somewhat confusing term, identifying a mechanism for dealing with circuit-switched wireless networks, like GSM, that can only deliver short asynchronous messages. In order to deliver larger documents or messages, users have to explicitly give the gateway permission to deliver the messages. In effect, users pull the notification to them by giving permission.

A pull notification has the same three components as a push notification: a subscriber ID, a URL, and an expiration time. The notification is sent to the Phone.com gateway, where it is queued for delivery. What happens next depends on whether the notification is being sent out on a circuit-switched network or another network. For a circuit-switched network, where users have to give explicit delivery permission, the gateway keeps the message queued until it expires or the users turn on their device and activate a network connection. At that point, the gateway fetches the contents of the URL and sends it on to the device's user agent as a multipart message. Waiting until the user opens the connection ensures that the document returned by the notification URL is the freshest.

For any other network, the gateway immediately fetches the notification URL and attempts to immediately send it on to the user agent as a multipart message. If it can't be sent immediately, it queues it and attempts to regularly resend it until it's successful or the notification expires.

There are two key distinctions between push and pull notifications:

- Push is appropriate for small messages, primarily alerts, and cache operations, which are always relatively small. Pull can be used for any size message.

- Push attempts to deliver notifications immediately. By contrast, there is no guarantee that pull notifications will be delivered immediately, although the gateway attempts to deliver all but circuit-switched pull notifications right away. You should use pull for information that is not time-sensitive.

There is one other interesting twist to notifications: security. To prevent rogue content servers from sending unsolicited intrusive notifications like advertisements, the Phone.com WAP gateway maintains an access control list that lists domains that can send notifications to its subscribers. In addition, the notification programming libraries, which are described next, have both non-secure and secure instantiations. The secure rendition uses a secure HTTP port number and requires a server certificate from an approved Internet Certificate Authority.

When sending notifications you can specify that they be sent secure, secure preferred (the gateway tries to create a secure connection on its first try), or non-secure. Secure-preferred mode is the only delivery method that guarantees delivery.

The C++ Notification APIs

To help you build notification applications, Phone.com supplies C++ (for Unix systems) and Component Object Model (COM) (for Windows systems) libraries that can be used with Visual Basic and Visual C++. The C++ functions fall into four categories, shown in Table 8.1: notification sending, notification management, user agent management, and gateway management.

Table 8.1   The Phone.com C++ Notification API

NOTIFICATION SENDING	
PostPrefetch	Post a pull notification.
PostAlert	Push an alert notification.
PostCacheOp	Push a cache notification.
PostAlertAndInvalURL	Push an alert/cache operation notification.
Push	Push a cache/alert notification.
NOTIFICATION MANAGEMENT	
ClearPendingNtfns	Delete all pending notifications for a subscriber/service combination.
DeleteNtfn	Delete a pending notification.
GetNtfnStatus	Get the status of a notification.
USER AGENT MANAGEMENT	
RemoveAlertFromInbox	Remove an alert from a subscriber's inbox.
GATEWAY MANAGEMENT	
GetCharset	Get the character set used for alert titles.
GetProtocol	Get the connection type (secure, non-secure) for a notification.
GetTimeout	Get the timeout period for HTTP requests to the gateway.
GetErrorDetail	Get the error string describing the error from the most recent gateway communication.
SetCharset	Set the character set used for alert titles.
SetTimeout	Set the timeout period for HTTP requests issued to the gateway.

The APIs are straightforward, although one detail needs explanation. There are actually two groups of functions for sending notifications. The first set includes **PostPreFetch**, **PostAlert**, **PostCacheOp**, and **PostAlertAndInvalURL**, with one function for each type of notification that can be sent. **PostAlert**, **PostCacheOp**, and **PostAlertAndInvalURL** all send push notifications. **PostPrefetch**, named for historical reasons, sends a pull notification.

There is also a **Push** function that you can use for sending cache and alert notifications. For a variety of reasons, Phone.com discourages use of this function and suggests you stick to the specialized sending functions.

The C++ Notification library contains three C++ classes:

- **TNtfnClientAPI**, the abstract base notification class;
- **TntfnClient**, the concrete non-secure notification class;
- **TntfnSClient**, the concrete secure notification class.

To send a non-secure notification, first you need to create a new notification object using code something like this:

```
TNtfnClient *client = new TNtfnClient( gatewayName );
```

gatewayName is the name of the Phone.com gateway that you want to send the notification to for dispatching.

Next, use **PostAlert**, **PostCacheOp**, or **PostPrefetch** to send the notification. Then, use the **GetNtfnStatus**, **GetPrefetchStatus**, and **GetAlertStatus** as needed to check the status of the notification. You can also use the notification and user agent management functions to delete or clear the notification.

Here are the definitions for the **PostXXXX** functions:

```
int PostPrefetch (
   const char *sub, const char *url, unsigned int ttlSecond );

int PostAlert (
   const char *sub, const char *url, unsigned int ttlSeconds,
   const char *alertType, const char *alertTitle, int len );

int PostCacheOp(
   const char *sub, const char *url,
   unsigned int ttlSeconds, const char *cacheOpCode);

int PostAlertAndInvalURL(const char *sub,
   const char *url, unsigned int ttlSeconds, const char *alertType,
   const char *alertTitle, int len);
```

Here are definitions of the parameters used for these functions and most of the other notification APIs.

sub. Subscriber ID.

url. URL of the notification content.

ttlSecond. Time to live (notification lifetime).

alertType. A null-terminated string specifying the type of signal to issue to the subscriber. See the Phone.com SDK for details.

alertTitle. The title to be displayed for the alert.

len. The title's length. This is required only for character encodings that don't terminate strings with a null character.

cacheOpCode InvalSvc. Invalidate all cache entries for the current service.

InvalURL. Invalidate only the cache entries with the specified URL.

That's all you really need to know to create, send, and manage non-secure notifications. The **PostXXXX** functions return an integer status code telling you if your notification was successfully sent; you can also query the gateway separately using **GetNtfnStatus**. The secure notification APIs are almost identical. Consult the Phone.com SDK for more details.

Nested Contexts

One of WML 1.1's limitations is its simplistic scope model. All variables are available to all decks at all times. This not only presents a security risk (decks from separate vendors can access each other's variables), but it also prevents you from preserving your state in the event that you invoke a deck from another vendor. Also, certain types of applications are easier to develop and maintain with a more sophisticated nested scope model.

To deal with some of these shortcomings, Phone.com added nested contexts to WML. A context, as defined by WML 1.1, is a user agent's variables and its history stack. With nested contexts, you can create a new context that has its own variables and history stack, and you can initialize variables in the new context as it starts executing. The new context is a child of the creating context. When the child finishes executing, its context disappears and the context of the parent is restored. You can also return values to the parent context, which it can assign to variables within its own context.

Nested contexts are similar to subroutines. They have their own, short-term scope that has no effect on the parent context. They also let you modularize your application. (You can modularize it using decks with WML 1.1, but you have no context control other than the **<newcontext>** element.) As all programmers know, modularization is a Good Thing.

In order to incorporate nested contexts into WML, Phone.com added some new WML elements, shown in Table 8.2. Note that there are elements for throwing and catching exceptions. These elements, coupled with the others, make it much easier than with WML 1.1 to create clean, efficient user interfaces for complex applications.

In addition to the new elements, Phone.com also defined two new intrinsic events, **<onexit>** and **<onthrow>**. You handle an **<onexit>** event with an **<onevent>** element inside a **<spawn>** element or with the **<spawn>**'s **onexit** attribute. You handle an **<onthrow>** event with a **<catch>** element inside a **<spawn>** element.

Creating a New Context

To create a new context, you need to use the **<spawn>** element, which is similar to the **<go>** element with a few added twists. A new child context, with a fresh history stack and no variables, is created, and the **<spawn>** URL is executed. If the URL points to a WML card or deck, the card is displayed. The child URL returns to the parent context using an **<exit>** element.

Like **<go>**, **<spawn>** allows both **<setvar>** and **<postfield>** elements, letting you set variables and define HTTP get/post variables. In addition, you can specify an HTTP request method using the **method** attribute. **<spawn>** lets you specify three additional elements within it: **<catch>** for catching exceptions thrown in the child context, **<onevent>** for catching and responding to the **<onexit>** intrinsic event created by the child, and **<receive>** for assigning variables being returned by the child.

Here's the complete syntax for **<spawn>**:

```
<spawn
  href=URL
  onexit=URL
  sendreferer=boolean
```

Table 8.2 Nested Context Elements

<spawn>	Create a new child context.
<exit>	Return from a child context.
<send>	Pass a value to the child context.
<receive>	Return a value to the parent context.
<throw>	Throw an exception.
<catch>	Catch an exception.
<reset>	Clear all variables in the current context.

```
  method="post" | "get"
  accept-charset=CharsetName
>
  <setvar>
  <postfield>
  <onevent>
  <catch>
<receive>
</spawn>
```

The only attribute that you haven't seen before is **onexit**, which is the URL to fetch after the child context is done executing. In addition to the familiar **<setvar>**, **<postfield>**, and **<onevent>** elements, the **<spawn>** body can contain one or more **<receive>** and **<catch>** elements.

The **<receive>** element is straightforward. It optionally specifies the name of a variable into which a child can return a value using a **<send>** element:

```
<receive name=varname/>
```

Returned values are assigned in the order in which they are listed in the **<spawn>** element. For instance, if the child returns the values 25, "testing," and "X," this code assigns those values to the variables var1, var2, and var3, respectively:

```
<spawn href="child">
  <receive name="var1"/>
  <receive name="var2"/>
  <receive name="var3"/>
</spawn>
```

You can also leave a **<receive>** element's **name** blank to bypass the return assignment. With the same three return values, this **<spawn>** element assigns the value 25 to var1 and "X" to var2:

```
<spawn href="child">
  <receive name="var1/>
  <receive/>
  <receive name=var2/>
</spawn>>
```

Finally, if the **<spawn>** element has more **<receive>** elements than the number of values returned by the child, the extra variables in those receives are set to empty strings.

The **<catch>** element is a bit more complicated. Here's its syntax:

```
<catch
  name=ExceptionName
  onthrow=URL
>
  <receive>
```

```
   <onevent>
   <reset>
 </catch>
```

name is the name of the exception being caught. **onthrow** is the URL to fetch when the exception is caught. A **<catch>** element can also include **<receive>** and **<onevent>** elements. Child contexts can return values in both **<exit>** and **<throw>** elements. **<throw>** returned values are assigned to the variables named in the **<catch>** **<receive>** elements.

The **<reset>** element clears all variables (but not the history stack) in the current context. When used in a **<catch>** element (you can also use a **<reset>** in other task elements), the **<reset>** takes place when the exception is caught. If the **<catch>** contains **<receive>** and **<reset>** elements, the **<reset>** is executed first.

Terminating a Context

There are two ways a child context can end: Either it executes an **<exit>** element or it throws an exception. The **<exit>** is simple. It contains zero or more **<send>** elements whose values get sent back to the parent context for (possible) assignment to parent variables. For instance, this **<exit>** sends three values back to the parent. The second value is a null string.

```
<exit>
  <send value="122.56"/>
  <send/>
  <send value="$X"/>
</exit>
```

When an **<exit>** is executed, the user agent first substitutes variable values in the **<send>** elements and stores all the **<send>** values temporarily. It then destroys the current context, including its variables and history, and sets the current context to the parent context. The **<send>** values are then assigned, in order, to the variables specified by the parent's **<receive>** elements. Finally, if there is an **onexit** intrinsic task handler specified in the current card of the parent deck, it is executed.

Here's a simple example that contains three cards. When the user presses the **accept** button on the first card, it creates a child context using the second card that returns a value. That value is displayed by the third card.

```
<wml>
  <card name="card1">
    <do type="accept">
      <spawn href="#card2" onexit="#card3">
        <receive name="var"/>
      </spawn>
```

```
    </do>
  </card>

  <card name="card2">
    <send value="some value" />
  </card>

  <card name="card3">
    <p>
      Card2 returned the value $var
    </p>
  </card>
<wml>
```

You can also write the first card with an explicit **<onevent>** element. The execution is the same; the code is just a bit more verbose.

```
<card name="card1">
  <do type="accept">
    <spawn href="#card2">
      <receive name="var"/>
      <onevent type="onexit">
        <go href="card2"/>
      </onevent>
    </spawn>
  </do>
</card>
```

You can also terminate a child by throwing an exception. Exceptions in nested contexts are very similar to Java and C++ exceptions: You throw an exception, it gets passed up the execution tree, clearing out contexts as it goes, until it is caught. If it is not caught, it bubbles all the way to the top of the execution hierarchy, where something happens. In the case of the Phone.com user agent, the user agent is reset.

Each exception has a required name that is used to identify it. You can also send one or more values with the exception. This input error exception includes a second message part plus the value that causes the exception.

```
<throw name="Invalid value>
  <send value="Nonumeric data expected"/>
  <send value=$x/>
</throw>
```

You catch an exception using a **<catch>** element inside the parent's **<spawn>**. This is unlike C++ and Java exceptions, where you can catch an exception in the same module that throws it. The nested context **<catch>** must happen at least one level above the scope level where the exception is thrown. Here's the full syntax for the **<catch>** element.

```
<catch
  name=ExceptionName
  onthrow=URL
>
  <receive>
  <onevent>
  <reset>
</catch>
```

Notice that, similar to how you handle an **<exit>** in a **<spawn>** element, you can specify a URL to execute using either the **onthrow** attribute or the **<onevent>** element in the body of the **<catch>**.

Here's a simple **<catch>** that handles the "Invalid value entered" exception in the previous example.

```
<catch name="Invalid value" onthrow="#errcard">
  <receive name="msg"/>
  <receive name="value"/>
</catch>
```

You can also write this using an **<onevent>** element. We also throw in a **<reset>** for demonstration purposes.

```
<catch name="Invalid value">
  <onevent type="onthrow">
    <go href="errcard"/>
  </onevent>
  <reset/>
  <receive name="msg"/>
  <receive name="value"/>
</catch>
```

That's a brief introduction to nested contexts, which you can use to make your Phone.com WAP applications more secure and also more modular. For more details on these WAP extensions and their current status, contact Phone.com.

WML Elements

DENTRY	Data-entry elements: <input>, <select>,and <fieldset>.
DOCHOICES	Valid <do> choices: accept, prev, help, reset, options, delete, and unknown.
FMTTEXT	Elements for formatting text: <b>, >big>, <em>, <i>, <small>, <strong>, <u>.
ID	An XML-compatible name that uniquely identifies an element within a document.
IEVENTS	Card-level intrinsic events: onenterforward, onenterbackward, and ontimer.
LENGTH	An integer to indicate length in pixels, or an integer plus a percent sign to indicate length as a percentage of the screen width.
NAME	A valid XML name—letters, digits, and underscore character.
NUMBER	A valid integer greater than or equal to zero.
STRING	Single-line Unicode 2.0 text that is not parsed.
TEXT	Multiline Unicode text that is not parsed.
VDATA	A STRING with possible variable references.
URL	An absolute or relative URI, URL, or URN, possibly containing variable references.

	ATTRIBUTES		ELEMENTS		
a	*href=URL*	id=ID	TEXT		
	title=VDATA	class=STRING	br		
	xml:lang=NAME		img		
access	domain=STRING	id=ID			
	path=STRING	class=STRING			
anchor	title=VDATA	id=ID	TEXT	go	img
	xml:lang=NAME	class=STRING	br	prev	refresh
b	xml:lang=NAME	class=STRING	TEXT	img	table
	id=ID		FMTTEXT	anchor	br
			a		
big	xml:lang=NAME	class=STRING	TEXT	img	table
	id=ID		FMTTEXT	anchor	a
			br		
br	xml:lang=NAME	class=STRING			
	id=ID				
card	title=VDATA	onenterbackward=URL	onevent (onenterforward | onenterbackward | ontimer)		
	newcontext=true | false	ontimer=URL	do	p	
	ordered=true | false	id=ID	timer		
	xml:lang=NAME	class=STRING			
	onenterforward=URL				
do	type=DOCHOICES	xml:lang=NAME	go	noop	
	label=VDATA	id=ID	prev	refresh	
	name=NAME	class=STRING			
	optional=true | false				
em	xml:lang=NAME	class=STRING	TEXT	img	table
	id=ID		FMTTEXT	anchor	a
fieldset	title=VDATA	id=ID	TEXT	img	table
	xml:lang=NAME	class=STRING	FMTTEXT	anchor	do
			DENTRY	a	
go	*href=URL*	accept-charset=STRING	postfield		
	sendreferer=true | false	id=ID	setvar		
	method=post | get	class=STRING			
head	id=ID	class=STRING	access	meta	
i	xml:lang=NAME	class=STRING	TEXT	img	table
	id=ID		FMTTEXT	anchor	a
			br		
img	*alt=VDATA*	height=LENGTH			
	src=URL	width=LENGTH			
	localsrc=VDATA	xml:lang=NAME			
	vspace=LENGTH (0)	id=ID			
	hspace=LENGTH (0)	class=STRING			
	align=top | middle | bottom				

	ATTRIBUTES		ELEMENTS		
input	*name=NAME* type=text | password value=VDATA format=STRING emptyok=true | false size=NUMBER	maxlength=NUMBER tabindex=NUMBER title=VDATA xml:lang=NAME id=ID class=STRING			
meta	http-equiv=STRING name=STRING forua=true|false *content=STRING*	scheme=STRING id=ID class=STRING			
noop	id=ID	class=STRING			
onevent	type=IEVENTS id=ID	class=STRING	go prev	noop refresh	
optgroup	title=VDATA xml:lang=NAME	id=ID class=STRING	optgroup option		
option	value=VDATA title=VDATA onpick=URL	xml:lang=NAME id=ID class=STRING	TEXT onevent (onpick)		
p	align=left | right | center mode=wrap | nowrap xml:lang=NAME	id=ID class=STRING	TEXT FMTTEXT DENTRY	img anchor a	table do br
postfield	*name=VDATA* *value=VDATA*	id=ID class=STRING			
prev	id=ID	class=STRING	setvar		
refresh	id=ID	class=STRING	setvar		
select	title=VDATA name=NAME value=VDATA iname=NAME ivalue=VDATA	multiple=true | false tabindex=NUMBER xml:lang=NAME id=ID class=STRING	optgroup option		
setvar	*name=VDATA* *value=VDATA*	id=ID class=STRING			
small	xml:lang=NAME id=ID	class=STRING	TEXT FMTTEXT br	img anchor a	table
strong	xml:lang=NAME id=ID	class=STRING	TEXT FMTTEXT a	img anchor	table br
table	title=VDATA align=STRING *columns=NUMBER*	xml:lang=NAME id=ID class=STRING	t r		
td	xml:lang=NAME id=ID	class=STRING	TEXT FMTTEXT	img anchor	br a
template	id=ID onenterforward ontimer	class=STRING onenterbackward	do onevent (onenterforward | onenterbackward | ontimer)		
timer	name=NAME *value=VDATA*	id=ID class=STRING			
tr	id=ID	class=STRING	t d		
u	xml:lang=NAME id=ID	class=STRING	TEXT FMTTEXT br	img anchor	table a
wml	xml:lang=NAME id=ID	class=STRING	head template	card	

WML Elements Cross Reference

Check the lefthand column and read across horizontally.

	a	access	anchor	b	big	br	card	do	em	fieldset	go	head	i	img	input	meta	noop	onevent	optgroup	option	p	postfield	prev	refresh	select	setvar	small	strong	table	td	template	TEXT	timer	tr	u	wml
a						x								x																		x				
access																																				
anchor						x					x			x									x	x								x				
b	x		x	x	x	x			x				x	x													x	x	x			x			x	
big	x		x	x	x	x			x				x	x													x	x	x			x			x	
br																																				
card								x										x			x												x			
do											x						x						x	x												
em	x		x	x	x	x			x				x	x													x	x	x			x			x	
fieldset	x		x	x	x	x		x	x	x			x	x	x										x		x	x				x			x	
go																						x				x										
head		x														x																				
i	x		x	x	x	x			x				x	x													x	x	x			x			x	
img																																				
input																																				
meta																																				
noop																																				
onevent											x						x						x	x												
optgroup																			x	x																
option																		x														x				
p	x		x	x	x	x		x	x	x			x	x	x										x		x	x	x			x			x	
postfield																																				
prev																										x										
refresh																										x										
select																			x	x																
setvar																																				
small	x		x	x	x	x			x				x	x													x	x	x			x			x	
strong	x		x	x	x	x			x				x	x													x	x	x			x			x	
table																																		x		
td	x		x	x	x	x			x				x	x													x	x				x			x	
template								x										x																		
timer																																				
tr																														x						
u	x		x	x	x	x			x				x	x													x	x	x			x			x	
wml							x					x																			x					

TEXT   Any valid Unicode string or WAP-defined character entity:

quot	&#34;	quotation mark
amp	&#38;	ampersand
apos	&#39;	apostrophe
lt	&#60;	less than
gt	&#62;	greater than
nbsp		nonbreaking space
shy	&#173;	soft hyphen (discretionary hyphen)

WML Attributes Cross Reference

Check the top row and read down vertically.

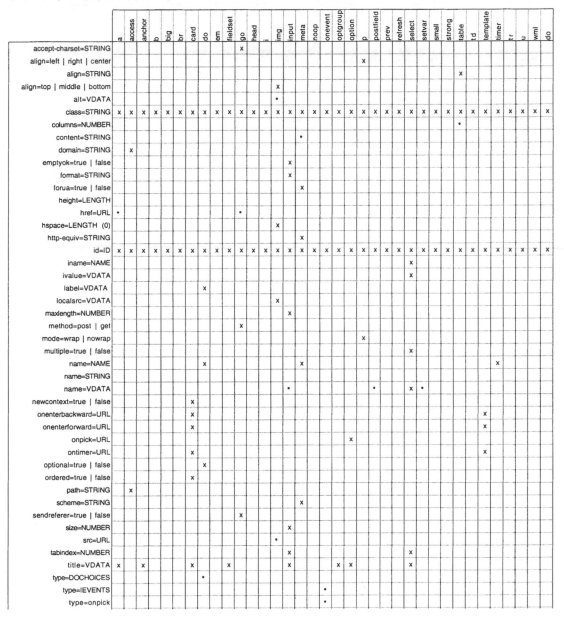

	a	access	anchor	b	big	br	card	do	em	fieldset	go	head	i	img	input	meta	noop	onevent	optgroup	option	p	postfield	prev	refresh	select	setvar	small	strong	table	td	template	timer	tr	u	wml	do
accept-charset=STRING											x																									
align=left | right | center																					x															
align=STRING																													x							
align=top | middle | bottom														x																						
alt=VDATA														•																						
class=STRING	x	x	x	x	x	x	x	x	x	x	x	x	x	x	x	x	x	x	x	x	x	x	x	x	x	x	x	x	x	x	x	x	x	x	x	x
columns=NUMBER																													•							
content=STRING																•																				
domain=STRING		x																																		
emptyok=true | false															x																					
format=STRING															x																					
forua=true | false																x																				
height=LENGTH																																				
href=URL	•										•																									
hspace=LENGTH (0)														x																						
http-equiv=STRING																x																				
id=ID	x	x	x	x	x	x	x	x	x	x	x	x	x	x	x	x	x	x	x	x	x	x	x	x	x	x	x	x	x	x	x	x	x	x	x	x
iname=NAME																									x											
ivalue=VDATA																									x											
label=VDATA								x																												
localsrc=VDATA														x																						
maxlength=NUMBER															x																					
method=post | get											x																									
mode=wrap | nowrap																					x															
multiple=true | false																									x											
name=NAME								x							x																	x				
name=STRING																																				
name=VDATA																•						•				•				•						
newcontext=true | false							x																													
onenterbackward=URL							x																								x					
onenterforward=URL							x																								x					
onpick=URL																				x																
ontimer=URL							x																								x					
optional=true | false								x																												
ordered=true | false							x																													
path=STRING		x																																		
scheme=STRING																x																				
sendreferer=true | false											x																									
size=NUMBER															x																					
src=URL														•																						
tabindex=NUMBER															x										x											
title=VDATA	x		x				x			x					x				x	x					x											
type=DOCHOICES								•																												
type=IEVENTS																		•																		
type=onpick																		•																		

continued

	a	access	anchor	b	big	br	card	do	em	fieldset	go	head	i	img	input	meta	noop	onevent	optgroup	option	p	postfield	prev	refresh	select	setvar	small	strong	table	td	template	timer	tr	u	wml	do
type=text | password															x																					
value=VDATA															x					x		•			x	•						•				
vspace=LENGTH (0)														x																						
width=LENGTH														x																						
xml:lang=NAME	x		x	x	x	x	x		x	x		x	x	x	x				x	x	x				x		x	x	x	x				x	x	x

•   Required attribute.

DENTRY	Data entry elements: \<input>, \<select>, and \<fieldset>.
DOCHOICES	Valid \<do> choices: accept, prev, help, reset, options, delete, and unknown.
FMTTEXT	Elements for formatting text: \<b>, \<big>, \<em>, \<i>, \<small>, \<strong>, \<u>.
ID	An XML-compatible name that uniquely identifies an element within a document.
IEVENTS	Card-level intrinsic events: onenterforward, onenterbackward, and ontimer.
LENGTH	An integer to indicate length in pixels, or an integer plus a percent sign to indicate length as a percentage of the screen width.
NAME	A valid XML name—letters, digits, and underscore character.
NUMBER	A valid integer greater than or equal to zero.
STRING	Single-line Unicode 2.0 text that is not parsed.
TEXT	Multiline Unicode text that is not parsed.
VDATA	A STRING with possible variable references.
URL	An absolute or relative URI, URL, or URN, possibly containing variable references.

WMLScript Library Functions

Lang
Arithmetic
  abs (num)   Return the absolute value of num.
  max (num1, num2)   Return the maximum of num1 and num2.
  min (num1, num2)   Return the minimum of num1 and num2.
Conversion
  isFloat (value)   Return true if value can be converted to float using parseFloat.
  isInt (value)   Return true if value can be converted to integer using parseInt.
  parseFloat (str)   Return the floating-point equivalent of str.
  parseInt (str)   Return the integer equivalent of str.
Environment
  characterSet ()   Return the IANA character set value.
  float ()   Return true if floating-point nums are supported.
  maxInt ()   Return the maximum integer.
  minInt ()   Return the minimum integer.
Flow Control
  abort (str)   Terminate, returning str.
  exit (value)   Terminate, returning value.
Random Number
  random (int)   Return a random integer between zero and int.
  seed (int)   Initialize the random num generator using int.

Float
Environment
  maxFloat ()   Return the maximum positive floating-point value.
  minFloat ()   Return the smallest positive floating-point value.
Arithmetic
  ceil (num)   Return the smallest integer not less than num.
  floor (num)   Return the greatest integer not greater than num.
  int (num)   Return the integer part of num.
  pow (num1, num2)   Return num1 to the num2 power.
  round (num)   Return the integer closest to num.
  sqrt (num)   Return the square root of num.

String
Basic
  charAt (str, num)   Return the str character at location num.
  compare (str1, str2)   Lexical comparison of str1 and str2.
  isEmpty (str)   Return true if str's length is zero.
  length (str)   Return the length of str.
  squeeze (str)   Remove all consecutive white space from str.
  trim (str)   Remove all leading and trailing white space from str.
Substring
  subStr (str, startNum, lenNum)   Return from str the substring starting at startNum and lenNum long.
  find (str, subStr)   Return the index of the first location of subStr in str.
  replace (str, oldStr, newStr)   Replace all oldStrs in str with newStr.
Element
  elementAt (str, num, sepStr)   Return the numth element in str that is separated by sepStr.
  elements (str, sepStr)   Return the number of substrings in str that are separate by sepStr.
  insertAt (str, elemStr, num, sepStr)   Insert elemStr in str at the numth element that is separated by sepStr.
  removeAt (str, num, sepStr)   Return str with the numth element separated by sepStr removed.
  replaceAt (str, elemStr, num, sepStr)   Return str with the numth element separated by sepStr replaced with elemStr.
Conversion
  format (fmtStr, value)   Convert value to a string using the formatting string fmtStr.
  toStr (value)   Return value converted to a string.

URL
  Managing
   escapeStr (str)   Return the escaped version of str.
   getBase ( )   Return the absolute URL of the current WMLScript compilation unit.
   getReferer ( )   Return the smallest URL of the resource that called the current compilation unit.
   isValid (str)   Return true if str is a valid URL.
   resolve (baseStr, embeddedStr)   Return a URL combining baseStr and embeddedStr.
   unescapeStr (str)   Return the unescaped version of str.
  Component
   getFragment (str)   Return the URL fragment portion of str.
   getHost (str)   Return the URL host portion of str.
   getPort (str)   Return the URL server port num from str.
   getParameters (str)   Return the URL parameters from str.
   getPath (str)   Return the URL path from str.
   getScheme (str)   Return the Internet protocol scheme from str.
   getQuery (str)   Get the URL query portion from str.
  Content
   loadStr (urlStr, cTypeStr)   Return the content of type cTypeStr specified by urlStr.

WMLBrowser
  Variables
   getVar (str)   Return the value of the variable str from the current context.
   setVar (str, value)   Set the value of the variable str to value.
  Tasks
   go (urlStr)   Queue deck urlStr for execution upon termination.
   prev ( )   Queue a prev task for execution upon termination.
   refresh ( )   Signal the WML user agent to do a <refresh>.
   newContext ( )   Clear the current WML user agent context.
  Query
   getCurrentCard ( )   Return the smallest possible URL of the current WML user agent card.

Dialogs
   prompt (str, defaultStr)   Display str and prompt for input using defaultStr as a default value.
   confirm (str, okStr, cancelStr)   Display str, okStr, and cancelStr, and return true if okStr is selected.
   alert (str)   Display str and wait for user confirmation.

Language Abbreviations Sorted by Language Code

LANGUAGE NAME	CODE	LANGUAGE FAMILY
Afar	AA	Hamitic
Abkhazian	AB	Ibero-Caucasian
Afrikaans	AF	Germanic
Amharic	AM	Semitic
Arabic	AR	Semitic
Assamese	AS	Indian
Aymara	AY	Amerindian
Azerbaijani	AZ	Turkic/Altaic
Bashkir	BA	Turkic/Altaic
Byelorussian	BE	Slavic
Bulgarian	BG	Slavic
Bihari	BH	Indian
Bislama	BI	[Not given]
Bengali; Bangla	BN	Indian
Tibetan	BO	Asian
Breton	BR	Celtic
Catalan	CA	Romance
Corsican	CO	Romance
Czech	CS	Slavic
Welsh	CY	Celtic
Danish	DA	Germanic
German	DE	Germanic
Bhutani	DZ	Asian
Greek	EL	Latin/Greek
English	EN	Germanic
Esperanto	EO	International
Spanish	ES	Romance

LANGUAGE NAME	CODE	LANGUAGE FAMILY
Estonian	ET	Finno-Ugric
Basque	EU	Basque
Persian (Farsi)	FA	Iranian
Finnish	FI	Finno-Ugric
Fiji	FJ	Oceanic/Indonesian
Faroese	FO	Germanic
French	FR	Romance
Frisian	FY	Germanic
Irish	GA	Celtic
Scots Gaelic	GD	Celtic
Galician	GL	Romance
Guarani	GN	Amerindian
Gujarati	GU	Indian
Hausa	HA	Negro-African
Hindi	HI	Indian
Croatian	HR	Slavic
Hungarian	HU	Finno-Ugric
Armenian	HY	Indo-European (other)
Interlingua	IA	International aux.
Interlingue	IE	International aux.
Inupia	IK	Eskimo
Indonesian	IN	Oceanic/Indonesian
Icelandic	IS	Germanic
Italian	IT	Romance
Hebrew	IW	Semitic
Japanese	JA	Asian
Yiddish	JI	Germanic
Javanese	JV	Oceanic/Indonesian
Georgian	KA	Ibero-Caucasian
Kazakh	KK	Turkic/Altaic
Greenlandic	KL	Eskimo
Cambodian	KM	Asian
Kannada	KN	Dravidian
Korean	KO	Asian

LANGUAGE NAME	CODE	LANGUAGE FAMILY
Kashmiri	KS	Indian
Kurdish	KU	Iranian
Kirghiz	KY	Turkic/Altaic
Latin	LA	Latin/Greek
Lingala	LN	Negro-African
Laothian	LO	Asian
Lithuanian	LT	Baltic
Latvian; Lettish	LV	Baltic
Malagasy	MG	Oceanic/Indonesian
Maori	MI	Oceanic/Indonesian
Macedonian	MK	Slavic
Malayalam	ML	Dravidian
Mongolian	MN	[Not given]
Moldavian	MO	Romance
Marathi	MR	Indian
Malay	MS	Oceanic/Indonesian
Maltese	MT	Semitic
Burmese	MY	Asian
Nauru	NA	[Not given]
Nepali	NE	Indian
Dutch	NL	Germanic
Norwegian	NO	Germanic
Occitan	OC	Romance
Afan (Oromo)	OM	Hamitic
Oriya	OR	Indian
Punjabi	PA	Indian
Polish	PL	Slavic
Pashto; Pushtu	PS	Iranian
Portuguese	PT	Romance
Quechua	QU	Amerindian
Rhaeto-Romance	RM	Romance
Kurundi	RN	Negro-African
Romanian	RO	Romance
Russian	RU	Slavic

LANGUAGE NAME	CODE	LANGUAGE FAMILY
Kinyarwanda	RW	Negro-African
Sanskrit	SA	Indian
Sindhi	SD	Indian
Sangho	SG	Negro-African
Serbo-Croatian	SH	Slavic
Singhalese	SI	Indian
Slovak	SK	Slavic
Slovenian	SL	Slavic
Samoan	SM	Oceanic/Indonesian
Shona	SN	Negro-African
Somali	SO	Hamitic
Albanian	SQ	Indo-European (other)
Serbian	SR	Slavic
Siswati	SS	Negro-African
Sesotho	ST	Negro-African
Sundanese	SU	Oceanic/Indonesian
Swedish	SV	Germanic
Swahili	SW	Negro-African
Tamil	TA	Dravidian
Telugu	TE	Dravidian
Tajik	TG	Iranian
Thai	TH	Asian
Tigrinya	TI	Semitic
Turkmen	TK	Turkic/Altaic
Tagalog	TL	Oceanic/Indonesian
Setswana	TN	Negro-African
Tonga	TO	Oceanic/Indonesian
Turkish	TR	Turkic/Altaic
Tsonga	TS	Negro-African
Tatar	TT	Turkic/Altaic
Twi	TW	Negro-African
Ukrainian	UK	Slavic
Urdu	UR	Indian
Uzbek	UZ	Turkic/Altaic

LANGUAGE NAME	CODE	LANGUAGE FAMILY
Vietnamese	VI	Asian
Volapuk	VO	International
Wolof	WO	Negro-African
Xhosa	XH	Negro-African
Yoruba	YO	Negro-African
Chinese	ZH	Asian
Zulu	ZU	Negro-African

Dialect Abbreviations Sorted by Country Name

COUNTRY	ISO CODE
Afghanistan	AF
Albania	AL
Algeria	DZ
American Samoa	AS
Andorra	AD
Angola	AO
Anguilla	AI
Antarctica	AQ
Antigua and Barbuda	AG
Argentina	AR
Armenia	AM
Aruba	AW
Australia	AU
Austria	AT
Azerbaijan	AZ
Bahamas	BS
Bahrain	BH
Bangladesh	BD
Barbados	BB
Belarus	BY
Belgium	BE
Belize	BZ
Benin	BJ
Bermuda	BM
Bhutan	BT
Bolivia	BO
Bosnia and Herzegovina	BA

COUNTRY	ISO CODE
Botswana	BW
Bouvet Island	BV
Brazil	BR
British Indian Ocean Territory	IO
Brunei Darussalam	BN
Bulgaria	BG
Burkina Faso	BF
Burundi	BI
Cambodia	KH
Cameroon	CM
Canada	CA
Cape Verde	CV
Cayman Islands	KY
Central African Republic	CF
Chad	TD
Chile	CL
China	CN
Christmas Island	CX
Cocos (Keeling) Islands	CC
Colombia	CO
Comoros	KM
Congo	CG
Cook Islands	CK
Costa Rica	CR
Côte d'Ivoire	CI
Croatia (local name: Hrvatska)	HR
Cuba	CU
Cyprus	CY
Czech Republic	CZ
Denmark	DK
Djibouti	DJ
Dominica	DM
Dominican Republic	DO
East Timor	TP

COUNTRY	ISO CODE
Ecuador	EC
Egypt	EG
El Salvador	SV
Equatorial Guinea	GQ
Eritrea	ER
Estonia	EE
Ethiopia	ET
Falkland Islands (Malvinas)	FK
Faroe Islands	FO
Fiji	FJ
Finland	FI
France	FR
France, Metropolitan	FX
French Guiana	GF
French Polynesia	PF
French Southern Territories	TF
Gabon	GA
Gambia	GM
Georgia	GE
Germany	DE
Ghana	GH
Gibraltar	GI
Greece	GR
Greenland	GL
Grenada	GD
Guadeloupe	GP
Guam	GU
Guatemala	GT
Guinea	GN
Guinea-Bissau	GW
Guyana	GY
Haiti	HT
Heard and McDonald Islands	HM
Honduras	HN

COUNTRY	ISO CODE
Hong Kong	HK
Hungary	HU
Iceland	IS
India	IN
Indonesia	ID
Iran (Islamic Republic of)	IR
Iraq	IQ
Ireland	IE
Israel	IL
Italy	IT
Jamaica	JM
Japan	JP
Jordan	JO
Kazakhstan	KZ
Kenya	KE
Kiribati	KI
Korea, Democratic People's Republic of	KP
Korea, Republic of	KR
Kuwait	KW
Kyrgyzstan	KG
Lao People's Democratic Republic	LA
Latvia	LV
Lebanon	LB
Lesotho	LS
Liberia	LR
Libyan Arab Jamahiriya	LY
Liechtenstein	LI
Lithuania	LT
Luxembourg	LU
Macau	MO
Macedonia, the Former Yugoslav Republic of	MK
Madagascar	MG
Malawi	MW
Malaysia	MY

COUNTRY	ISO CODE
Maldives	MV
Mali	ML
Malta	MT
Marshall Islands	MH
Martinique	MQ
Mauritania	MR
Mauritius	MU
Mayotte	YT
Mexico	MX
Micronesia, Federated States of	FM
Moldova, Republic of	MD
Monaco	MC
Mongolia	MN
Montserrat	MS
Morocco	MA
Mozambique	MZ
Myanmar	MM
Namibia	NA
Nauru	NR
Nepal	NP
Netherlands	NL
Netherlands Antilles	AN
New Caledonia	NC
New Zealand	NZ
Nicaragua	NI
Niger	NE
Nigeria	NG
Niue	NU
Norfolk Island	NF
Northern Mariana Islands	MP
Norway	NO
Oman	OM
Pakistan	PK
Palau	PW

COUNTRY	ISO CODE
Panama	PA
Papua New Guinea	PG
Paraguay	PY
Peru	PE
Philippines	PH
Pitcairn	PN
Poland	PL
Portugal	PT
Puerto Rico	PR
Qatar	QA
Reunion	RE
Romania	RO
Russian Federation	RU
Rwanda	RW
Saint Helena	SH
Saint Kitts and Nevis	KN
Saint Lucia	LC
Saint-Pierre et Miquelon	PM
Saint Vincent and the Grenadines	VC
Samoa	WS
San Marino	SM
Sao Tome and Principe	ST
Saudi Arabia	SA
Senegal	SN
Seychelles	SC
Sierra Leone	SL
Singapore	SG
Slovakia (Slovak Republic)	SK
Slovenia	SI
Solomon Islands	SB
Somalia	SO
South Africa	ZA
Spain	ES
Sri Lanka	LK

COUNTRY	ISO CODE
Sudan	SD
Suriname	SR
Svalbard and Jan Mayen Island	SJ
Swaziland	SZ
Sweden	SE
Switzerland	CH
Syrian Arab Republic	SY
Taiwan, Province of China	TW
Tajikistan	TJ
Tanzania, United Republic of	TZ
Thailand	TH
Togo	TG
Tokelau	TK
Tonga	TO
Trinidad and Tobago	TT
Tunisia	TN
Turkey	TR
Turkmenistan	TM
Turks and Caicos Islands	TC
Tuvalu	TV
Uganda	UG
Ukraine	UA
United Arab Emirates	AE
United Kingdom	GB
United States	US
United States Minor Outlying Islands	UM
Uruguay	UY
Uzbekistan	UZ
Vanuatu	VU
Vatican City State (Holy See)	VA
Venezuela	VE
Vietnam	VN
Virgin Islands (British)	VG
Virgin Islands (U.S.)	VI

COUNTRY	ISO CODE
Wallis and Futuna Islands	WF
Western Sahara	EH
Yemen	YE
Yugoslavia	YU
Zaire	ZR
Zambia	ZM

[ECMA] Standard ECMA-262: "ECMAScript Language Specification", ECMA, June 1997. www.ecma.ch/stand/ECMA-262.htm.

[HTML4] "HTML 4.0 Specification, W3C Recommendation 18-December-1997, REC-HTML40-971218", Raggett et al., September 17, 1997. www.w3.org/TR/REC-html40

[HUNTER] Hunter, Jason et al, *Java Servlet Programming*, O'Reilly & Associates, Inc., ISBN 1-56592-381-X.

[IANA] "(Internet Assigned Numbers Authority) Official Names for Character Sets", Simonsen et al. ftp://ftp.isi.edu/in-notes/iana/assignments/character-sets.

[ISO639] Code for the representation of names of languages—The International Organization for Standardization, 1st edition, 1988.

[ISO3166] Codes for the representation of names of countries—The International Organization for Standardization, 3rd edition, 1988-08-15.

[ISO10646] "Information Technology—Universal Multiple-Octet Coded Character Set (UCS)—Part 1: Architecture and Basic Multilingual Plane", ISO/IEC 10646-1:1993.

[ISO8879] "Information Processing—Text and Office Systems—Standard Generalised Markup Language (SGML)", ISO 8879:1986.

[JAVASCRIPT] Flanagan, David, *JavaScript, The Definitive Guide*, O'Reilly & Associates, Inc., ISBN 1-56592-234-4.

[NAIK] Naik, Dilp, *Internet Standards and Protocols*, Microsoft Press, ISBN 1-57231-692-6.

[RFC822] "Standard for the Format of ARPA Internet Text Messages", STD 11, RFC 822, Crocker, August 1982. ftp://ds.internic.net/rfc/rfc822.txt

[RFC1123] "Requirements for Internet hosts—application and support", STD 3, Braden, IETF, October 1989.

[RFC1766] "Tags for the Identification of Languages", H. Alvestrand, March 1995. ftp://ds.internic.net/rfc/rfc1766.txt

[RFC2045] "Multipurpose Internet Mail Extensions (MIME) Part One: Format of Internet Message Bodies", Freed and Borenstein, November 1996, ftp://ds.internic.net/rfc/rfc2045.txt

[RFC2070] "Internationalization of the Hypertext Markup Language", Yergeau et al, January 1997, ftp://ds.internic.net/rfc/rfc2070.txt

[RFC2396] "Uniform Resource Identifiers (URI): Generic Syntax", Berners-Lee et al., August 1998. ftp://ds.internic.net/rfc/rfc2396.txt

[RFC2616] "Hypertext Transfer Protocol—HTTP/1.1", Fielding et al., June 1999. ftp://ds.internic.net/rfc/rfc2068.txt

[ROBERTS] Roberts, Dave, *Internet Protocols Handbook*, Coriolis Group Books, ISBN 1-883577-88-8.

[SELF] Ungar, David, and Smith, Randall B., "Self: The Power of Simplicity", OOPSLA '87 Conference Proceedings, pp. 227-241, Orlando, FL, October, 1987.

[STEVENS] Stevens, Richard, TCP/IP Illustrated, Volume 3, Addison-Wesley, ISBN 0-201-63495-3.

[UNICODE] *The Unicode Standard: Version 2.0*, The Unicode Consortium, Addison-Wesley Developers Press, 1996. www.unicode.org/

[VCAL] "vCalendar—the Electronic Calendaring and Scheduling Format, version 1.0", The Internet Mail Consortium (IMC), September 18, 1996. www .imc.org/pdi/vcal-10.doc

[VCARD] "vCard—The Electronic Business Card, version 2.1", The Internet Mail Consortium (IMC), September 18, 1996. www.imc.org/pdi/vcard-21.doc.

[WAP] *Official Wireless Application Protocol*, Wireless Application Protocol Forum Ltd., John Wiley & Sons, Inc. ISBN 0-471-32755-7. www.wiley.com/comp-books/WAP.

[WONG] Wong, Clinton, *Web Client Programming*, O'Reilly & Associates, ISBN 1-56592-214-X.

[XML] "Extensible Markup Language (XML)", W3C Proposed Recommendation, PR-xml-971208, T. Bray, et al, December 8, 1997. http://www.w3.org/TR/PR-xml

To use this CD-ROM, your system must meet the following requirements:

Platform/Processor/Operating System. Pentium or faster Intel processor with Windows 95, Windows 98 or Windows NT 4.0, or later.

RAM. 32 MB of RAM recommended.

Hard Drive Space. Approximately 20MB or free disk space.

Peripherals. None.